新编
第二语言习得概论

（第二版）

张宏武　编　著

A New Course on
Second Language Acquisition (2nd Edition)

暨南大学出版社
JINAN UNIVERSITY PRESS

中国·广州

图书在版编目（CIP）数据

新编第二语言习得概论 = A New Course on Second Language Acquisition：英文/张宏武
编著 . —2 版 . —广州：暨南大学出版社，2023. 11
ISBN 978 - 7 - 5668 - 3817 - 9

Ⅰ . ①新…　Ⅱ . ①张…　Ⅲ . ①第二语言—概论—英文　Ⅳ . ①H003

中国国家版本馆 CIP 数据核字（2023）第 227799 号

新编第二语言习得概论（第二版）
XINBIAN DI-ER YUYAN XIDE GAILUN（DI-ER BAN）
编著者：张宏武

··

出 版 人：阳　翼
策划编辑：杜小陆
责任编辑：康　蕊
责任校对：苏　洁　王燕丽　黄亦秋
责任印制：周一丹　郑玉婷

出版发行：暨南大学出版社（511443）
电　　话：总编室（8620）37332601
　　　　　营销部（8620）37332680　37332681　37332682　37332683
传　　真：（8620）37332660（办公室）　37332684（营销部）
网　　址：http：//www. jnupress. com
排　　版：广州良弓广告有限公司
印　　刷：佛山市浩文彩色印刷有限公司
开　　本：787mm×960mm　1/16
印　　张：19. 5
字　　数：400 千
版　　次：2016 年 12 月第 1 版　2023 年 11 月第 2 版
印　　次：2023 年 11 月第 1 次
定　　价：68. 00 元

（暨大版图书如有印装质量问题，请与出版社总编室联系调换）

前　言

第二语言习得作为一门独立学科始于 20 世纪 60 年代，它的历史不算太长，但在近五六十年间，该学科取得了快速发展。学者们从不同的视角、在不同的层面上、以不同的方法对第二语言习得进行了大量研究，出版了大量文献，提出了大量宝贵的理论假设和习得模式。随着研究的不断深入，第二语言习得与语言学、心理学、社会学、教育学、认知科学、哲学等学科的关系日趋密切，从而逐渐发展成为一门跨学科的科学。掌握和了解一定的二语习得知识，不仅对英语专业的学生来说必不可少，而且对从事外语教学、科研工作的广大教师，包括从事汉语作为第二语言教学的教师来说也十分必要。近年来，虽然从国外引进了许多研究和介绍二语习得的著作，但是由于偏重理论、内容深奥、术语繁多、语言难懂，这些著作往往使初次接触该学科的学生望而生畏，对二语习得产生畏难情绪。为此，我们编写了这本教程，供初次接触二语习得的中国学生，尤其是英语专业的学生使用。

本书是在 2016 年 12 月暨南大学出版社出版的《新编第二语言习得概论》第一版的基础上修订而成，在原有内容的基础上做了必要的调整和补充，增加了新的知识和理论。对一些重要术语，如中介语假说、中介语语用学、话语行为、社会语用能力、语用语言能力、标记、普遍语法、类型普遍性、信息加工理论、竞争模式、可教性/可学性假说、关注形式教学等的解释补充了新的诠释和观点；增添了技能习得理论、中介语话语、社会教育模式、实践共同体、二语习得的生态学、动态系统理论、课堂二语习得理论、强化输入、结构输入、二语语用教学等新内容。

本书用英文编写而成，讲解过程主要以英语为例，间或借用汉语、法语、西班牙语例句，但都有英文解释。全书共有七章：第一章介绍二语习得及其相关术语。第二章呈现中介语研究成果。第三、四、五章分别从语言学、心理学、社会学视角介绍第二语言习得领域取得的主要研究成果以及重要的理论知识和二语习得模式。第六章涉及课堂教学与二语习得的关系，主要探讨关注形式教学、外显教学/内隐教学、增强意识、加工教学、语用教学、语法讲解等课堂教学行为对二语习得的作用和影响。第七章简要介绍二语习得研究中的数据收集和数据分析的方法。各章之间既存在有机联系，又各自具有相对的独立性。为帮助读者克服理解上的困难，本书采用通俗易懂的语言撰写，书后又附有英语术语解释及其汉语翻译。为便于自学，本书增添了部分练习的参考答案。由于目前许多术语尚无统一的翻译标准，该书中专业术语的翻译仅供参考。

第二语言习得的研究成果颇丰。作为一本入门教程，本书只是选择性地介绍较有影响的、较有代表性的理论和模式，使初学者能够对该学科的基本知识和研究动向有一个概括了解和宏观认识，同时也期望对我国外语教学与研究带来有益的启发。

第二语言习得研究经历了半个世纪的发展，内容浩瀚，不同流派对语言习得过程和习得机制又有不同的解释和描述。要为初学者编写一本简明扼要的读本，绝不是一件容易的事情。我们尽自己最大努力作了尝试。本书在编写过程中，由于水平有限，难免出现谬误，诚恳期望读者不吝指正。

张宏武

2023 年 9 月 20 日于嘉园

About the Book

This book is intended for both undergraduates and graduate students majoring in English language and literature. There are three main reasons for me to write this course book.

One is that I feel necessary to give a brief introduction to the studies in second language acquisition (SLA) for English majors, especially those who are going to be, and have the potential to be English teachers after graduation. I have learned from my own teaching experience that knowing the basic rationale in SLA is of great help for second/foreign language teaching. SLA is the right course to acquaint us with such fundamental principles so that we can be competent in second language teaching. SLA offers us from different perspectives the process of learning a second language, and knowing this enables us to have an integrative concept of what it is to be learned, how to learn it and why some learners are more competent than others.

Second, while teaching this subject, I have found it hard to cope in one semester with all those wonderful achievements in the field of SLA research. Also, I think it unnecessary to do this, especially for undergraduate students, because it is impossible for them to master everything within such a short period of time. A brief introduction, then, is necessary. The reason is that few undergraduates will be second language acquisition researchers; many of them will be English teachers after graduation. In addition, having a better understanding of SLA may as well pave the way for further in-depth research in the future. Therefore, it is my goal to make the course book more concise so that it is suitable for one-semester classroom teaching.

The third reason is related to the difficulty of the subject. Many books are imported directly from English speaking countries, and most of them are strongly theoretical and are written for researchers in the field of second language acquisition. They are excellent academic works, but not suitable as textbooks for Chinese students, who learn English mainly for communicative purpose. In most cases, students are daunted by the difficulty in comprehending the contents, either because it is too technical or because it gives too detailed an account of the development in SLA research. These books are thick, even containing more than 500 pages, which is a great challenge for readers, who spend endless hours wrestling with special terms and complex syntax in them. This is why I was determined to write this short course book.

When I had the idea of writing a course book on SLA, I realized I needed to touch upon this subject in a way that differs from the academic way of dealing with linguistic issues. Rather than discuss in detail, I intended to introduce briefly the main findings in SLA research from four major perspectives: linguistics, psychology, sociology, and pedagogy. The goals of this course book can be summarized as follows: it is concise and reader-friendly with little jargon. If there are special terms, they are given clear definitions.

This book can be used as the textbook for one semester. However, the major points in the field can be covered two periods a week, for eighteen or so weeks in a semester all together.

The textbook has seven short chapters. Chapter 1 gives a brief introduction to the study of SLA, and presents some fundamental terms in SLA. The second chapter discusses the characteristics of and the major findings in the study of interlanguage. A brief introduction is also given to interlanguage pragmatics, which has become a major concern in recent years. Chapter 3, 4, and 5 are the major parts of the book, discussing SLA from linguistic, psychological, and socio-cultural perspectives respectively. Chapter 6 covers the relationship between classroom instruction and SLA. The last chapter is about second language data collection and analysis. This final part is specially designed for those whose job is related to second language acquisition research.

The features of the book can be briefly summarized as follows:

(1) Brief and concise. The principle I followed throughout the whole course of writing this book is brevity and conciseness. Each chapter is designed to introduce briefly the major and the most recent findings in the field of SLA so that the readers may feel easy to have a quick glimpse of the recent contributions made by devoted SLA researchers. It will also be rather comfortable for classroom instruction in one semester.

(2) Reader-friendly. Another principle I followed while writing this book is that the language is made easy for readers to understand. Without losing, or distorting the main theme of each SLA theory, I tried my best to make the language as plain as possible, so that

readers will not be daunted by linguistic barriers and will have easy access to the content.

(3) Well-designed assignment. In order that readers will have a better understanding of the thoughts and ideas presented in each chapter, I have designed different kinds of exercises at the end of each chapter, including "Questions for self-study", "Blank-filling", and "Open discussion for pair or group work". These exercises are intended to bring readers a refreshing review of the key issues touched upon in each chapter. The open questions can be done in pairs or in groups. Some of the questions in the "Open discussion" section are especially designed for those who are interested in L2 acquisition research. These questions and topics provide them a chance of further exploration.

Zhang Hongwu
September 20, 2023

A NEW COURSE ON SECOND LANGUAGE ACQUISITION
(2nd Edition)

目录

ENG

A NEW COURSE ON ACQUISITION

A NEW COURSE ON
ACQUISITION

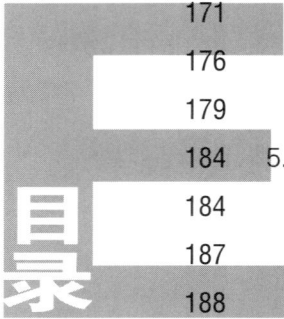

目录

ENG

A NEW COURSE ON
ACQUISITION

LISH 目录

SECOND LANGUAGE

LISH目录

SECOND LANGUAGE

Chapter One   An Introduction to Second Language Acquisition

As a relatively young field of enquiry, the study of second language acquisition (SLA) has expanded and developed significantly in the past 60 years. When you turn to this page, you are approaching this young field of second language acquisition. In this opening chapter, we provide a general introduction to second language acquisition, beginning with the definition of SLA and the aims of SLA research. Then, we introduce some basic terminologies in the field of second language acquisition, and discuss the external and internal factors which affect second language learning. Finally, we give a brief review of first language acquisition (particularly child language acquisition), because a knowledge of child language development will pave the way for a better understanding of second language acquisition.

1.1   Definition of Second Language Acquisition (SLA)

What is a second language? A second language can be defined as any language that is learned after the acquisition of the mother tongue, or the first language. In this context, learning of a second language refers to the learning of a third, a fourth or even a fifth language. A second language (L2) is commonly called a target language in a learning situation. Next, what does it mean by second language acquisition, or what does an SLA researcher do in this field? Before we define this term, let us look at the definitions given by some early scholars:

"Second language acquisition research" refers to studies which are designed to investigate questions about learners' use of their second language and the processes which underlie second language acquisition and use （Lightbown，1985）.

SLA is thought of as a discipline devoted to discovering and characterizing how it is that a human being is able to learn a second language：what pre-knowledge does he or she bring to the task，what set of learning procedures does he or she use，what strategies are appropriate for certain phenomena and not others，etc （Schachter，1993）.

［SLA］is concerned with what is acquired of a second language，what is not acquired of a second language，what the mechanisms are which bring that knowledge （or lack thereof）about and ultimately，an explanation of the process of acquisition in terms of both successes and failures （Gass，1993）.

By SLA we mean the acquisition of a language after the native language has already become established in the individual （Richie and Bhatia，1996）.

From the above definitions，it is easy for us to see a duel purpose in SLA：all definitions agree that the goals of SLA are to study，discover and characterize what is acquired of an L2 and how it is acquired. We have three main concerns in this coursebook. First，we focus on the question of "what"，that is the developing knowledge and use of the second language being learned. This scope of SLA includes informal L2 learning taking place in naturalistic contexts，formal L2 learning taking place in classrooms，and L2 learning that involves a mixture of these settings and circumstances. In addition to what is learned of a second language，we are equally interested in what is not learned in these contexts.

Second，we focus on the question of "how"，that is the study of how a second language is learned. We are interested in how learners create a new language system with limited exposure to a second language，and how they make hypotheses about the rules of a second language. Considering how the rules are constructed in the learner's mind，the study of second language acquisition is closely related to other areas of study such as linguistics，psychology，psycholinguistics，sociology，sociolinguistics，discourse analysis，conversational analysis，education，and so forth.

In addition to the questions of "what" and "how"，our third concern is "why"：why some learners achieve more proficiency than others do. It is a fact that in any situation，there must be some learners who are more successful in learning an L2 than others. The research of "why" tries to answer this question.

The field of SLA research has both theoretical and practical importance. The theoretical importance is associated with our understanding of how language is represented in the mind and whether there is a difference between the way language is acquired and processed and the way other kinds of information are acquired and processed. The practical importance arises from the assumption that an understanding of how languages are learned will lead to more effective teaching practices. In a broader context, a knowledge of second language acquisition may help educational policy makers set more realistic goals for programs for both foreign language courses and the learning of the majority language by minority language children and adults (Spada and Lightbown, 2008).

1.2   The Aims of SLA Research

Second language acquisition research covers not only the study of those people who are learning an L2, but also the process of learning that language. In trying to probe into the process of learning a second language, researchers are seeking to answer the following three fundamental questions (Saville-Troike, 2008: 2):

(1) What does the L2 learner come to know?
(2) How does the learner acquire the knowledge?
(3) Why are some learners more successful than other learners?

SLA research aims to seek answers to the above questions. In order to answer the first question, researchers collect samples of leaner language and try to describe their features. Learner language is full of errors, and researchers usually start their study by classifying those errors. Also, researchers may record learners' speech while they are communicating with native speakers or other learners, and then produce transcriptions of the recordings. By studying the transcriptions, researchers identify specific grammatical features such as negatives or interrogatives in the data, and describe the "rules" which could account for the learner's productions. The goal of research is essentially descriptive, that is, to record the learner language, to try to establish whether it manifests regularities of some kind, and to find out how it changes over time.

The second aim of SLA is to explain how the learner acquires the L2 knowledge. For example, does the learner depend on his innate ability to acquire L2 rules? How does he process language input? How does restructuring of L2 system take place? Does the learner acquire L2 knowledge by explicit or implicit means? How does he learn by interacting with others? Why do learners produce the L2 in the way they do? Why does learners' language exhibit marked "rules"? Why does the learner language change systematically over time? These are only a few questions, and there are more to be raised.

In order to answer these questions, researchers may consider both external and internal factors which affect L2 acquisition. The external factors are concerned with the social situation in which learning takes place. Researchers who are searching for external explanations of learner language make comprehensive use of ideas and methods from the sociolinguistic study of language. The internal factors which also make contributions to L2 acquisition are rooted in the mind of the learner, who employs mental processes to convert input into knowledge. The mental processes can be regarded as learning processes. By means of the learning processes, the learner constructs his or her L2 knowledge.

Another aim of SLA is connected with the third question as to why some L2 learners perform better than others, which focuses on the individual language learner. Although the basic assumption in SLA research is that learner language offers evidence of universal learning processes, learners do vary significantly in their rate of learning, in their approach to learning, and especially in their final achievements. The study of individual learner differences seeks to document the factors which contribute to different kinds of variation.

1.3　Basic Terminologies in SLA

Every subject, or area of study, has its terminology. The terminology of a subject refers to the set of special words and expressions used in connection with it. The main purpose of this chapter is to set the scene for the rest of the book. We have discussed what is meant by the term Second Language Acquisition, and declared the main objectives of the study of SLA. Here we think it necessary to examine a few key terms relating to the research of SLA. Understanding these terms will pave the way for a better understanding of what SLA is about.

1. 3. 1   Native language and target language

Native language refers to the mother tongue, or the first language (L1) spoken by native speakers. For example, English is the native language for American and British people; Chinese is the native language for Chinese people and Japanese for Japanese people. Native language is "picked up" in naturalistic environment and in an informal manner. People generally learn to speak and use the language in real communicative contexts, and the primary focus is on meaning instead of linguistic forms. Native language is also tightly bound to native culture, and because of this, it is often difficult to decode a person from another culture. However, target language refers to any language that is the aim of learning. A second or foreign language which is being learnt can be called a target language. A target language, unlike native language, is often learned in classrooms in a formal way. People learn to speak it in an inauthentic context. While people are learning it, their primary focus is on linguistic forms first, and then move on gradually toward interactive communication.

1. 3. 2   Second language and foreign language

A second language, in a broad sense, refers to any language learned after one has acquired one's native language. However, when compared with a foreign language, it refers more narrowly to a language which plays a dominant role in a particular country or region though it may not be the first language of many people who use it. A second language is often acquired by minority group members or immigrants who speak another language natively. However, a foreign language is not the native language of large numbers of people in a particular country or region. It is not used as a medium of instruction in schools, nor is it widely used as a medium of communication. A foreign language is typically taught as a school subject for the purpose of communicating with foreigners or for reading printed materials in the language. English, for instance, is a second language for Chinese immigrants in the U. S. A. , but it becomes a foreign language for Chinese people in China.

Similar distinction should also be made between the second language context and foreign language context. In a second language context, the language is spoken in the country or area where it is being learnt. In a foreign language context, the language is not normally spoken outside the classroom, as is the case of learning English in China. In this book and in the field of SLA in general, a second language refers to any language other than a person's first language. Therefore, for a learner of English in China, the field of SLA research would say that English is a second language being learned in a foreign language context.

1.3.3 Library language, auxiliary language and language for specific purposes

A library language is one which functions primarily as a tool for further learning through reading, especially when books or journals in a desired field of study are not commonly published in the learners' native language. An auxiliary language is one which learners need to know for some official functions in their immediate political setting, or will need for purposes of wider communication, although their first language serves most other needs in their lives. Both library language and auxiliary language belong to a second language, the only difference being in the function of each type.

Other restricted or highly specialized functions for second languages are designated language for specific purposes, such as French for Hotel Management, English for Aviation Technology, Spanish for Agriculture, and so on. The learning of each of these languages typically focuses only on a narrow set of occupation-specific uses and functions. One such prominent area is English for Academic Purposes (EAP).

1.3.4 Bilingualism and multilingualism

Bilingualism refers to the use of two (or at least two) languages either by an individual, or by a group of speakers, such as the inhabitants of a particular region or a country. Bilingualism is the normal linguistic phenomenon in most of the countries of the world. In everyday use, a bilingual person is one who can speak, read, or understand two languages equally well. But the ability to read and write a second language or foreign language does not necessarily imply a degree of bilingualism. That is, bilingual is an end point, usually referring to someone who can use two languages with some degree of proficiency. However, SLA researchers are interested in individuals who are in the process of learning.

Multilingualism refers to the use of three or more languages by an individual, or by a group of inhabitants of a particular region or country. Usually, a multilingual person does not know all the languages equally well. For example, he or she may speak and understand one language best, or may be able to write in only one of them. Or he or she may use each language for different communicative purposes: one language at home, one at work, and one for shopping. Multilingualism and multilingual acquisition are complex phenomena. They implicate all the factors and processes associated with SLA and bilingualism as well as unique and potentially more complex factors and effects associated with the interactions that are possible among the multiple languages being learned and the processes of learning them (Gass and Selinker, 2008: 21). It must be pointed out that both bilingualism and multilingualism overlap to some extent with second language acquisition.

1.3.5　Acquisition and learning

In order to investigate how learners acquire an L2, we need a clear, operational definition of what is meant by the term "acquisition". Unfortunately, researchers have been unable to agree on such a definition. A distinction is made between "acquisition" and "learning". According to Krashen (1982), "acquisition" refers to the subconscious process of "picking up" a language through exposure and "learning" refers to the conscious process of studying it. According to this view, it is possible for learners to acquire or learn L2 features independently and at separate times. Although this distinction is favored particularly by teachers, it is problematic mainly because of the difficulty of demonstrating whether the processes involved are conscious or not. In this coursebook, the two terms "acquisition" and "learning" will be used interchangeably.

1.3.6　Second language acquisition and foreign language learning

Second language acquisition, generally, refers to the learning of a new language after the native language has been learned. Sometimes the term refers to the learning of a third or fourth language. It also means both the acquisition of an L2 in a classroom setting and in the natural environment. Foreign language learning, however, is different. It refers to the learning of a nonnative language in the environment of the learner's native language. For example, French speakers learn English in France or Chinese speakers learn Spanish in China. Second language acquisition, in contrast, refers to the learning of a nonnative language in the environment in which the language is spoken. For example, if German speakers learn Japanese in Japan, Japanese is their second language. Such a process of learning may or may not take place in a classroom situation. An important distinction is that learning in a second language environment has considerable access to speakers of the language being learned, whereas learning in a foreign language environment usually does not have such an advantage.

1.3.7 Input and output

In the area of SLA, input refers to the language which a learner hears or receives and from which they can learn. In contrast, the language a learner produces is called output. Both input and output are important for L2 learning. In second language acquisition, one learner's output can be another learner's input.

As for "input" in SLA, it must be pointed out that the language a learner hears or reads must have some kind of communicative intent. That is, there must be a message in the language. A learner's job is to understand the message, to comprehend the meaning of the utterance or sentence. Therefore, input is related to comprehension in that whenever a learner of a language is engaged in actively trying to comprehend something in the L2, he or she is getting input and that input serves as the basis for acquisition. The definition of input here is different from the common, everyday use of the term.

Input for acquisition is not information about the language. Learning a rule is not input. Input for acquisition is not drilling or filling out an exercise to practice verb forms. When learners produce language, they are not getting input. Language used for display purposes or for correction is not input. Thus, when a teacher corrects a student who pronounces the -ed ending of the past tense as a full syllable by saying "Not 'talkED'. Talk [t]. Talk [t]", this speech is not input for acquisition. Only instances of the L2 that are used to communicate information or to seek information can be considered as input for acquisition (VanPatten, 2007: 36). Another feature of input that is important for acquisition purposes is that it must somehow be comprehensible. Language that is completely incomprehensible to the learner will not be of much use.

Input can be conversational and non-conversational. Conversational input refers to the language learners hear in communicative contexts. It is language directed to the learners to which some kind of response is expected. The learner is part of the interaction. Everyday conversations, classroom conversations in the L2, and playing games are all examples of such contexts in which learners can receive conversational input. Non-conversational input is language that a learner hears when he or she is not part of the interaction. It is not directed to an individual learner. When a learner listens to the radio, watches TV, or attends a lecture, he gets non-conversational input, in which the learner does not participate in communicative conversations. Input can also be visual as well as aural. Reading, for example, is an important means of input, especially for adult language learners. But for child language learners, oral input is the most important type.

As for "output" in SLA, it is not language production without meaning. Meaningless utterances and imitations are not output. Output in SLA means language that has a communicative purpose. It is the language that learners produce to convey certain kind of meaning. It can be the output of an immigrant in a grocery store or bakery, an ESL student trying to register for classes in Kansas, a learner of German on a study-abroad experience who is trying to buy a certain medication, a foreign language student in a classroom who is answering a question, and so on. So, when we discuss issues related to output, we are speaking of the same kind of language that we speak of when we talk about input-language that has some kind of communicative intent (VanPatten, 2007: 80).

1.3.8 Competence and performance

Philosophers and scientists have dealt with the difference between competence and performance for centuries. Competence refers to a person's underlying knowledge of a system, event, or fact. It is the non-observable ability to do something. Performance is the observable and concrete realization of competence. It refers to the actual doing of something, such as walking, singing, dancing, and speaking. In western society, competence-performance distinction is used in all walks of life. For example, children in schools are assumed to possess certain competence in given areas and that this competence can be measured and assessed by means of observation of elicited samples of performance.

As for language, competence refers to one's knowledge of the system of a language, that is, the rules of grammar, its vocabulary, all the pieces of a language and how these pieces fit together. Performance, however, is the actual comprehension (listening, reading) or production (speaking, writing) of linguistic events. According to Chomsky, competence is the mental representations of linguistic rules that constitute the speaker's internal grammar. The internal grammar is implicit rather than explicit. The speaker has the intuitions about the grammaticality of sentences. That is, they know whether an utterance is grammatically correct or not. The competence-performance distinction has been extended to cover communicative aspects of language.

The term *communicative competence* is used in contrast to Chomsky's term *linguistic competence*. Hymes (1979: 15) referred to communicative competence as "rules of use without which the rules of grammar would be useless". This means besides grammatical rules, language use is governed by rules of use. Based on these rules of use, the desired or intended functions are performed and the language used is appropriate to the context. Some scholars have distinguished communicative competence and communicative performance. The former includes both linguistic and pragmatic knowledge. That is, the speaker has knowledge of what is the appropriate and correct language behavior and what is effective language behavior in relation to particular communicative goals. The latter, communicative performance, is the actual use of these two types of knowledge in understanding and producing speech.

In light of this distinction, the principal goal of SLA is to describe and explain the learners' linguistic competence. This is usually done by studying the samples of their performance, for the mental knowledge is not open to direct inspection. As for research method, some SLA researchers analyze the actual utterances learners produce in speech and writing. Some try to tap learners' intuitions about what is correct or appropriate by means of judgment tasks. Others rely on the introspective and retrospective reports that learners provide about their own learning (Ellis, 1994: 13). One thing we think necessary to point out here is that none of these research methods can provide a direct window into competence. It is not easy to extract underlying grammatical knowledge from the subjects, especially children, as for whether it's better to say "two foots" or "two feet". Children may have no interest in the researcher's grammatical question and therefore say whatever they want to. Researchers then have to design indirect methods of inferring competence, among which are tape recording and transcription of countless hours of speech followed by studious analysis.

1.3.9　Comprehension and production

Comprehension refers to the identification of the intended meaning of written or spoken communication. It can be a bottom-up process, drawing on information contained in the message, or a top-down process, which draws on information contained in the background knowledge, information from the context and from the listener's and speaker's purposes or intentions. Production refers to the output of language, such as speaking and writing. In child language, most evidence points to the general superiority of comprehension over production. They seem to understand "more" than they actually produce. A good example can be found in a child's phonological development. Look at the following example from a dialogue between a 3-year-old child and Miller (Brown, 2021: 38):

(C = Child; M = Miller)
C: *My name is Litha.*
M: *Litha?*
C: *No, Litha.*
M: *Oh, Lisa.*
C: *Yes, Litha.*

Obviously, the child can perceive the contrast between two English sounds: /θ/ as in Litha and /z/ as in Liza, though she could not produce the contrast herself. Similarly a beginning English learner may understand a sentence with an embedded relative clause, but they may not able to produce one in speaking or in writing. Look at the following example:

(T = Teacher; L = Learner)
T: *Which girl is your sister, the girl who is standing under the tree or the girl who is talking with the tall man?*
L: *The girl is standing under the tree. She is my sister.*

How do we explain this difference? It is known that even adults understand more words than they can use in speech; they also perceive more sentences than they can speak out. Can we say that comprehension ability is somewhat separate from production ability? Can we say comprehension indicates more of our overall competence, and production, a smaller portion? Definitely not. It is necessary to distinguish production competence from comprehension competence. A theory of language must include some explanation of the separation of two kinds of competence.

1. 3. 10　Explicit learning and implicit learning

These two terms are widely used in cognitive psychology and have become increasingly common in current accounts of second language acquisition. Explicit learning is a conscious process and is likely to be intentional. It can be investigated by giving learners an explicit rule and asking them to apply it to data or by inviting them to try to discover an explicit rule from an array of data provided. Implicit learning, however, is typically defined as learning that takes place without intentionality or awareness. It can be investigated by exposing learners to input data, which they are asked to process for meaning, and then investigating whether they have acquired any L2 linguistic properties as a result of the exposure. For example, learners could be asked to read a book and then tested to see if they had acquired any new vocabulary in the process.

1.3.11　Naturalistic and instructed second language acquisition

This distinction is made in accordance with where second language acquisition takes place. Naturalistic second language acquisition takes place in naturally occurring social situations while instructed second language acquisition often takes place in classrooms, with the help of or "guidance" from reference books and language teachers. The learning occurs differently in the two situations. In the former case, the learner focuses on communication and thus learns incidentally, whereas in the latter case, the learner typically focuses on some aspect of the language system. Not all SLA researchers favor the terms "naturalistic" and "instructed". Some prefer to use "untutored" / "tutored" or "uninstructed" / "instructed". The point has been made that there is really nothing "unnatural" about classrooms. It should be noted that learners often do not belong exclusively to the "naturalistic" or "instructed" categories but rather to a third category, often called "mixed". In this coursebook, we will discuss, in chapter six, instructed second language acquisition in more detail by examining how it affects L2 acquisition.

1.4　The External and Internal Factors in SLA

When we try to explain why learners acquire a second language in a certain way, we need to consider the external and internal factors which affect the learning of a second language. External factors relate to the environment in which learning takes place. However, the role and the importance of external factors in L2 acquisition remain a controversial issue. Behaviourists regard them as important factors. Mentalists think internal factors are central to acquisition, believing that the Language Acquisition Device (LAD) enables learners to extract "rules" from input. Cognitive theorists, then, emphasize the joint contribution of both external and internal factors in second language acquisition.

1. 4. 1   External factors

One of the external factors is the social environment in which second language learning takes place. Social factors probably have an indirect rather than a direct effect on the learning of an L2. These factors are likely to be mediated by the attitudes held by learners. Social factors shape learners' attitudes, which, in turn, decide the learning outcomes. This influences the opportunity to hear and speak and the attitudes towards the language. For example, when you respect or are respected by native speakers, you may learn it well. But when you are disliked by or hate native speakers, or when you want to distance yourself from native speakers, you may not learn it well.

A second external factor is the input and interaction. Acquisition cannot take place without a learner's access to input in the L2, which may come in spoken or written form. Spoken input may occur in the context of interaction in which a learner talks with somebody else or in the context of non-reciprocal discourse such as listening to radio or watching TV. The kind of input received by a learner in an interactive context may have been adjusted, and this can be found in language addressed to learners, such as foreigner talk and teacher talk, much of which is simplified input. The input received in a non-reciprocal context is the authentic input from the real world.

1. 4. 2   Internal factors

Unlike external factors, internal factors are not directly observable. They are covert and can only be inferred by studying learner's production and their report of how they learn an L2. A few internal factors to be discussed here include L1 transfer, cognitive mechanism, communication strategies, general world knowledge, and linguistic universals.

1. 4. 2. 1   L1 transfer

L1 transfer implies the important role the mother tongue plays in the acquisition of a second language. Before a learner learns a second language, he has already acquired his mother tongue, which may be considered a source of learning. Beginners draw on their first language when learning an L2. L1 transfer refers to the incorporation of features of the L1 into the knowledge systems of the L2 which the learner is trying to construct. The learner uses his previous L1 experience as a means of organizing the second language data.

There are two kinds of transfer: negative and positive. Negative transfer occurs in cases where the L2 differs from the mother tongue, as is also called interference. In contrast, positive transfer occurs in cases where the patterns of the L1 and the L2 are similar. Therefore, it can be said that L1 both facilitates and impedes L2 learning. In order to make predictions about the occurrence of L1 interference, researchers carried out contrastive analyses of the native language and the target language. It was found that transfer errors are more frequent with beginners than with intermediate L2 learners. This is because the beginners have less previous L2 knowledge to draw on in making hypotheses about rules, and might therefore be expected to make more use of their L1 knowledge.

It is, of course, economical and productive for L2 learners to transfer their L1 knowledge to the new task. They do not have to discover everything from zero. L1 provides a rather rich and specific set of hypotheses which learners can use. For many aspects of the L2, these hypotheses will be confirmed, because of the similarities that languages share. The L2 learner is likely to feel that everything he learns is different from his mother tongue. In fact, there are many ways in which his L1 knowledge can be directly transferred. Negative transfer often results in erroneous utterances.

However, the results of error analysis studies done by researchers (such as Dulay and Burt 1974) showed that transfer did not necessarily take effect even if there were differences between L1 and L2. Also, many errors made by learners seem to reflect intra-lingual processes rather than L1 interference. That is, they were the result of processes based on the learner's existing knowledge of the L2. But this does not affect the interest in studying transfer. More findings have been made. For example, transfer exists in all aspects of language—phonology, syntax, semantics, and pragmatics; transfer may not always manifest itself as errors, but also as avoidance, overuse, and facilitation. It is generally acknowledged that transfer works in complex ways and that it constitutes only one of the processes involved in L2 acquisition. In a word, L1 transfer is used as a learning process and an aid to communication.

1. 4. 2. 2　Cognitive mechanisms

Cognitive mechanics refer to the underlying processes which enable humans to acquire, process, store, and retrieve information, as well as solve problems and make decisions. Perception, attention, memory, reasoning are important cognitive mechanics in language learning. We've just noted that learners use L1 as a means of learning. This learning process consists of cognitive mechanisms which enable learners to extract information about the L2 from input and build their own language system—noticing features in the input, comparing these features with those in learners' mental grammars, and integrating new features into their interlanguages. For example, learners may notice that -s indicates plurality, relative pronoun *who* substitutes human nouns and *which*, non-human nouns.

1. 4. 2. 3　Communication strategies

When L2 learners are engaged in communication, they often have communicative intentions which are difficult to express, because the needed linguistic items are absent in their minds. This problem can often be anticipated by the learner in advance, who may be able to avoid communication or modify what he intended to say. If the learner is already engaged in speaking, he must try to find an alternative way of getting the meaning across. Such a way, in either of the above two cases, of coping with the situation is what is called "communication strategy". William Littlewood (2000) has summarized some communication strategies as follows:

(1) Avoid communicating. Learners may avoid discussing topics when they know that they lack the necessary vocabulary for those topics. This strategy would be more frequent with learners who dislike risks or uncertainty.

(2) Adjust the message. When it is too late to avoid a problem in an on-going communication, learners may decide to alter the meanings they intended to communicate. They may omit some information, make the ideas simple or less precise, or say something slightly different.

(3) Use paraphrase. In order to communicate a meaning, learners may also use a means of paraphrasing what they want to say, such as circumlocution or description. For instance, a learner might say "*I'd better tie myself in*" if he could not recall the word for "*car seat - belt*". In this way learners develop their ability to use the L2 fluently or

compensate for inadequate knowledge when communicating a particular message. This communicative strategy helps learners make effective use of L2 knowledge. A learner may also invent his own term "*picture place*", if he has not learned the word "*art gallery*".

(4) Use approximation. Learners may decide to use words which convey the meaning as closely as possible. One may use a less specific word than the intended meaning ("*some fruit*" instead of "*pineapple*", for example).

(5) Create new words. To express the desired meaning, a learner may use a new word or phrase, which might be the result of literal translation of a native language word. A German learner of English, who did not know the word for a "*bedside table*", coined the word "*night-table*" which is a literal translation for the German *Nachttisch*.

(6) Switch to the native language. Sometimes learners may decide to lift a word from his own native language instead of trying to create a new one with second language material. For example, a Chinese-speaking learner of English produced "*I saw the film Hua Pi yesterday afternoon and had a Er Meng last night.*" This strategy is most likely to succeed in situations where the hearer knows the speaker's native language. Learners in the classroom situation often use this strategy.

(7) Use non-linguistic resources. Even in our native language, we often use non-linguistic resources to make our meanings clearer. Gesture, mime, and imitation are often used in daily communications. For example, we don't have to say "*Please put the vacuum cleaner beside the table*". Instead, we may point and say "*Put it here, please.*" It is believed that L2 speakers can profit more from these non-linguistic means for complementing their linguistic resources.

(8) Seek help. When a communicative breakdown occurs, learners may seek help from outside. They may use a bilingual dictionary. They may rely on the co-operation of the listener by signaling that he is in difficulty directly or indirectly by means of hesitation.

1.4.2.4　General world knowledge

General world knowledge forms the fundamental background upon which the learner depends while learning an L2. Such knowledge helps learners understand L2 input. This is because human beings, whatever nationality they are from and whichever cultural background they possess, have much in common in understanding the outside world. General world knowledge can be conducive to understanding what other people are talking about.

1.4.2.5   Linguistic universals

Just as all human beings possess biological properties and cultural properties, they are equipped with knowledge of how language in general works. This general language knowledge is called language universals. According to mentalist theories, people have innate knowledge of language, which takes the form of Language Acquisition Device (LAD). Within this device stays the knowledge of linguistic universals. People, somehow, know what is grammatically possible and what is grammatically impossible.

There have been two approaches to the study of linguistic universals in SLA: typological universals and universal grammar (UG). The former is devoted to discovering structural similarities among languages. For example, it is found that all languages have nouns and verbs, with nouns functioning as subjects and objects of verbs, and verbs expressing tense, aspect, and modality. This universal knowledge of language is helpful in language learning. The latter probes into one language in great depth to search for language universals, for it is believed that language is species-specific, and the universality of language can be studied by looking closely at one's mother tongue. For example, one of the findings of UG, the Phrase Structure Principle, claims that all languages are made up of phrases consisting of a head and a complement, such as the prepositional phrase *in the classroom* and verbal phrase *have breakfast*, within which *in* and *have* are head words and *the classroom* and *breakfast* are complements. The only difference is that in some languages, the head precedes the complement, while in others, it may come after the head. Such knowledge affects the learning of an L2.

1.5   A Review of First Language Acquisition

During 1960s and 1970s, when SLA was beginning to establish itself as a research discipline, there also existed an increased pace of research on first language acquisition. We discuss first language acquisition here because much SLA research parallels the developments in first language acquisition research, and over the years has drawn on concepts from first language acquisition area to understand L2 phenomena. There has been an influence of first language acquisition research on the study of L2 learning, and this influence can be felt both at the theoretical level and at the practical level.

At the theoretical level, researchers have been working with exciting new ideas about language and the learning process. Concepts such as imitation and habit – formation have to a large extent been replaced by notions which emphasize the child's own creativity in constructing his knowledge of the language. These concepts and ideas have been employed to view second language learning from the same perspective and to find evidence to support this view. At the practical level, first language researchers have developed new techniques for collecting and analyzing children's speech. These techniques have also been used in the field of L2 learning, to gather data and accumulate evidence about the sequences and processes that are involved.

A large amount of research on children's grammatical development has been conducted since 1960s. Here we introduce some gains in such research, which we hope will enable us to understand how children's grammatical competence grows.

1.5.1　From babbling to words

The first characteristic of children's speech can be described as "babbling", produced by infants at about six months. Babbling most commonly consists of consonant-vowel sequences, such as *baba*, *dada*, and later *bada*. These early babbling sounds are often taken to be "words" by parents, with *mama*, for instance, referring to the infant's mother. In order to communicate with others, children use intonation to express meaning. They can use proper stress and intonation contours of their language to distinguish among statements, questions, and requests. For example, a child can say *dada* with the stress on the second syllable. We can imagine the child stretching out her arms with the intention of a request, something like "Pick me up, daddy"! Or when a child hears a door open and says *dada* with rising intonation, this can be interpreted as a question such as "Is that daddy"?

After using babbling to express meaning, children are beginning to use single words to express their ideas. A marked feature of children's utterances is that they are frequently missing smaller parts—particularly the past tense marker -*ed*, the verb *be*, the possessive marker -*'s*, the plural ending -*s*, the definite article *the*, and the indefinite article *a*. Such early speech of children can also be described as "telegraphic speech", because children's speech lacks inflections and those small function words such as articles and prepositions, and because of its resemblance to the style of writing used in telegrams and classified ads. When one sends a telegram or runs a classified ad, they have to pay by the word; so there's a good reason to use as few words as possible. Children in the early stages of language learning also have to "pay by the word" as they struggle to put together their first sentences, and they too see the advantage of communicating as economically as possible (O'Grady, 2005). The following are some examples taken from a stage when children are already joining two words to form an utterance:

Allgone sticky (after the child had washed her hands)
Allgone outside (after closing the door)
More page (asking an adult to continue reading)
Sweater chair (indicating where the sweater is)

(Littlewood, 2000: 7)

As can be seen, children's first sentences are mostly two words in length. Many of children's early sentences seem to be built around a small number of pivot words, such as *allgone* in the above examples. These pivot words serve as hooks to which other words can be attached. They show up over and over again in the company of a variety of different words. More examples are: *see boy*, *see sock*, *see hot*; *push it*, *move it*, *close it*, *do it*.

It can be seen clearly that the situation plays an important role in conveying meaning since the utterances are so reduced. The result is that the same two words might convey different meanings in different situations. For instance, when a child picks up his mother's sock and says *mommy sock*, he expresses the relationship between the two words, as in the sentence *This is mommy's sock*. In another situation, for example, when the mother is dressing the baby, who might also say *mommy sock*, this time he means *Mommy is putting on my sock*. Even at this stage, we can see that children use the language creatively, since they use utterances which have never been heard. The above examples such as *allgone sticky* and *allgone outside* are children's own creations. Children, just like adults, are making use of an ability to combine items from a limited set so as to communicate meanings.

Researchers attempted to write "grammars" for children's two-word utterances in terms of two main classes of word: a restricted "pivot" class and a much larger open class. However, these attempts have not managed to account for all the two-word utterances which children have been heard to produce. A more fruitful approach has been to focus on the meanings expressed by these utterances. Lois Bloom (1970) found that utterances containing two nouns were used to express five kinds of relationship, as can be shown in Table 1.1. The interpretations depended on her observation of the child in an actual situation.

Table 1.1   Five Relationships Between Children's Two-word Utterances

Relationship	Examples	Possible Meaning
conjunction	cup glass	cup and glass
description	party hat	a party hat
possession	daddy hat	daddy's hat
location	sweater chair	The sweater is on the chair.
agent − object	mommy book	Mommy is reading a book.

Dan Slobin (1979), similarly, studied the communicative functions performed by two-word utterances in the speech of children who were acquiring six different languages. He found seven main types of function, as illustrated in Table 1.2.

Table 1.2   Seven Functions of Children's Two-word Utterances

Communicative Functions	Examples	Possible Meaning
locating or naming	there book	The book is there.
demanding or desiring	more milk	Give me more milk.
negating	not hungry	I am not hungry.
describing an event or situation	block fall	A block falls.
indicating possession	my shoe	This is my shoe.
describing a person/thing	pretty dress	The dress is pretty.
questioning	where ball	Where is the ball?

Another well-known analysis of the communicative function of children's speech is that of Michael Halliday (1975) . Halliday argued that language acquisition takes place because the child realizes he can do certain things with language, and that he learns these different functions in a predictable order. First, the child uses language to get what he wants ("instrumental" function); next, he uses language to control other people's behaviour ("regulatory" function), and so on. Halliday's "functional" approach to language and language learning has had considerable influence on second language teaching.

It should be noted that the study on the meanings and functions of children's speech has led many people to play down the role of a specific language-acquisition capacity in explaining children's development. They prefer to account for it more in terms of the child's growing mental capacity and communicative needs. The universal features in all languages are then seen as resulting from the common ways in which people think and interact—that is, from universal features of human cognition and social development.

1.5.2 Development of inflections and function words

As children's processing capacity grows, the telegraphic speech extends beyond the two-word stage, and longer utterances appear, which are still telegraphic. Examples are: *Andrew want that* and *Cat stand up table*. At this stage, children are on the way to acquiring inflections and function words. These small items are usually called *morphemes*. Here, we introduce Roger Brown's study (1973) about how three children acquired morphemes in their first language.

The findings came to have a wide influence for studies in both first language acquisition and second language learning. It was found that children do not master each morpheme suddenly, from one day to the next, but gradually, over a period of time. One problem is to decide at what point a morpheme should be counted as "acquired". Brown's criterion is that a child should produce it on 90 percent of the occasions when the adult grammar requires it. Based on this criterion, Brown found that the 14 morphemes were acquired in a sequence which was remarkably similar for the three children. Table 1.3 illustrates the "average" order of acquisition of morphemes.

Table 1. 3   Average Order of Acquisition of Morphemes

Order	Morphemes	Examples
1	present progressive *-ing*	Girl playing
2	preposition *on*	Boy on horse
3	preposition *in*	Truck in water
4	plural *-s*	cats，boys，fishes
5	irregular past forms	came，fell，went
6	possessive *'s*	Jack's，Bob's，Chris'
7	un – contractible copula	I am happy. He is happy. You are happy.
8	articles *the* and *a*	a dog，the dog
9	regular past *-ed*	lumped，jogged，wanted
10	regular third-person-singular *-s*	talks，sings，watches
11	irregular third-person-singular forms	He does. She has.
12	un-contractible auxiliary *be*	I am playing. She is playing. You are playing.
13	contractible copula	I'm happy. Pat's happy. Joe's happy. You're happy.
14	contractible auxiliary *be*	I'm playing. Pat's playing. Joe's playing. You're playing.

Brown also calculated the relative frequency of these morphemes in the speech of the children's parents. It was found that the order of frequency does not correlate with the order of acquisition, which therefore cannot be explained in simple habit-formation terms. This evidence shows that the child is an active contributor to the acquisition process.

Brown's research was longitudinal. That is, he studied the three children's performance over the actual period of time when they were mastering the morphemes. There were also cross-sectional studies of children's acquisition of the same morphemes. For example, one such a study was conducted on twenty-one children's use of these morphemes. The researchers examined how well the children performed with the morphemes and "scored" each morpheme according to how accurately it is produced by children. As a result, they found that the accuracy order was similar to the acquisition order which Brown had obtained（Littlewood，2000：10）.

Children's acquisition of verb inflections offers evidence for their active contribution to the learning process. Before mastering the regular past inflection *-ed* (for example, *she walked*), children produce a number of common irregular past forms, such as *came* and *went*. At this stage, these forms are simply individual words for children, not the result of a productive rule for forming the past tense. Then comes a stage in which children produced erroneous utterances such as *Where it goed?* and *It comed off*. This actually does not mean that children's acquisition order is from irregular to regular verb past forms. Nor is it a sign of regression. Instead, it is a sign of progress in children's developing system. The truth is that they have now mastered a rule for forming the past tense. It is this rule that leads children to produce *goed* and *comed*. Only later will he learn that *go* and *come* have irregular past tense, and they are exceptions to the rule. This will be further discussed in the coming chapter.

1.5.3 Development of negatives and interrogatives

While children are mastering morphemes, they are increasing their ability to produce more complicated utterances. The development of negatives and interrogatives has aroused researchers' interest. For both structures, children seem to follow similar sequences of development.

The sequence of children's acquisition of negatives has been observed and can be illustrated as follows: At first, the negative element is not part of the structure of the sentence, but is attached to the beginning or end, as in *No singing song*, and *No the sun shining*. Then comes the second stage, in which the negative element is inserted into the sentence, as in *I no want envelope*, *He no bite you*, and *He don't want it*. Children also begin to produce the appropriate part of *do*, *be*, or the modal verbs, to suit the person or tense, such as *You don't want some supper*, *Paul didn't laugh*, and *I am not a doctor*.

As for acquisition of interrogatives, there is also a predictable development for all children. Lightbown and Spada (2006) provided the examples of the acquisition of question formation. In stage 1, children use intonation in yes/no questions, as in *Cookie? Mommy book?* In stage 2, they use intonation with sentence complexity. For yes/no questions, they use declarative sentence order with rising intonation as in *You like this?* For *wh-* questions, a question word with declarative order is used as in *Why you catch it?* In stage 3, children begin to use inversion in yes/no question, but keep declarative order in *wh-* questions. Examples are *Can I go? Is that mine? Why you don't have one?* Stage 4 is

inversion. The auxiliary word *do* is used in yes/no questions, but still not in *wh-* questions. Children may say *Do you like ice cream? Where I can draw them?* In stage 5, inversion is used with *wh-* questions as in *Why can he go out?* But when negation needs to be included, the declarative form is maintained, as in *Why he can't go out?* In stage 6, children may over-generalize the rule for forming questions by saying, for example, *I don't know why can't he go out.*

Listed above are some findings in studying children's language development in first language acquisition. It must be pointed out that the evidence is not sufficient to determine whether all children pass through these same stages. When discussing second language acquisition, we will also see that, in the development of interlanguage, adults learning a second language go through such predictable sequences while acquiring certain structures. However, the situation with adult second language learning is more complex due to possible interference of their mother tongue.

Assignment

1. Questions for self-study.

(1) What is second language?

(2) What is second language acquisition?

(3) What are the aims of studying second language acquisition?

(4) What are the differences between second language acquisition and foreign language learning?

(5) What is the difference between "conversational input" and "non-conversational input"?

(6) How do you define "competence" and "performance"?

(7) What are the internal factors influencing the learning of a second language?

(8) What does "linguistic universals" mean?

(9) What's your understanding of cognitive mechanism in L2 learning?

(10) What are the characteristics of children's telegraphic speech? Give example to illustrate.

(11) What is the sequence of children's acquisition of morphemes found in Brown's study?

（12） How do native English children develop their interrogative structures? Give examples to illustrate.

2. Fill in the blanks with the right words.

Native language is "picked up" in _____ environment and in an informal manner. People generally learn to speak and use the language in real communicative contexts, and the primary focus is on _____ instead of linguistic forms. Native language is also tightly bound to native _____ , and because of this, it is often difficult to decode for a person from another culture. A target language, unlike native language, is often learned in classrooms in a _____ way. People learn to speak it in an unauthentic context. While people are learning it, their primary focus is on linguistic _____ first, and then move on gradually toward interactive communication.

The underlying knowledge of language is called _____ , while the actual use of language is called _____ .

3. Match the following terms in column I to the definitions in column II.

I	II
（1） first language	a. any language that is the aim of learning
（2） target language	b. a language which is acquired during childhood
（3） second language	c. a language that has no immediate practical application, which might be used later for travel or be required for school
（4） foreign language	d. an officially or socially dominant language, which is not the speaker's L1, but needed for education, employment or other basic purpose

4. Open discussion for pair or group work.

（1） Try to list all of the languages that you can use. First classify them as L1s and L2s, and then further classify the L2s as "second", "foreign", "library", "auxiliary", or "for special purposes". Then, distinguish between the ways you learned each of the languages: through informal exposure, formal instruction, or some combination of these.

（2） Think about the distinction between second language acquisition and foreign language learning as discussed in this chapter. Let's assume that they are fundamentally different. How would you explain the differences? Now take the opposite position, and defend your position. Also look at the distinction from a social point of view. Discuss in terms of specific examples from your experience, such as learning English in an English-speaking country, such as the United States or Great Britain, or learning English in a non-English country such as China.

(3) Discuss with your classmates the following statements, telling whether they are true or false. Give reasons or examples to justify your answers.

a. A second language refers to the language that is not spoken in the community where the learner is living.

b. A foreign language is the one that is learned and used in the classroom setting, but seldom used in real communicative environment outside the classroom.

c. Native language is acquired in the natural context, and it is not taught by a parent or a teacher in any formal way.

d. The purpose of studying second language acquisition is to improve teaching efficiency.

e. External factors that influence second language learning refer to those factors in the social surrounding, such as input and the learning environment.

f. A learner's first language system and the general world knowledge belong to the internal factors influencing the second language learning.

g. A second language learner often comprehends more than he or she can produce.

h. All children can learn a second language accent-free.

i. No adult can learn a second language accent-free.

j. Teaching a second language is as effective as learning a second language in the natural environment.

k. A person who speaks two languages equally well is bilingual.

l. A person who speaks three or more languages for different communicative purposes is multilingual.

m. Competence refers to the ability of using the language in a social context, while performance refers to the way a person behaves while communicating with others.

n. Language teaching in the classroom is a waste of time.

o. Everyone has a language acquisition device in the brain, so everyone can learn any language successfully.

p. General world knowledge is of great help to the learner, even if he or she is learning a foreign language.

(4) In Section 1.4, we discussed two external factors and five internal factors which may exert an influence upon an L2 learner. What other factors might there be that affect L2 learning in addition to those factors mentioned in the text?

(5) According to the L1 transfer, as is discussed in 1.4, there are two kinds of transfer: positive and negative. Study each of the following two sentences. Is it a result of negative transfer? If not, what causes the error?

a. *He comed late.*

b. *Give me two apple.*

(6) We have discussed two kinds of input in this chapter: conversational input and non-conversational input. Do you think there are any linguistic differences between conversational input and non-conversational input? Some hints are given below and think about the differences in the following aspects:

—level of formality

—length of utterances

—relative number of questions versus statements

—incomplete sentences

—range or type of vocabulary

(7) When defining "input" and "output", we hold a view that both input and output must be language that has certain kind of communicative intent. Why should it be so? Do you think the kind of language produced by learners during drills in the classroom is the same as the kind of language they produce when they are engaged in communicating an idea? Why or why not?

Chapter Two   The Study of Interlanguage

The notion of "interlanguage" (IL) has been central to the development of second language acquisition research. Interlanguage is viewed as a separate linguistic system which is different from both the learner's native language and the target language. The fundamental assumption in second language acquisition research is that while learners are acquiring a second language, they are creating their own language system. In light of this concept, the learner's speech is not a deficit system, filled with random errors, but a system of its own with its own structure. In this chapter we first give an introduction of interlanguage hypothesis, including its background and development. Then, we will briefly discuss the characteristics of interlanguage and present the major findings in interlanguage studies, in particular the developmental patterns of the learner language. Finally, we will present some recent studies in interlanguage pragmatics.

2. 1   Background to the Study of Interlanguage

The study of SLA started from the study of the language that learners produce at different stages of their development. The study of learner language (interlanguage) is necessary because it can provide researchers with important information about how learners learn an L2. An understanding of interlanguage and its characteristics is fundamental to the study of SLA. It paves the way for further investigation of SLA from linguistic, psychological, and socio-cultural perspectives in the following chapters.

It is necessary to briefly review the background to the study of interlanguage. In the late 1960s, researchers began to show considerable interest in the empirical study of L2 acquisition. Why did this happen? Two main reasons could explain such a phenomenon. One was related to the need to investigate the claims of competing theories. According to the early contrastive analysis hypothesis (CAH), L2 learners were strongly influenced by their L1. Thus, some researchers (for example, Lado, 1957), contended that errors were mainly the result of transfer of L1 habits. This theory of learning was challenged by Chomsky's attack on behaviorism and by the research on L1 acquisition. According to research on first language acquisition, children did not seem to learn their mother tongue as a set of habits but rather seem to construct mental rules. This challenge to CAH created the necessary climate for empirical study of L2 acquisition. Researchers asked, and attempted to find answers to, questions such as: Were learners' errors the result of L1 transfer? Did L2 learners, like L1 learners, construct unique mental rules? These questions could not be answered without the study of interlanguage.

The second main reason was directly connected with language pedagogy. Audiolingual method and oral/situational approach were the prevailing methods of the day. They both emphasized structuring the input to the learner and controlling output in order to minimize errors. However, it was noted that children were successful in acquiring L1 without such a structured learning environment. Also, many L2 learners seemed to be successful in learning an L2 in natural settings. Thus, it was even argued that the teacher's "interference" impedes, rather than facilitates, L2 learning in the classroom. But how did L2 learners learn in natural settings? What strategies did they use? What made some learners more successful than others? All these questions invite empirical enquiry. Many early SLA studies investigated L2 learners in naturalistic or mixed settings in order to find what experiences worked for them, so that suitable copies could be introduced into the language classroom.

The empirical studies, though mainly descriptive, were theoretical. In the late 1960s and 1970s a growing consensus was reached that behaviorist theories of L2 learning were inadequate. It was argued that learners' L2 development was guided by a "built-in-syllabus". The term "interlanguage" was coined to refer to the special mental grammars that learners constructed during the course of their development. Learners are playing an active role in constructing these grammars. Their behavior, including their errors, is rule-governed, and the language they produce—interlanguage—reflected the strategies they used to construct temporary grammatical rules.

2. 2　The Interlanguage Hypothesis

2. 2. 1　Definition of interlanguage

It is assumed that while a learner is learning a second language, he is building his own language system of abstract linguistic rules which serve as a base for his comprehension and production of the L2. This particular language system constructed by the learner is different from both his mother tongue and the target language. The American linguist, Larry Selinker (1972) introduced the term "Interlanguage" to refer to the system of a learner's language as it moves gradually from the L1 toward the target L2. The development of IL is considered a creative process, which is driven by inner forces in interaction with environmental factors and which is influenced both by L1 and by the input from the target language. A learner's interlanguage is a unique language system. The interlanguage is also called learner language since it is constructed by the learner.

There have been some slightly different conceptualizations of learner language. For example, Nemser (1971) referred to it as "approximative system", while Corder (1981) termed it "transitional competence". However, the notion of "interlanguage" seemed to prevail and was used in the literature on second language acquisition in the 1990s.

2. 2. 2　Development of the interlanguage hypothesis

The term interlanguage was defined as the separate linguistic system which could be evidenced when adult L2 learners attempt to express meaning in a language they are in the process of learning. The linguistic system includes not only phonology, morphology, and syntax, but also the lexical, pragmatic, and discourse levels of the interlanguage. Interlanguage is usually thought of as characteristic only of adult second language learners, who have passed puberty and thus cannot be expected to employ the language acquisition device (LAD) —the innate language learning structure that was instrumental in the acquisition of their native language. Children acquiring second languages are thought to have the ability to re-engage the LAD. Second language learners who begin their study of the L2 after puberty, however, do not succeed in developing a linguistic system as children do when acquiring that language natively. This observation led Selinker (1972) to hypothesize that adults use a latent psychological structure, instead of an LAD, to acquire second languages. Selinker claimed that interlanguage depends on five central processes that are part of the "latent psychological structure":

(1) Native language transfer. Although L1 transfer is not the only process involved, ample research evidence shows that it does play an important role in shaping learners' interlanguage systems. Selinker suggested that the way in which this happens is that learners make "interlingual identifications" in approaching the task of learning a second language: they perceive certain units as the same in their NL, IL and TL. For example, they may perceive NL "开" as exactly the same as TL "open" as in the expression "open the door", and develop an interlanguage in which "open" can be used (erroneously in terms of the TL) in expressions like "*open* the light", "*open* the meeting", and so on.

(2) Overgeneralization of target language rules. This psycholinguistic process is also widely observed in child language acquisition. The learner shows evidence of having mastered a general rule, but does not yet know all the exceptions to that rule. A well-known example is that the learner may use the past tense marker -*ed* for all verbs, regular and irregular alike. They may say "I *walked* to school", and "He *laughed*"; they may also say "I *goed* to school", and "He *drinked* beer".

(3) Transfer of training. Transfer of training occurs when L2 learners apply rules learned from teachers or textbooks. Sometimes such learning is successful; that is, the resulting interlanguage rule is the same as the target language rule. But sometimes errors occur. For example, a lesson plan or textbook that describes the past perfect tense as the "past past" can lead the learner to erroneously use the past perfect for the distant past. So, for example, they may say "*I had learned English in the 1980s*". Such errors are also called "induced errors".

(4) Strategies of communication. Strategies of communication are often used by L2 learners to resolve communication problems. When the learner attempts to communicate meaning and feels that the linguistic item needed is not available, he can resort to a variety of strategies of communication in getting the meaning across. We discussed eight communication strategies in chapter one, which are treated as the internal factors affecting L2 learning. In communicating meaning, L2 learners create linguistic forms and patterns which are different from idiomatic target language expressions. These linguistic forms and patterns used in such attempts may become more or less permanent parts of the learner's

interlanguage.

（5）Strategies of L2 learning. L2 learners use learning strategies in a conscious attempt to master the target language. One such strategy is simplification. For example, the learner "simplifies" English so that all verbs may occur in the present continuous, yielding sentences like "*I'm hearing him*". Another strategy is learners' conscious comparison of what they produce in the IL with the NL, setting up interlingual identifications. Other examples of learning strategies are the use of mnemonics to remember target vocabulary, the memorizing of verb declensions or textbook dialogues, the use of flash cards, and so on. Research evidence showed that all five of these psycholinguistic processes could affect the construction of interlanguages.

2.2.3　The revised interlanguage hypothesis

Since its first detailed proposal in 1972, the interlanguage hypothesis has experienced some modifications and expansions. The first expansion is the inclusion of children's second language acquisition. The original interlanguage hypothesis was restricted to apply only to adults acquiring second languages. However, evidence emerged that children in language immersion programs also produced interlanguages, resulting from L1 transfer. There appear to be sociolinguistic reasons for this phenomenon. The children receive native-speaker input only from their teacher, and give one another non-native input. Therefore, they did not have enough opportunity or incentive to produce what Swain calls "comprehensible output". To the extent that these children produce interlanguages in these contexts, there is some question whether they are using LADs to internalize the target language or whether they are using those psycholinguistic processes described as more characteristic of adults learning second languages. More research is needed to find out how they differ from adult learners.

A second expansion of the interlanguage hypothesis has occurred in response to the growing interest in the influence of universal grammar (UG) on the development of interlanguage. The crucial question was this: UG is assumed to be central to the development of natural languages, but is interlanguage a natural language? Two positions are taken in response to this question. The first position, as Selinker's initial hypothesis takes, is that it is not, at least as the notion "natural language" has been defined in linguistics. This early position argues that natural languages are produced by LADs; language universals exist in human languages by virtue of the way in which the language acquisition device is structured;

but interlanguages fossilize and evidence native language transfer; interlanguages therefore are a product of latent psychological structures, not LADs; so, interlanguages do not have to obey language universals. The opposing position holds that interlanguages are natural languages, and have to obey language universals. Central to this position is the view that interlanguages are products of the same language acquisition device that produces native languages. In this view, interlanguages fossilize because of complex changes in cases where parameters have already been set for one language and a second language must be learned. The debate on this issue is still going on.

A third modification has been a growing emphasis on the way in which interlanguage development seems to vary in different social context, or discourse domains. Increasing evidence seems to show that learners can produce more fluent, grammatical, and transfer-free interlanguage in some social contexts than in others. For example, international teaching assistants may be more fluent and grammatical in lecturing on their academic field than when talking about an everyday topic like favorite foods or bicycling. Key processes such as fossilization may be more prominent for a given learner in one context than in another.

A fourth issue centers on the phenomenon of fossilization itself and whether it is inevitable. It was argued by Selinker that no adult learner can hope to speak a second language in such a way that he or she is indistinguishable from the native speakers of that language. There are inevitable forces leading to the cessation of learning. There are neurolinguistic reasons for this inevitability. There is a very common case where an adult learner's phonological system may fossilize, but the morphology, syntax, and lexicon may not, continuing to develop until reaching full identity with the target language. Scovel (1988), like Selinker, argued that the causes of phonological fossilization are neurolinguistic in nature and related to the process of cerebral lateralization, which is completed at puberty. Those who claim that fossilization is caused by sociolinguistic forces argued that fossilization is not an inevitable process. Such researchers suggest that if learners can identify with the target social group, or if the need is great enough, they will be able to continue learning the second language until their production and perception is indistinguishable from that of native speakers. It should be noted that this issue also is far from settled since it relates to matters of human potential rather than human's actual behavior.

Finally, research on interlanguage has expanded far beyond its original focus on phonology, morphology, syntax, and lexis, to include the sociolinguistic component of communicative competence. Research on interlanguage includes comparative work on the way in which learners execute speech acts across three linguistic systems. For example, Cohen and Olshtain (1981) have studied the way learners attempt to apologize, using their interlanguage, in target language social contexts, and compared this to the way native speakers apologize in the same contexts.

In short, the interlanguage hypothesis provided the initial spark that ignited a field of research on SLA, and it continues to provide what some feel to be the most productive framework for research.

2.3 Characteristics of Interlanguage

In the previous section we had a brief review of the development of interlanguage hypothesis. Now we are looking at the basic features of interlanguage. As a unique type of language, interlanguage has its own characteristics:

(1) Interlanguage consists of errors.

The reason why we pay much attention to errors is that they are an obvious feature of learner language. Errors are evidence of the state of a learner's knowledge of the L2. An error is different from what we call a "mistake". A mistake is akin to slips of the tongue. They are generally one-time-only events. The speaker who makes a mistake is able to recognize it as a mistake and correct it if necessary. An error, however, is systematic. That is, it is likely to occur repeatedly and is not recognized by the learner as an error. The learner in this case has incorporated a particular erroneous form (from the perspective of the TL) into his own system.

Errors are not only systematic; many of them are also universal. That is, a kind of error found in one learner's speech is often attested in the speech of many other learners. What's more, some errors are common only to learners who share the same mother tongue. Errors can have different sources. Learners may commit errors of omission when they attempt to make the task of learning and using the L2 simpler. For example, they may leave out articles "a" and "the" and leave the -s off plural nouns. They may make overgeneralization errors when they overgeneralize forms that they find easy to learn, as in using "eated" instead of "ate". Learners also make transfer errors when they attempt to make use of their L1 knowledge. By studying errors, we can see that learners are actively involved in shaping the "grammars" they are learning, and that they are "creating" their own rules. To understand how learners acquire an L2, researchers use error analysis as a tool. This will be discussed in more detail in chapter three.

(2) The learner's grammar is dynamic.

The second language learner's interlanguage is constantly changing. However, he does not jump from one stage to the next, but rather slowly revises the interim system to accommodate new hypotheses about the target language system. This change is described as discontinuous progression "from stable plateau to stable plateau" (Selinker, 1992: 226). For example, at the beginning, learners may build a very simple grammar in which only one form of the verb is used, such as "walk" used in all cases. But over time, they learn more other forms, such as "walking" and "walked", gradually sorting out the functions these verbs are used to perform. In such a process, an old "rule" is superseded by a new "rule".

A new rule spreads in the sense that its coverage gradually extends over a range of linguistic contexts. For example, early WH questions are typically non-inverted (for example, "What you want?"), but when the learner acquires the subject inversion rule, he may first apply the rule to a limited number of verbs and WH pronouns such as "who" and "what". Later he extends the rule, by making it apply both to an increasing range of verbs and to other WH pronouns. Such a process of constant revision and extension of rules is a feature of the inherent instability of interlanguage and its built-in propensity for change. This results in a succession of interim grammars. That is, learners change their grammar from one time to another by adding rules, removing rules and reorganizing the whole system.

(3) Interlanguage is a reduced system.

It was suggested that the L2 learner' starting point is the same as in L1 acquisition. It is a "basic" system consisting of lexical items and a few simple rules for sequencing them. This system constitutes the "initial hypothesis" and may be universal (that is, all languages, when stripped down, result in the same basic system). The fact that IL is a reduced system can be proved by the errors learners produce while constructing their grammars. For example, learners who make omission errors are in some way simplifying the learning task by ignoring more complicated grammatical features. In this case, interlanguage is a reduced system, both in form and function. The characteristic of reduced form refers to the less complex grammatical structures that typically occur in an IL compared to the TL. Examples like *he borrow a book yesterday* belong to reduced form since there is an omission of past tense suffix after the verb *borrow*. The characteristic of reduced function refers to the smaller range of communicative needs typically served by an IL, especially if the learner is still in contact with members of the L1 speech community. For example, when they want to ask for help, they may use the L1 to perform the function.

(4) Interlanguage is likely to fossilize.

According to Selinker, only about five percent of learners go on to develop the same mental grammar as native speakers. Most learners stop some way short, making no further progress. This kind of phenomenon is called fossilization. The *Random House Dictionary of the English Language* defines fossilization of a linguistic form, feature, rule, and so forth in the following way: "to become permanently established in the interlanguage of a second language learner in a form that is deviant from the target-language norm and that continues to appear in performance regardless of further exposure to the target language."

A central characteristic of any interlanguage is that it fossilizes, that is, it stops to develop at some point, falling short of full identity with the target language. Unlike children acquiring their native language, the adult second language learner never achieves a level of facility in the use of the target language. Fossilization refers to a process in second or foreign language learning, in which incorrect linguistic features become a stabilized part of the way a person speaks or writes a language. Aspects of pronunciation, vocabulary usage, and grammar may become fixed or fossilized. Fossilization does not occur in L1 acquisition. It is unique to L2 grammars.

2.4 Major Findings in Interlanguage Studies

The research in interlanguage has yielded substantive findings. We firmly believe that these findings in IL studies are invaluable in producing indirect implications for second language learning and teaching. In this part, we will summarize some main findings in terms of three principles governing IL developments: systematic change in grammar, acquisition orders and developmental sequences, and influence of learners' L1.

2.4.1　Systematic change in grammar

In the studies of interlanguage, one of the focuses was on whether interlanguage grammar is systematic. Despite the variability of interlanguage, it is possible to detect the rule-based nature of learners' use of L2. In this section we mainly focus on the systematicity of interlanguage grammar. First, look at the following examples:

No look my card.
Don't look my card.

The above two examples are from Ellis' (1984) study of a 10-year-old Portuguese child. This boy produced two negative utterances within minutes during the same game of word bingo, for the same purpose and in the same context, while he was addressing the same person and with similar amount of planning time. Learners such as the boy begin to use two more forms of grammar freely, that is, in a non-systematic way. Other examples are from Wagner-Gough (1975):

Giving me the book.
Give me the book.

Obviously, the speaker uses *v-ing* form and simple verb form to perform the same function of request. The random changes in grammar are called free variation. It characterizes a learner's interlanguage at the early stage of second language learning. However, later on, it can be found that the changes in learner grammar are not random, but systematic. This is because different changes take place at different stages of development. Initially, it can be assumed that learners begin by acquiring a single form (such as simple form of a verb) and use it for a variety of functions (such as referring to future, present, and past time). Later, they acquire other verb forms but use them interchangeably with the simple form. For example, when learners first acquire the past tense form of a verb (for example, "painted"), they are likely to use it in free variation with the simple form of the verb "paint". Shortly after that, they begin to use the forms systematically. For example, they use "painted" in planned discourse and "paint" in unplanned discourse. Finally, they eliminate the non-target form and use the target-language form to perform the same function as native speakers, using "painted" consistently to refer to past time.

By systematic change, we mean that the change is rule-governed. That is, we may be able to explain and even predict when learners use one form and when another. But what are the rules? Three key points illustrate the contexts upon which changes in IL grammar depend: linguistic context, situational context, and psycholinguistic context.

2.4.1.1 Linguistic context

Some research findings show that interlanguage changes are affected by linguistic context. These changes may occur at the level of phonology. An early study (Dickerson, 1975) investigating phonological variation by native Japanese speakers learning English found that the sound /r/ was more frequently used before a low vowel, for example /a/, than before a mid-vowel, for example /ɛ/, or /ɔ/, and more frequently before a mid – vowel than before a high vowel such as /i/ or /u/. Similarly, another study (Sato, 1984) considered the reduction of consonant clusters in English by two Vietnamese children. A difference was noted in the TL production of consonant clusters depending on whether the cluster was at the beginning of the syllable or at the end. Syllable-initial clusters were more accurately produced than syllable-final clusters.

More interlanguage changes could be found at the level of morphology. One of the findings is that learners' choice of past tense marker depends partially on the type of the verb, e.g., whether it is an event verb, an activity verb or a state verb. Learners find it easier to mark verbs for past tense if the verb refers to events (for example, "arrive"), somewhat more difficult to mark verbs that refer to activities (for example, "sleep"), and most difficult to mark verbs referring to states (for example, "seem"). The kind of verbs affects the kind of errors made by learners. With activity verbs, learners tend to use the progressive form instead of the past tense. With state verbs, they tend to use the simple form. For example:

He _arrived_ at noon. (event verb)
After that we _sleeping_ in the tent. (activity verb)
Last night everything _seem_ very quiet and peaceful. (state verb)

A similar interesting finding in an investigation (Wolfram, 1989) was that Vietnamese learners of L2 English in the United States were more likely to manifest past tense marking on suppletive forms (such as *go/went*) than on replacive forms (such as *make/made*). This change may be caused by a "principle of perceptual saliency" as suggested by Wolfram. That is, the more distant the past tense form is phonetically from the present tense form, the more likely it is to be marked for the past tense.

Another finding is that learners may behave differently depending on whether or not an adverb of frequency (for example, *every day* or *usually*) occurs with an activity verb. In a sentence which refers to past time but which does not have an adverb of frequency, learners are likely to use a progressive marker. For example, a learner may say *John watching TV* to mean "John watched TV all the time". However, in a sentence with such an adverb, learners are more likely to use the base form of the verb. Thus, one may say *John usually watch TV every day* instead of *John usually watched TV every day*. From these two examples, we can see one linguistic form can trigger the use of another form.

Evidence of interlanguage variation caused by linguistic context can also be found at the level of syntax. For example, the effects of linguistic context are also felt in learners' use of the verb "to be". Learners sometimes use full "be" (such as *is*), sometimes contracted "be" (such as *'s*), and sometimes omit "be" entirely. Which one is used is also determined by the linguistic context. It is found that the choice of the three forms is related to the type of subject of a sentence. If the subject of the sentence is a pronoun, the learner may use the full "be" form or its contracted form, as in the sentence *He is not here* or *He's not here*. If the subject is a noun, "be" is more likely to be omitted as in *Teacher not here*. More examples:

—*Is Tom here?*
—*He is not here. /He's not here.*
......
—*Some didn't come. Can you name a few?*
—*Tom not here. Jack not here...*

2. 4. 1. 2　Situational context

Learners change their use of language according to the situation they are involved in. Just like native speakers, L2 learners are influenced by situational factors, and in particular, by their addressee. That is, they are sensitive to the person they are talking to. For example, in an interview, the interviewees, Chinese-Thai bilinguals adapt their speech by using more Thai phonological variants with the Thai interviewer, and more Chinese variants with the Chinese interviewer. Another aspect of the situation to which learners are sensitive is topic. It is found in a study by Selinker and Douglas (1985) that Polish ESL learners vary their learner language noticeably on a number of linguistic features according to whether the discourse is concerned with an everyday topic or a specialized, technical topic. Besides, the attitude which learners have towards a topic also affects their language behavior. If they see themselves as experts, for example, they may be more likely to interrupt.

The study of interlanguage variation is greatly influenced by the study of style shifting. For example, according to Tarone (1983), L2 learners possess a continuum of styles, ranging from careful style to vernacular style. The former reflects the kind of language in formal situations that require careful language use, while the latter is evident in informal situations in which there is more spontaneous language use. Each style has its linguistic norms, and learners change their style in accordance with the demands of the situation. Learners are more likely to use the correct target-language forms in formal contexts and non-target forms in informal contexts.

2. 4. 1. 3　Psycholinguistic context

Another factor which accounts for the systematic change in IL grammar is the psycholinguistic context. There are some important factors. One of them is attention. If learners focus more attention to linguistic forms, accuracy will increase. Another important factor is planning time. This is related to whether learners have the opportunity to plan their speech production or not. A second language learner will be more careful in selecting grammatical forms and is more likely to produce correct speech when he has time to prepare what he is going to say. On the other hand, when he is making a spontaneous speech or having an online talk, more errors would occur since he does not have time to plan his speech. However, if the effort and time is required to plan the propositional content or to produce complex sentences, learners may be inhibited from attending to specific linguistic forms.

The above findings may provide some insights into the process of SLA. It reveals the way form-function relationships in IL evolve over time, partly reflecting patterns of variable use at an earlier point of time. They also have implications for language teaching and testing. The fact that ILs are shown to be partly systematic, even in those areas where they are variable, means that they are potentially susceptible to systematic change through instruction.

2.4.2 Acquisition order and sequence of acquisition

Interlanguages also exhibit common acquisition order and the sequence of acquisition. Acquisition order concerns whether learners acquire the grammatical structures of an L2 in a definite order. For example, do they learn a feature before another? The sequence of acquisition, however, concerns the learning of a particular grammatical feature. The relevant question is whether learners acquire a grammatical structure in a single step or proceed through a number of interim stages before they master the target structure.

2.4.2.1 The order of acquisition

In order to " discover " the order of acquisition, researchers choose a number of grammatical structures to study. They collect samples of learner language and identify how accurately each feature is used by different learners. Then they get an accuracy order by ranking the features according to how accurately each feature is used by learners. It is argued that the accuracy order must be the same as the order of acquisition, for the more accurately learners are able to use a particular feature the more likely they are to have acquired that feature early. Roger Brown's (1973) morpheme order studies within the context of child language acquisition became the cornerstone of early work in SLA. He observed that there was a predictable order of acquisition of certain inflectional morphemes in English.

In SLA, early learner language is characterized by a silent period, extensive use of formulaic expressions, and structural and semantic simplification, particularly in natural learning context. Early studies of the order of acquisition of grammatical morphemes produced mixed results. The difference was in whether learners focused on form or meaning. It was reported that there is a consistent accuracy order when the learners focus on communicating meaning (while a different order occurs only when the learners are able to focus on form rather than the meaning of their utterances）. More other studies showed that there is a definite accuracy order and that this order remains more or less the same regardless of the learners' mother tongue, their age, and whether or not they have received formal language instruction. Based on these studies, Krashen（1977）even proposed a "natural order" of acquisition, which can be roughly described as three layers of order as shown below, the first layer of inflections being the easiest, while third layer being the most difficult to learn：

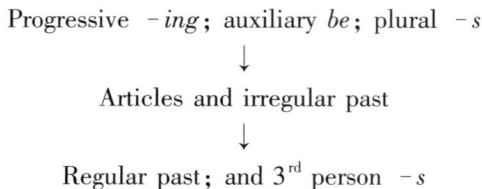

Progressive *-ing*; auxiliary *be*; plural *-s*

↓

Articles and irregular past

↓

Regular past; and 3rd person *-s*

It should be noted here that the above research on the order of acquisition has been criticized on a number of grounds. Some say it is wrong to assume that the order of accuracy is equal to the order of acquisition. Others have shown that the order does change somewhat according to the learner's first language. There may also be a misunderstanding that the research treats acquisition as if it is a process of accumulating linguistic structures, with one to be learnt before or after another. The truth might be that even the learning of the simplest structure goes through a process of gradual development. This can be shown by the study of sequence of acquisition.

Whereas the early findings of order of acquisition of morphemes were not fully convincing, more recent studies of the acquisition of tense and aspect and syntactical structures lend strong support to the existence of development sequences. Learners of different L2s manifest similar patterns of development when acquiring tense and aspect. This is evident in both meaning-based and form-based analyses. For example, a constant order of acquisition reported by Klein（1995）is：①third person -s and present tense copula, ②irregular past tense forms and *v-ing*, ③present perfect forms, ④regular past tense forms, ⑤future with "shall" or "will", ⑥ past perfect forms. Bardovi‐Harlig（2000）reported a similar acquisition order in her longitudinal study of 16 learners of L2 English from 4 different language backgrounds：past → past progressive → present perfect → past perfect. She also identified 4 general principles：First, acquisition is slow and gradual. Second, form often precedes function. That is, when a given morpheme first appears it is overgeneralized and thus lacks a clear contrast with existing forms. Third, irregular morphology precedes regular morphology. This is likely to reflect the fact that irregular forms are acquired as distinct lexical items. Fourth, when learners are acquiring compound verb tenses such as the present/past progressive and the present/past perfect, they begin by using a verb with verbal suffix (for example, "eating") and only subsequently produce verbs with auxiliaries (for example, "is eating").

2. 4. 2. 2 Sequence of acquisition

The process of learning a particular grammatical structure is seen as a process which involves reconstruction or reorganization. A well-known learning pattern during the process of learning an L2 is called a U-shaped pattern. The U-shaped pattern reflects three or more stages of linguistic use. Lightbown's study (1983) of the use of the -*ing* form from French learners of English showed a three-stage U-shaped learning sequence. At the beginning, learners produced error-free forms like *He is taking a cake*. At stage 2, learners appear to lose what they knew at the first stage. A typical utterance is *He take a cake*, which is different from the TL norm. The final stage looks just like stage one; the correct TL usage appears again. The whole process can be illustrated in Figure 2. 1.

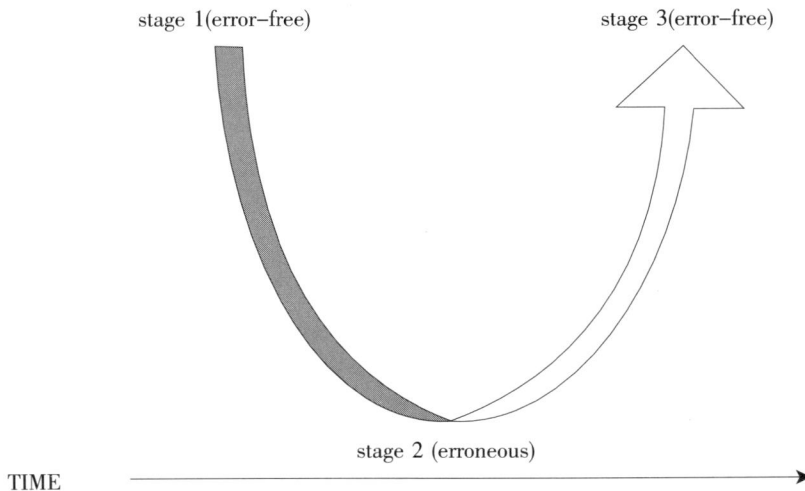

Figure 2. 1   **U-shaped Learning Pattern**

Ellis (2000) cited another example to show how L2 learners acquire irregular past tense form "ate" and discovered a five-stage U-shaped learning process. At stage 1, learners fail to mark the verb for past tense, using "eat" in all cases. At stage 2, they begin to produce the correct form "ate". At stage 3, however, learners overgeneralize the regular past tense form, and begin to use "eated". Next, some learners produce the hybrid form "ated", and finally at stage 5, they master the correct irregular past tense form. The whole process is shown in Figure 2.2.

The sequences of learning are instructive because they reveal that the correct initial use of a form, such as stage 2, does not always mean that the form is "acquired". Learners who produce "eated" and "ated", in fact, are more advanced than those at stage 2 who produce "ate". Indeed, learners follow a U-shaped course of development. This is so because learners reorganize their existing knowledge in order to accommodate new knowledge. Thus stages 3 and 4 arise when learners have begun to acquire the regular -ed form such as *jumped*. Forms like "eated" and "ated" show an overgeneralization of the regular -ed past tense. This is called restructuring. When they restructure the grammatical system, they may seem to slip back. But in fact, they are advancing on the way of learning.

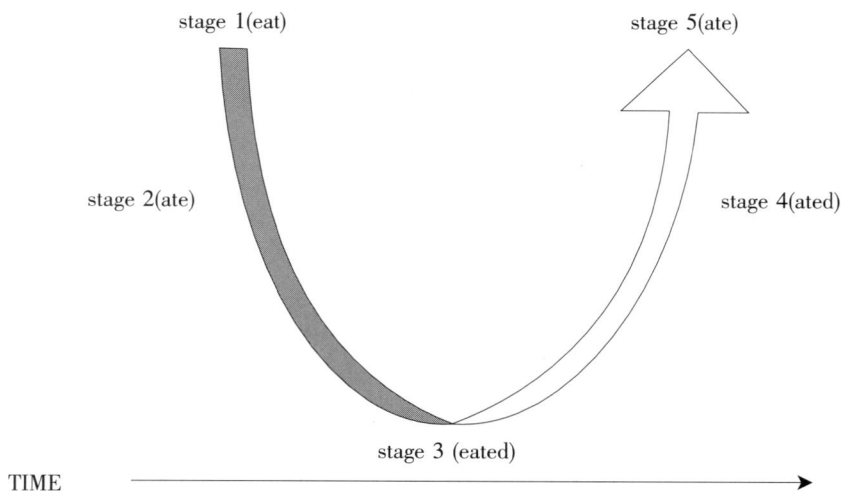

stage 1(eat)   stage 5(ate)

stage 2(ate)   stage 4(ated)

stage 3 (eated)

TIME ⟶

Figure 2.2   U-shaped Learning Process of "Ate"

In case of syntactic structures, regularities are also evident. The acquisition of English and German negation involves a series of transitional stages in which learners gradually switch from external negation (for example, "No you are playing here") to internal negation (for example, "Mariana not coming today") and from preverbal to post-verbal negation. The sequence is shown in Table 2.1.

Table 2.1 General Stages in the Sequence of Acquisition of L2 English Negation (Ellis, 2013: 93)

Stage	Description	Example
1	External negation (i. e. "no" or "not" is placed at the beginning of the utterance)	No you are playing here.
2	Internal negation (i. e. the negator— "no", "not" or "don't" is placed between the subject and the main verb)	Mariana not coming today.
3	Negative attachment to modal verbs	I can't play that one.
4	Negative attachment to auxiliary verb as in target language rule	She didn't believe me. He didn't said it.

The study of L2 phonology has provided evidence of developmental sequences. Various influences—the learners' L1, the universal properties of language, and uniquely developmental processes—conspire to shape the path of acquisition. Thus, learners' acquisition of closed syllable structure shows a staged progression: consonant deletion→ epenthesis→feature substitution→target form.

A comparison of developmental patterns found in L1 (as shown in chapter one) and L2 acquisition lends partial support to the L1 = L2 hypothesis. Some striking similarities have been found in syntactic structures such as negatives, though there are differences. When engaging in informal learning, adult L2 learners are more likely to manifest similar patterns of acquisition to children acquiring their mother tongue, but differences occur when they use formal learning strategies.

2.4.3 L1 influence

L1 influence has been a key issue in SLA for a long time. According to Contrastive

Analysis Hypothesis （CAH）, developed early in the 1950s and 1960s, it was widely believed that L1 played a decisive and negative role in SLA. This was called 'interference', and interference could be predicted by systematically comparing and contrasting the learner's L1 and L2, looking at the points of difference between the two. However, this strong view of CAH has not been supported by research findings. The following quotations may enable us to see whether language transfer is important in forming interlanguages:

Interference, or native to target language transfer, plays such a small role in language learning performance. （Whiteman and Jackson, 1972: 40）

Direct interference from the mother tongue is not a useful assumption. （George, 1972: 45）

Language background did not have a significant effect on the way ESL learners order English morphemes. （Larsen – Freeman, 1978: 372）

Since the late 1970s, research on the role of the native language has taken on a different view, advocating a non-behaviorist position and questioning the assumption that language transfer has to be part of behaviorism. Transfer can be viewed as a creative process. Researchers interested in SLA were less interested in a wholesale acceptance or rejection of the role of the native language. Rather, the emphasis was on the determination of *how* and *when* L1 influences SLA and on the explanations for the phenomenon. Most important in this discussion is the broadening and reconceptualization of language transfer. The term *cross-linguistic influence* is suggested to refer to the general influence of L1 on learners' IL. Here we will discuss some relevant issues related to L1 influence.

2.4.3.1 Avoidance

When speaking or writing in a second language, a learner may often try to avoid using a difficult word or structure, and will use a simpler word or structure instead. This is called avoidance in SLA. For example, a learner who is not sure of the use of the relative clause in English （such as *That's the building where I live*） may avoid using it and use two short sentences instead: *That's my building. I live there.*

How does this occur? There is evidence in SLA research that native language may influence which structures a learner produces and which are not produced. However, the source of avoidance is disputable. It may be that the differences between L1 and L2 are the major source of avoidance. There is also evidence that the opposite occurs. That is, when great similarities exist between L1 and L2, the learner may doubt these similarities are real.

Another view holds that avoidance has less to do with NL-TL differences, but rather is based on the complexity of the L2 structures in question. This is supported by a study conducted by Dagut and Laufer (1985). They found that Hebrew-speaking learners of English (Hebrew has no phrasal verbs) generally preferred the one-word equivalent of the phrasal verbs. For example, they use *enter*, *remove*, *save*, *stop*, *disappoint*, *confuse* instead of *come in*, *take away*, *lay aside*, *shut off*, *let down*, *mix up*. Within the category of phrasal verbs, they preferred those that are semantically more transparent (for example, *come in*, *take away*) to those that are less transparent (for example, *let down*, *mix up*). Therefore, it was concluded that the complexity of the target language structure had a greater impact on the issue of avoidance than did L1-L2 differences.

In another study of Swedish learners of English (Laufer and Eliasson, 1993), attention was focused on the use or avoidance of English phrasal verbs (*pick up*, *put down*). Two tests (a multiple-choice test and a translation test) were given to advanced Swedish-speaking learners of English (Swedish is a language with phrasal verbs). The researchers considered whether the responses to (or translations of) Swedish phrasal verbs consisted of single-verb synonyms or English phrasal verbs. The results were compared with the results from Hebrew-speaking learners of English. Different types of phrasal verbs were considered, including figurative ones (for example, back up = support, turn up = arrive) and literal ones (for example, come down = descend, put in = insert). It was found that the best predictor of avoidance is the L1-L2 differences. Although L1-L2 similarity and L2 complexity have a role, the only factor that consistently predicts avoidance is the L1-L2 difference.

2.4.3.2 Different paths

The influence of L1 can also be felt in the direction of interlanguage development. Here we review a study done by Zobl (1982) first. In Zobl's study, there were two subjects, a Chinese-speaking child and a Spanish-speaking child, who were acquiring the definite article *the*. The Chinese child tended to use *this* to serve the function of a definitizer. When even there is native speaker modeling of the definite article *the*, it is deleted or changed to *this*, as can be seen from the following data:

NS	**Chinese-speaking child**
Is this airplane your brother's?	*This airplane is…*
Show me the airplane.	*Show me airplane?*
Put it on the chair.	*Chair? This one?*
Ask Jim "Where's the turtle?"	*Jim, where's turtle?*
You want to push the pen.	*I want to push pen. Push, pencil.*
Is this table dirty?	*Yes, this is dirty. Table is dirty.*
Whose bike is this?	*This…Edmond's. Mark, I want this bike.*
What are you going to do with the paper?	*I want this paper school.*
Ask Jim if he can play with the ball.	*Jim, can you play the ball?*
Ask Jim if you can have the pencil?	*Jim, you want this pencil?*
Is he washing the car? What's he doing?	*Washing car.*

However, from the data with the Spanish-speaking child, both *this* and *the* were frequent, as can be seen in the samples below:

Hey hey this. Here the toy.
The car.
Lookit this. Lookit this cowboy.
Here. This cowboy.
Indians D'Indians. That d'Indians.
This one…that truck.
I gonna open that door.
Get the car.
Shut the door.
Same thing this car.

It can be seen that the differences between these two children suggest that facts of native languages lead them down two different paths—the Chinese child through a stage in which *this* occurs before the definite article, and the Spanish child to a starting point in which the definite article and the demonstrative *this* co-occur.

2. 4. 3. 3　Overproduction

Not only are there different paths for development, but also there are different uses of forms depending on the native language. For example, it was found from the English compositions written by Chinese and Japanese speakers that they overproduced extraposed structure (for example, "*It is very unfortunate that…*") and existential structures (for example, "*There is a small restaurant near my house in my country. May things of the restaurant are like those…*"). It was claimed that these structures were being used to carry the weight of a particular discourse function, even though the TL makes use of other forms for that same function.

Schachter and Rutherford (1979) hypothesized that the native language plays a role here. That is, there is an influence of L1 function (the need to express topic-comment type structures) to L2 form. Both Chinese and Japanese contain the type of sentence that heavily relies on the concept of topic. Sentences are organized around a topic – comment structure (for example, "*As for meat* [topic], *we don't eat it anymore* [comment]."). Han (2000) refers to this structure as a pseudo-passive and claimed that it becomes more like a target-like passive as learners become more syntactically sophisticated. She examined the spontaneous writing of two advanced Chinese learners of English and found both a true passive and a structure that looks more like a topic-comment structure in the same writing, as is shown below:

They told me that the attractive offer will be sent to me a bit later since what I sent them have not received.

The first part of the sentence includes a target-like passive, whereas the second part, *what I sent them have not received*, is more L1-like. *What I sent them* is the topic, and *have not received* is the comment. What is noteworthy, however, is that the first part of the sentence may be somewhat formulaic and may have been used as a formulaic chunk from a letter the writer had received. Obviously, this example shows that L1 exerts a subtle influence even at later stages of proficiency. Overproduction of certain structures by L2 learners is the result of influence of L1 function.

2.4.3.4　Differential learning rates

L1 transfer can be viewed as a facilitation of learning. This hypothesis is supported by Ard and Homburg (1992) who advocated a return to the original concepts embodied in the terminology of the psychology of learning. In a study, they compared the responses of two groups of learners (Spanish and Arabic) to the vocabulary section of a standard test of English. The response patterns were of major interest. One would expect differences in response patterns to those items in which a Spanish word and an English word were cognates, as in the following example.

It was the first time I ever saw her *mute*.

> (a) shocked
> (b) crying
> (c) smiling
> (d) silent

but not to items in which all words were equally distant from the native languages of the learners, as in the example below.

The door swung slowly on its old _____.

> (a) fringes
> (b) braids
> (c) clips
> (d) hinges

It was found that the Spanish learners did consistently better on this latter type of item than did the Arabic speakers. Ard and Homburg discussed this in light of learning time and hence accelerated learning rates. Because so many cognates exist between their NL and the TL, the Spanish speakers can focus more of their learning time on other aspects of language (other vocabulary items). It is the concentration on other vocabulary which results in a facilitation of learning. Thus, knowing a language that is related in some way to the TL can help in many ways, only some of which can be accounted for by the mechanical carryover of items and structures.

There is another perspective on the concept of differential learning rates. An NL structure that corresponded to a TL developmental sequence was a factor in preventing learners from moving on to the next sequential stage. In other words, the learners' L2 internal grammar system exhibited delayed reorganization. The evidence from Henkes' study could lend support to this view. Three children (French, Arabic, Spanish) were observed in their acquisition of English copula -*be*. Zobel (1982) pointed out an interesting fact that whereas the Arabic child continued to use the copula variably, even at an advanced state of syntactic acquisition, the other two children regularly employed the copula at this stage. Thus, although the same pattern of copula use was observed in all three children, it took the Arabic child longer to get the facts of English straightened out due to the absence of the category in the native language. The influence of different L1s (Spanish, French, and Arabic) on the acquisition of the English copula -*be* can be attributed to the following facts:

Spanish: *Su casa es vieja.* (His house is old.)
French: *Sa maison est vieille.* (His house is old.)
Arabis: *baytuhu qadimun.* (House his old.)

2.5   Interlanguage Pragmatics

Above we have discussed the unique interlanguage system inside the learner's mind, its characteristics and systematic variation. In this part, we will look at the "outside" use of the interlanguage in a particular social context, the interlanguage pragmatics. Interlanguage pragmatics deals with both the acquisition and use of L2 pragmatic knowledge. As is known, learning a second language not only involves the learning of pronunciation, lexical items, sentence construction, but also involves the learning of the appropriate way of using these words and sentences in the second language. For example, when we hear *Is George there?* on the telephone, we know that this question is not only a request for information, but also a request to speak with that person. If an L2 learner responds to the question on the basis of an information request, saying *Yes*, without calling that person to the phone, it can be said that he or she has failed to understand the pragmatic force beyond the literal meaning of the utterance *Is George there*. Look at another example:

Context: It is raining hard. Mary is leaving her office, but she doesn't know where her umbrella is. She looks worried, saying:

I can't find my umbrella.

How do you respond to this utterance? Does Mary simply utter a fact that she can't find her umbrella, or she has lost it, as is shown in the following conversation:

—*Can you find your umbrella?*
—*No. I can't find my umbrella.*

If you think so, you have not understood the intention of Mary's utterance. In this particular context, Mary's utterance is a request for help rather than a statement of a fact. What she needs urgently is the hearer's help of looking for the umbrella. Therefore, the following response proves to be socially "wrong", though it is grammatically correct.

—*I can't find my umbrella.*
—*Oh, I'm sorry to hear that.*

2.5.1 Second language speech act

According to speech act theory, the performance of a speech act involves the performance of three types of act: a locutionary act (the act of saying), an illocutionary act (the performance of a particular language function by what is said) and a perlocutionary act (the achieving of some kind of effect on the addressee). The term speech act is generally used to refer exclusively to "illocutionary act". Much of the research in interlanguage pragmatics has been conducted within the framework of speech acts. Speech acts can be thought of as functions of language. For example, requesting, inviting, complaining, thanking, apologizing, refusing are speech acts as well as functions of language. To communicate means to perform linguistic acts. It must be pointed out that all languages have a means of performing speech acts, and presumably speech acts themselves are universal, yet the form used in specific speech acts varies from culture to culture (Gass and Selinker, 2008: 288). Therefore, to study second language speech acts, we have to take into consideration whether there are linguistic forms available in language to realize speech acts, and how cross-cultural differences affect both second language performance and the interpretation by native speakers of second language speech acts.

If the form of speech act differs from culture to culture, miscommunication and misunderstandings will occur. We can see why the above assumed conversation is a failure through a brief analysis: Mary performs a speech act (requesting) by saying *I can't find my umbrella* in a particular context. When one says *Oh, I'm sorry to hear that*, he or she only understands the literal meaning of Mary's utterance, but fails to decode her real intention, i. e., asking for help. Therefore, miscommunication takes place. When breakdowns happen, native speakers do not usually attribute it to linguistic cause, but to individual or cultural causes, by thinking that the interlocutor is rather rude or uncooperative. This kind of misunderstanding can be best shown in the following conversation between a British tourist and a native Finnish speaker:

British tourist: *We're trying to find the railway station. Could you help us?*
Native Finnish speaker: *Yes.*

(Gass and Selinker, 2008: 288)

As far as language learning is concerned, the area of pragmatics is perhaps one of the most difficult areas, because learners are generally unaware of this aspect of language; they might be equally unaware of the negative perceptions that native speakers may have of them as a result of their pragmatic errors. In cross-cultural communication, if a native speaker has a negative perception of a relatively proficient non-native speaker, the miscommunication is often serious in terms of personal relations. This is because the cause of breakdown is more likely to be attributed to personal defect or culture than to the non-native speaker's inability to map correct linguistic forms onto corresponding pragmatic intentions. The most dangerous communicative situation is such that interlocutors assume that they understand each other, and because of this, they are less likely to question interpretations. As is described by Varonis and Gass (1985), when one interlocutor confidently (but inaccurately) interprets another's utterance, it is likely that participants will run into immediate problems because they do not share a common discourse space.

2.5.2 Production of speech acts: differences between L2 learners and L1 speakers

Evidence shows that native speakers (NSs) and non-native speakers (NNSs) have different systems of pragmatics. There are many ways in which NNSs differ from NSs in the production of speech acts. In this part, we will discuss four areas of differences: they may use different speech acts; if the same speech acts are used, they may differ in semantic formula, content, or form (Bardovi-Harlig, 2006: 14).

Different speech acts may be a significant difference in language use between NSs and NNSs. Even in the same context, NNSs may perform different speech acts than the NSs. Alternatively, they may choose not to perform any speech act at all. For example, in the same context of deciding what courses to take, NSs and NNSs prefer different speech acts. NSs tend to use more suggestions than NNSs, while NNSs produce more rejections than NSs. These two speech acts may serve the same function of control. While the NSs exercise control over their course schedules by making suggestions, NNSs control the course schedules through rejections, by blocking their advisors' suggestions. Although the context is the same, such a difference in choosing speech act may cause different feelings of harmony in the hearts of advisors.

A second way in which NSs and NNSs may differ is in the choice of semantic formulas. Formulas are those fixed expressions used in a particular situation. Semantic formulas refer to the means by which a particular speech act is accomplished in terms of the primary content of an utterance. For example, the speech act, apology, may contain the following various components:

an illocutionary force indicating device: *I'm sorry*;
an explanation or account of the situation: *The bus was late*;
an acknowledgment of responsibility: *It's my fault*;
an offer of repair: *I'll pay for the broken vase*;
a promise of forbearance: *It won't happen again.*

In a study of complaints (Murphy and Neu, 1996) in which both 14 NSs and 14 NNSs take a role of a student whose assignment was unfairly graded by his professor, it was found that all the NSs and only three NNSs used a complaint. The majority of the NNSs used a criticism instead of a complaint, as can be seen below:

NSs' complaint: *I think, uh, maybe it's my opinion. Maybe the grade was a little low.*
NNSs' criticism: *But you just look at your point of view and, uh, you just didn't recognize my point.*

A third way in which NSs and NNSs may differ is in the content of their contribution. While a semantic formula gives the type of information, content stands for the specific information given by a speaker. Even if the NSs and NNSs use the same semantic formulas, the content may be strikingly different. An example is the content of explanations, a semantic formula found in refusals. Uliss-Weltz (1990) has compared the explanations offered by Americans and Japanese ESL users, and characterized the Americans' explanations as being more detailed, and the explanations of Japanese as being vague according to the American standard:

American: *I have a business lunch that day.*
Japanese speaker: *I have something to do.*

The fourth way in which NNS production may differ from NS norm is in the form of a speech act. For example, in a longitudinal study of pragmatic development in the context of the academic advising session, it is found that in early sessions, NSs and NNSs differed in the speech acts, while in later sessions they produced the same speech acts, but in different forms. Learners do not often use the mitigators used by their NSs. What's more, they often use aggravators which were never used by NSs. Compare the following two groups of suggestions made by NSs and NNSs (Bardovi-Harlig, 2006: 19):

NS1: *Perhaps I should also mention that I have an interest in sociolinguistics and would like, if I can, to structure things in such a way that I might do as much sociolinguistics as I can.*
NS2: *I was thinking of taking sociolinguistics.*

NS3: *I have an idea for spring. I don't know how it would work out, but...*

......

NNS1: *In the summer, I will take language testing.*

NNS2: *So, I, I just decided on taking the language structure.*

2. 5. 3 Sociopragmatic competence and pragmalinguistic competence

We can distinguish two ways of examining illocutionary acts in SLA. The first way belongs to error analysis and thus focuses on learners' failure to perform acts in native-like ways. The second way reconceptualizes illocutionary acts as part of communicative competence. Two kinds of failure were distinguished by Thomas (1983): socio-pragmatic failure and pragma-linguistic failure. The former takes place when a learner fails to perform the illocutionary act required by the situation, while the latter occurs when a learner tries to perform the right speech act but uses the wrong linguistic means. The alternative view of illocutionary acts involves viewing them in terms of knowledge rather than failure. Kasper (2001), for example, reformulated Thomas' distinction in the following way:

Pragma-linguistic knowledge requires mappings of form, meaning, force, and context... Socio-pragmatics refers to the link between action-relevant context factors and communicative action and does not necessarily require any links to specific forms at all.

Seen in this way the ability to perform illocutionary acts constitutes part of communicative competence. This ability is included in sociolinguistic competence, which is defined as "the extent to which utterances are produced and understood appropriately in different sociolinguistic contexts" (Canale, 1983: 7). Canale continued to point out that appropriateness involves both appropriateness of meaning and appropriateness of form. The former constitutes sociopragmatic competence and the latter pragma-linguistic competence. Research has begun to cover the use and acquisition of a number of illocutionary acts. Much of the research focused on requests, apologies, refusals, complaints, thanking, invitations, suggestions, compliments, greetings, criticisms, and disagreements. Ellis (2013: 171–172) summarized two common characteristics shared by many of these acts: First, they constitute relatively well-defined acts in the sense that they are realized by means of a small set of easily recognizable linguistic elements (formulaic expressions). Second, many of these acts are face-threatening in nature and, therefore, provide a means of studying to what extent L2 learners with different L1 backgrounds are able to use native-like politeness strategies.

2.5.4 Comments on L2 speech act research

To learn a language means to learn how to use the language. Learning to produce the right speech act is an important part of learning a second language. There have now been a considerable number of studies of L2 learners' perceptions and performances of a range of speech acts. However most of these studies have been cross-sectional, making it difficult to reach reliable conclusions about developmental sequences. Below are some general conclusions supported by the current studies:

(1) Learners make pragmatic errors just as they make linguistic errors. These errors fall into two types: sociopragmatic errors and pragmalinguistic errors. It appears that learners are better able to overcome their pragmalinguistic than their sociopragmatic errors. Learners make rapid progress in developing strategies for performing illocutionary acts and in learning how to perform them using different linguistic means. However, it takes a long time to learn the sociocultural rules and many learners may never do so.

(2) A linear relationship does not seem to exist between how learners perform specific speech acts and their general proficiency. For example, Matsumara's (2003) study of Japanese university students' advice-giving in English showed that proficiency had only a weak effect. Advanced learners are more native-like but tend to be verbose in giving advice.

(3) L1 transfer is also a major factor identified. It is hypothesized that the more proficient the learner the more likely transfer occurs. Another hypothesis is that the more proficient the learner the greater the positive transfer but the less the negative transfer.

(4) It is disputable whether staying longer in L2 environment assists learners to approximate more closely to native-speaker pragmalinguistic and sociopragmatic norms. Some studies (for example, Matsumara, 2003) found that the length of stay or amount of exposure to the L2 has a greater effect than linguistic proficiency. However, some researchers (for example, Rose, 2002) did not find length of residence a reliable predictor of L2 pragmatic ability.

(5) Learners' ability to encode illocutionary acts in socially appropriate ways may

depend on psycholinguistic factors. According to research（Kasper, 1984a）, when learners were under communicative pressure they tended to engage in modality reduction. That is, they omitted grammatical features such as modal verbs and adverbials associated with the expression of modal meanings like possibility and tentativeness.

2.5.5　The relationship between linguistic and pragmatic competence

Despite the abundant research mentioned above, what is not clear about interlanguage pragmatics is the extent to which the acquisition of pragmatic knowledge is different from or related to the acquisition of linguistic knowledge. This raises the key question of the relationship between pragmalinguistic development and grammatical development: Do learners acquire grammar and then put this to use to convey pragmatic meanings? Or do these two types of developments take place simultaneously with each supporting the other? It is not easy to answer such questions because the majority of the studies have been comparative rather than acquisitional. That is, they compared L2 and native-speaker pragmatic behavior rather than investigated how learners develop pragmatic competence over time.

However, relevant research provides important evidence and food for thought for us to find tentative answers to the above-mentioned key question. There are two assumptions regarding the relationship between linguistic and pragmatic development: pragmatics-precedes-grammar sequence and grammar-precedes-pragmatics sequence.

First, there is evidence to support the separateness of pragmatic and grammatical development in second language context. Schmidt's（1983）longitudinal study of Wes documented considerable development in pragmatic competence without any equivalent development in linguistic competence. Wes was a 33-year-old Japanese artist, who left school at 15 and had little formal instruction in English. It was only when he began to visit Hawaii that he had opportunities to use English. Thus, he is an example of a naturalistic learner who learns an L2 at the same time as learning to communicate in it. Schmidt commented that Wes "developed considerable control of the formulaic language that acts as social grease in interaction". This enabled him to show pragmatic development while not advancing much linguistically. In another longitudinal study, Ellis（1992）found that ESL classroom learners relied extensively on formulaic expressions especially in the early stages of their pragmatic development of L2 requests. These and other studies of naturalistic learners suggest that the early stage of acquisition is essentially pragmatic rather than grammatical. Learners grab at the slender linguistic resources at their disposal, such as formulaic sequences, simple lexis, and intonation, to perform the illocutionary acts that are communicatively important to them. If lexis, and formulaic sequences serve as the foundation for the development of grammar, then, at least in the case of learners in L2 context, the development of some minimal pragmatic competence can be seen as the basis for the subsequent development of grammar. This development pattern can be called the pragmatics-precedes-grammar sequence.

Second, there is also evidence indicating that acquisition of grammar serves as the condition for pragmatic development. Learners with very advanced overall proficiency may still be lacking in pragmatic skills. Takahashi's (1996) study showed that unlike native speakers who preferred biclausal request formulas (for example, "I was wondering if you could...") , Japanese university students chose monoclausal formulas. This finding can be easily explained by the fact that they had not yet acquired the biclausal constructions involved. Grammar serves as a resource for encoding different kinds of meaning—semantic meaning as well as pragmatic meaning. For example, the modal verb *can* serves to convey ability (semantic meaning) as in *I can swim one hundred meters* and to perform a request (pragmatic meaning) as in the formulaic expression *Can I have a...?* When learners acquire new grammatical forms they may do so either in conjunction with their symbolic/semantic meaning or indexical/pragmatic meaning. In the later stages of development, grammatical forms may be first acquired in relation to their core semantic meanings and only take on a pragmalinguistic function later. If this argument is accepted, then, it can be said that grammatical development precedes pragmatic development. Such a development pattern is the grammar-precedes-pragmatics sequence.

In spite of the above two assumptions, it is still too early to reach any definite conclusion about the relationship between grammatical and pragmatic competence. In order to have a clear picture of the issue, we should take into consideration the context of acquisition. In a second language context, where learners are exposed to communicative uses of the L2, the pattern of development may be described above. However, in a foreign language context, learners may have both limited opportunity and limited need to develop pragmatic competence while the type of instruction they receive may prioritize grammar. In such a context, grammatical development is likely to precede pragmatic development even in the early stages. These learners acquire grammar and only later learn how to put this to use pragmatically. Therefore, differences might exist in the kind of competence demonstrated by second and foreign language learners.

Bardovi-Harlig and Dörnyei's (1998) study investigated whether this is the case. They elicited judgements of English utterances from high- and low-proficiency ESL and EFL learners. The judgements required the participants to indicate whether each utterance was appropriate or correct and in the case of negative judgements to assess the severity of the deviation. Clear differences were found in the judgements of the ESL and EFL learners. The ESL learners identified more pragmatic errors and rated them as more severe than the grammatical errors, whereas the EFL learners found more grammatical errors which they rated as more serious than the pragmatic errors. We also might expect differences in the kind of competence revealed by naturalistic learners and foreign language learners. In naturalistic learners, pragmatic development precedes grammatical development in the early stages but subsequently grammatical development is required to perform in pragmatically sophisticated ways. However, in foreign language learners, grammatical development may precede pragmatic development from the beginning.

The problem of the relationship between pragmatic and grammatical competence has not been fully solved. However, clear answers will only be forthcoming when there are more studies of beginning-level learners, when elicitation procedures appropriate to such learners are available, when there are more longitudinal studies, and when researchers specifically set out to integrate the study of emergent grammar and pragmatic ability.

2.5.6 Future research in interlanguage pragmatics

Interlanguage pragmatics deals with the study of non-native speakers' use and acquisition of linguistic action patterns in a second language. It must take into account not only how language is used, but also what it is being used for and who it is being used with. Much research on interlanguage pragmatics has focused on pragmatic use rather than on acquisition. Therefore, some researchers such as Bardovi – Harlig (1999) and Kasper and Schmidt (1996) pointed out that there is a lack of studies on changes in or influences on pragmatic knowledge.

According to Bardovi-Harlig (2004), at the heart of interlanguage pragmatics is the question of native-like attainment: whether, or to what extent, adults can acquire the pragmatics of a second language. There is also the necessity to consider the relationship between L2 learners' pragmatic knowledge and grammatical knowledge. If L2 learners do not have a variety of verbal forms in their minds, their use of verbal forms to express pragmatic functions will be limited. It was found that low level learners relied on imperatives when making requests in every situation. As their proficiency increased, however, they limited the use of imperatives appropriately to subordinates and intimates. Thus, it seems that there is a certain order L2 learners follow in acquiring pragmatic functions of verbal forms.

Another example given by Bardovi-Harlig is the context where graduate students talk with a faculty advisor about what course to take the next semester, the NNS says *I will take syntax* while the NS says *I was thinking of taking syntax*. This example suggests that the NNS has learned the core meaning of *will* as an indicator of the future, but he does not understand the subtlety of using the progressive as a marker of the future. What's more, he has not yet acquired the pragmatic function of the progressive as a means of mitigation in such a talk about a tentative selection of a course for the next semester. Compared with the NNS's definite answer, the NS's utterance sounds more flexible and more acceptable, because it allows further considerations and reconsiderations. Therefore, the pragmatic extension of progressives to refer to the future is a later developmental stage.

Another attention that should be given in the future research is the role that the acquisitional context plays in learners' pragmatic development. The effects of acquisitional context need to be explored at the micro-rather than macro-level, that is, in terms of the specific types of input and interaction learners are exposed to. In this respect, the study of pragmatic development lags behind that of linguistic development. So far interlanguage pragmatics research has focused more or less exclusively on learners' perceptions and productions.

A final suggestion for future interlanguage pragmatics research is that more attention should be paid to writing instead of spoken medium (Ellis, 2013: 198) . This is particularly the case with illocutionary acts. Although we know something about how contextualized acts such as requests, apologies, and refusals are acquired, we know little about how learners acquire the ability to perform acts found in decontextualized, written language. Research suggests that the ability to perform speech acts like requests, apologies, and refusals in face-to-face interaction may be distinct from the ability needed to perform speech acts like definitions in writing.

Assignment

1. Questions for self-study.

（1） What is interlanguage? What are the characteristics of interlanguage?

（2） What are the five psycholinguistic processes of the latent psychological structure used by adult L2 learners in shaping interlanguage, according to Selinker's hypothesis?

（3） What's the difference between free variation and systematic variation in interlanguage development? Give examples to illustrate.

（4） Give examples to show that interlanguage grammar is dynamic.

（5） Give examples, or find examples in your or somebody else's utterances to illustrate that interlanguage is a reduced system.

（6） What are the factors (contexts) which affect the systematic change of interlanguage?

（7） What is the difference between the acquisition order and the sequence of acquisition? Give examples to illustrate.

（8） How does L1 influence the learner's interlanguage?

（9） What is second language speech act?

（10） How does L1 and L2 speech act production differ from each other?

（11） What is the relationship between linguistic competence and pragmatic competence?

2. Fill in the blanks in the following short passage with proper words.

Errors are evidence of the state of a learner's knowledge of the L2. An error is different from what we call a "mistake". A mistake is akin to _____ of the tongue. They are generally one-time-only events. The speaker who makes a _____ is able to recognize it as a mistake and correct it if necessary. An error, however, is _____. That is, it is likely to occur repeatedly and is not recognized by the learner as an error. The learner in this case has incorporated a particular erroneous form (from the perspective of the TL) into his own _____. Errors are not only systematic; many of them are also _____.

3. Open discussion for pair or group work.

（1） Have you ever reached a stage of fossilization or stabilization of progress, where you seemed to just stall for weeks or more? If so, describe that experience to your classmates. Then tell about what propelled you out of those doldrums, or determine what might have helped you if you stayed there or are still there.

(2) Think about the phenomenon of avoidance we discussed in this chapter. It has been primarily investigated in syntax. Why do you think such an emphasis has occurred? Can avoidance take place in phonology? In vocabulary? Why or why not?

(3) There are many speech acts in verbal communications, such as complaining, insulting, thanking, apologizing, requesting, refusing, complimenting, suggesting, and so on. These speech acts can be studied as part of second language use. Choose one of the above speech acts, and gather data from L2 speakers in their use of it. While you are gathering data, take into account such factors as gender, status, and familiarity. Give an analysis of how these factors affect your results?

(4) Speech acts are of interest to language teachers and learners because there are multiple ways to accomplish one particular speech act. How you accomplish a speech act can also be different from language to language. Think of how many different ways you can refuse a dinner invitation in English. The following factors can be taken into consideration:

—the person who made the invitation
—the reason why you could not, or did not want to, attend
—different levels of formality
—consequences for refusal
—expression of regret
—length of utterances

(5) One reason why speech acts can be challenging for L2 learners is that the function of the speech acts does not always match the syntactic structure. Learners are generally taught that declarative sentences are statements, interrogative sentences are questions, imperatives are commands, and exclamatives are exclamations. However, a declarative speech act does not always use declarative syntax, and a questioning speech act does not always appear in the form of a question. To understand the differences between speech acts and syntactic structures, choose one speech act, such as "command", and brainstorm together as many different ways as you can to command somebody to do a particular task (for

example, close the door). The brainstorm can range from delicately polite to downright offensive ways to command someone. Then, identify the different syntactic structures used, grouping them together into categories. After discovering about the vast array of syntax that can accomplish the same speech act, answer the following questions:

—Does using more words sound more polite?

—Does commanding someone using a question sound more polite than a straightforward one?

—Does this differ between your mother tongue and the target language?

Chapter Three Linguistic Aspects of SLA

In the previous chapter we discussed interlanguage, a unique language system constructed by L2 learners in a second or foreign language context. An obvious characteristic of IL is that it is deviant from the normal TL. The study of SLA can be seen, to a certain extent, as the study of IL. Interlanguages, considered to be "natural languages", consist of "a set of linguistic rules which can generate novel utterances". Like natural languages, interlanguages can be idealized to make them amendable to linguistic analysis. In this and the following two chapters, we focus on three areas in which the SLA's relationship with other academic disciplines has been most heavily felt: linguistics, psychology, and sociolinguistics. It does not mean that these are the only areas in which SLA has strong ties. Rather, they are selected as representative.

With regard to the influence each field has on SLA, the difference can be found in general emphasis: linguistics focuses on the products of acquisition (a description of the linguistic systems of L2 learners), psychology focuses on the process by which those systems are created (a description of the process of the way in which learners create learner systems), and sociolinguistics focuses on social factors that influence the acquisition of the linguistic system and the use of that system. However, all areas concern one and the same learning problem: how is it that learners acquire the complexities of a second language?

Linguistics has impacted the research in L2 acquisition since the early days of SLA research. Virtually every theory of linguistics has had some relevance to SLA research. In this chapter we present a linguistic approach to the study of second language acquisition. Specifically, we first review the nature of language and the early approaches to the study of SLA, including contrastive analysis, error analysis, and the monitor model. Then we survey the study of SLA from different linguistic approaches including typological universals, universal grammar, and functional approaches.

3.1 The Nature of Human Language

In order to have a better understanding of SLA, it is necessary to understand what it is that needs to be learned. A simple answer to this question might be that an L2 learner needs to learn the grammar of the target language. But what is meant by this? What is language? All those who grow up in a normal way can acquire their mother tongue in the first few years of life. The acquired knowledge of language is largely of an unconscious kind. A native English-speaking child, for example, learns how to use particular grammatical structures, such as the relative clause. He learns that the relative clause has a modifying function. However, he may not know, in a conscious sense, that it is a relative clause; nor can he tell what a relative clause is used for. For example, a child can utter the following sentence with a relative clause *I want that toy that that boy is playing with*, without knowing its function, and without being able to divide the sentence into component parts. It is in this sense that the complex knowledge that man has about his native language is largely unconscious.

3.1.1 Common characteristics of language

It is widely accepted that language is unique to human beings. With language, we convey thoughts and feelings to each other, and transmit our knowledge and beliefs to our children. With language, we are able to change the world. With language, we uniquely possess power and intelligence among all the creatures on earth. Most linguists agree that all languages in the world share the same characteristics. We mainly touch upon the following three:

First, language is symbolic. Meaning is not inherently conveyed by a sequence of sounds or letters. It comes from the unspoken agreement of a group of speakers that certain sounds represent certain persons, things, or activities outside the language system. This symbolic connection is always arbitrary, and there is no logical relationship between the sound that stands for a thing and the actual thing itself. For instance, a dog is called a *dog* not because the sound suggests the four-legged animal. It is just symbolic. English speakers agree that the animal is called a *dog*. Chinese call it *gou*, and Spanish people call it *perro*.

Second, language is systematic. A language is made up of recurring elements which appear in regular patterns of relationship. Any one of the world languages has an infinite number of possible sentences, which are created according to rules and principles which speakers are unconscious of. Every one uses language creatively. Although we use the same stock of words again and again, most particular combinations of words making up the sentences may have never been used before. However, we can understand them well, because we understand the rules by which the words are combined to express meaning. To put it in another way, this is so because language is systematic. Even the sounds produced in speaking, and the orders in which they occur are systematically organized in ways that most of us are unaware of.

Third, language is social. A very important function of language is that we use it to communicate, to categorize and catalogue objects, events, and processes of human experience. Although the ability to acquire L1 depends on inherent neurological device, no one can develop that potential without interaction with others in the society they grow up in. Language can be described partially as "the expressive dimension of culture."

3.1.2 Different aspects of language

Language consists of multiple layers, much like a layered cake, each layer of it serving an important function. But to get the full experience, you need all these components in order for a language to be a language. When you know a language, you have to know a portion of all of those layers. Linguists have traditionally divided a language into different aspects for systematic description and analysis. Here we briefly deal with phonology, morphology and lexicon, syntax, semantics, and pragmatics.

3.1.2.1 Phonology (sound system)

The study of phonology focuses on a few fundamental questions such as when to combine sounds and when not to, which sounds are possible and which are impossible, and what sounds are found in what parts of words. For example, if a person wants to express the meaning of "writing a letter", he, especially an American speaker, would say the following in normal speech: *I'm gonna wriDa leDer.* However, in clearer, more articulated speech, he may say: *I am going to write a letter.* This can be understood in the following conversation between Tom and Sally:

（T ＝ Tom；S ＝ Sally）

T：*What are you gonna do?*

S：*I'm gonna wriDa leDer.*

T：*You're gonna do what?*

S：*I'm gonna wriDa leDer.*

T：*What? I can't hear you.*

S：*I'm going to write a letter.*

（Gass and Selinker, 2008：9）

Here we can clearly see that speakers know when to combine sounds and when not to. This happens according to a particular conversational context. In addition to knowing sound variation, native speakers also know which sounds are possible and which are impossible. For example, it is known that the English sound /b/ can be blended with /r/, as in *brain*, but can not with the sound /n/, as in *bnick*. In Chinese, a single vowel, or a blend of consonant-vowel combination, can stand alone, as in 啊（ah!）or 拉（la），but there isn't any vowel-consonant combination in the syllable of a single Chinese character.

3.1.2.2　Morphology and lexicon

The study of morphology is the study of word formation, which mainly deal with morphemes, inflections that carry grammatical information, and affixes which may be added to change the meaning of words or their grammatical category. A morpheme is a minimal unit of meaning. There are two kinds of morphemes：bound morpheme and free morpheme. A bound morpheme is one that can not be a word itself such as *un* in *unfair*. A free morpheme is one that is a word, such as *table*, and *book*. We can create words by adding morphemes. For example, the word *unluckiness* is a combination of un + luck + y (i) + ness. Similarly, the word *disestablishmentarianism* is created by putting morphemes together：dis + establish + ment + ari + an + ism. Not only do we have knowledge of word formation, but we also know which words can go together with other words. For example, we know we are right in saying that *Mt. Everest is a high mountain*, but wrong in saying that *The Empire State Building is a high building*. Similarly, Chinese native speakers say 国家大 but not *人口大. They say 一匹马，but not *一匹牛；一只羊，but not *一只猪.

3. 1. 2. 3 Syntax

Knowledge of syntax of a language refers to the knowledge we have of the order of elements in a sentence. Syntax is a branch of grammar dealing with the ways in which words are arranged to show connections of meaning within the sentence. A sentence is a sequence of words arranged in a certain order in accordance with grammatical rules. Those sequences of words which conform to the rules are well-formed; those that do not are not acceptable to native speakers. Native speakers have an unconscious knowledge of what strings of words are grammatical and what are ungrammatical. For example, English speakers know the sentence *The black bike is under the big tree* is acceptable, while *The big tree is the black under bike* is unacceptable. Chinese speakers know 上海是个大城市 is grammatical, while 大城市是个上海 is not.

Not only do people know which sentences are acceptable in their language, they also know which are approximately the same in terms of meaning. For example, the two sentences *Tom broke the window* and *The window (it) was broken by Tom* have the same general meaning in that they refer to the same event. But when someone asks, "Who broke the window?", the most likely answer is "*Tom broke the window*" rather than "*The window was broken by Tom*". If the question is, "What happened?" or "What's wrong with the window", the answer is likely to be "*The window was broken by Tom*" instead of "*Tom broke the window*". Thus, native English speakers know not only what patterns are similar to each other, but also when to use different grammatical patterns.

Another aspect of language is how the meaning of the whole sentence is influenced by moving the elements in it. For example, adverbs can be moved in a sentence without changing the meaning, as in the two sentences: *Yesterday Tom met Mary* and *Tom met Mary yesterday*. However, when the nouns move, the meaning will be changed. For example, *Yesterday Tom met Mary* and *Yesterday Mary met Tom* do not share a common meaning. Therefore, knowing a language entails knowing a set of rules with which we can produce an infinite set of sentences.

3. 1. 2. 4 Semantics

Semantics deals with meaning. This does not only relate to grammatical sentences, since many ungrammatical sentences are meaningful. The sentence *That girl beautiful is my sister* is not grammatical but meaningful. In contrast, some sentences are grammatical, but meaningless, such as *The blind man saw the red light and stopped*.

Knowledge of the semantics of a language entails knowledge of the referential meaning of words. For example, if one can distinguish the meaning of the *leaf of a tree* and the *leaf of a table*, he can understand an advertisement on the television for a table with extra leaves. However, this is not enough. Referential meaning is not the only way of conveying meaning, the way elements in a sentence are combined also affects the meaning of the sentence. For example, the following two sentences differ in meaning:

The man bit the dog.
The dog bit the man.

3.1.2.5 Pragmatics

Pragmatics deals with the way in which language is used in real contexts. This is part of what L2 learners should learn. For example, when we answer a question on the phone *Is Mike there?* it would be strange to say Yes, with the person on the other end saying *Thank you*. Similarly, the following conversation taking place between a stranger and a city dweller also sounds ridiculous:

(S = Stranger; D = Dweller)
S: *Excuse me, can you tell me the way to the railway station?*
D: *Yes, I can. / No, I can't.*

The two questions above are not information questions, which call for a *yes or no* response. Instead, they are requests, to speak to Mike in the first case, and to ask for direction in the second case. Clearly, the speakers have their intentions behind the words. However, if, in the first case, the speaker's intention is a parent checking on the whereabouts of a child, then it would be another case:

(M = Mother)
M1: *This is Mike's Mum. Is Mike there?*
M2: *Yes.*
M1: *Oh! Thanks, I just want to know where he was.*

To sum up, learning a language does not only involve the learning of how to express ideas by means of sounds, words, sentences, but it also involves understanding the meaning of utterances and appropriate use of the language in real contexts.

Charles Morris (1938: 30) defined pragmatics as "the science of the relation of signs to their interpreters". In other words, pragmatics is concerned not with language as a system or product, but rather with the interrelationship between language form, messages and language users. It explores the following questions:

—How do people communicate more than what the words or phrases of their utterances might mean by themselves, and how do people make these interpretations?

—Why do people choose to say and /or interpret something in one way rather than another?

—How do people's perceptions of contextual factors (for example, who the interlocutors are, what their relationship is, and what circumstances they are communicating in) influence the process of producing and interpreting language?

3. 2　Early Approaches to SLA

3. 2. 1　Contrastive analysis hypothesis (CAH)

Before the SLA field was established, scholars from the 1940s to the 1960s had conducted contrastive analyses by comparing two languages. They believed that L2 teaching would be more effective if similarities and differences between L1 and L2 could be identified. This belief was best summarized by Lado (1957):

Individuals tend to transfer the forms and meanings and the distribution of forms and meanings of their native language and culture to the foreign language and culture—both productively when attempting to speak the language and to act in the culture and receptively when attempting to grasp and understand the language and the culture as practiced by natives.

It was possibly because of the occurrence of transfer that Lado further claimed that "those elements that are similar to his native language will be simple for him, and those elements that are different will be difficult". The assertion that linguistic differences could be used to predict learning difficulty led to the emergence of CAH: Where two languages were similar, positive transfer would occur; where they were different, negative transfer, or interference, would result. Then followed a detailed structure-by-structure comparison of the sound system, morphological system, syntactic system, and even the cultural system of two languages, just for the purpose of discovering similarities and differences. Lado gives examples in Spanish and English for some of the types of contrasts he describes below in Table 3.1.

Table 3.1　Contrastive Analysis: Spanish and English (from Saville-Troike, 2008: 36)

Types of Contrasts	Contrastive Analysis	
Same form and meaning, different distribution	**Spanish**: *la paloma blanca* " the dove white"; *las palomas blancas* " the (pl) doves whites" **English**: *the white dove*; *the white doves*	The form *-s* and the meaning "plural" are the same in both languages, but the distribution of occurrence is different. Spanish attaches the *-s* to articles, modifiers, and nouns, but English attaches it only to nouns. This is the same contrast which was illustrated in the early expressions of *moderns languages* and *greens beans*. (The difference in word order is a contrast in form at another level of analysis.)
Same meaning, different form	**Spanish**: *iré* " (I) will go" **English**: *I will go*.	The meaning "future" is expressed by different grammatical elements in the two languages. In Spanish, it is conveyed by the future tense suffix *-é* added to the infinitive form of the verb *ir*, while it is conveyed by the auxiliary verb *will* in English. (The first-person subject is another contrast in form, also conveyed by the Spanish suffix *-é* while the overt pronoun *I* is required in English.)

(To be continued)

Types of Contrasts	Contrastive Analysis	
Same meaning, different form and distribution	**Spanish**: *agua* "*water*" **English**: *water*	The English word *water* may occur as a noun in *a glass of water*, as a verb in *water the garden*, and as a modifier noun in the compound *water meter*. The Spanish word *agua* may occur only as a noun unless its form is changed: i. e. its distribution is more limited than that of the equivalent in English.
Different form, partial overlap in meaning	**Spanish**: *pierna* "*leg of humans*"; pata "*leg of animals or furniture*"; etapa "*leg of a race or trip*" **English**: *leg*	The scope of meaning for the English word *leg* covers the scope of three different words in Spanish; no single equivalent term can be used in both languages.
Similar form, different meaning	**Spanish**: *asistir* "to attend" **English**: *assist*	Similar words like these are sometimes called "false friends", and are predicted to cause great difficulty for speakers of one language learning the other. Since the words look and sound so much alike, L2 learners are likely to assume that they also share meaning.

CAH was heavily influenced by structuralism and behaviorism, which were dominant in linguistics and psychology in USA through 1940s and 1950s. The ultimate goal is to predict areas that will be either easy or difficult for learners. Teaching of a second language under the influence of contrastive analyses at that time was based on the following assumptions:

(1) Language is a habit and language learning involves the establishment of a new set of habits.

(2) The major source of error in the production or reception of an L2 is the L1.

(3) One can account for errors by considering differences between L1 and L2.

(4) The greater the differences, the more errors that will occur.

(5) One who learns an L2 learns the differences. Similarities can be ignored.

(6) Difficulty and ease in learning is determined respectively by differences and

similarities between the two languages.

There were two versions of CAH, the strong and the weak. In the strong view, it was held that one could make predictions about learning and hence about the success of language-teaching materials based on a comparison between the two languages. The weak version gained credence largely due to the failure of predictive contrastive analysis, and then became part of error analysis.

After the appearance of the strong version, criticisms followed. Those who argued against the strong version of CAH pointed out that many areas where predictions made did not appear in actual learner production: predicted errors did not occur. Besides, errors which occurred in learner production had not been predicted by the theory. That is, the theory did not actually predict what was happening in nonnative speech. For example, one difference between French and English is that the object pronoun precedes the verb in French, while in English, the object pronoun follows the verb. However, the fact is that the French learners of English produced *I see them* instead of *I them see*, as predicted by CAH (Zobl, 1980). In other words, French learners of English never pre-pose the object pronoun. Rather, they correctly follow English word order.

Another criticism of CAH is related to the concept of difficulty. A fundamental concept of the CAH was that differences signified difficulty and similarity signified ease. Difficulty in this view was equated with error. That is, an error produced by a learner was a signal that the learner was having difficulty with a particular structure being learned. Actually, this is not always so. Let us look at an example from Kellerman (1987), a sentence written by a student:

But in that moment it was 6: 00.

When asked to comment on the use of the preposition *in*, the student insisted that the *in* was correct but questioned whether it should be it **was** 6: 00 or it **had been** 6: 00. Obviously, the learner had some difficulty in tense usage even though there was no error reflecting that difficulty. On the contrary, there seemed to be no doubt in her mind about the correctness of the preposition *in*. From this example, one of many, we find that difficulty cannot be simply equated with errors, which is a predicted result of linguistic differences. The difference described by a linguist or a teacher through CA is not a real measure of difficulty in reality. In short, what is different in two languages is not necessarily difficult for learners, and what is similar not necessarily easy.

Contrastive analysts' claims were made on logical grounds and supported by reference to anecdotal evidence. It must be pointed out that these claims were not supported by data obtained from the systematic study of learner language itself, but usually only by utterances that analysts happened to have noticed and remembered. Unfortunately, it is likely that analysts tend to notice data that their theories predict and not to notice the data that do not fit their theories. Learner utterances that were clear evidence of transfer were noticed and quoted, but learner utterances that did not provide evidence of transfer went unnoticed. Thus, in the late 1950s and the 1960s, there were virtually no systematic attempts to observe learner language and to document scientifically the way in which learner language developed, or to independently and objectively verify the strong claims of the CAH that language transfer was the sole process shaping learner language.

Although the CAH has some problems, the above discussion does not mean that NL does not play any role in SLA. What is implied is that there are other factors affecting second language development and that the role of the L1 is far more complex than the simple 1 : 1 correspondence suggested by CAH.

3.2.2　Error analysis（EA）

3.2.2.1　The significance of errors

We have just discussed CAH and its shortcomings. Now we are going to focus on errors made by L2 learners, so as to learn more about second language development. It may appear unusual to focus on what learners get wrong rather than what they get right. However, studying errors can be beneficial to teaching and learning of an L2. First, errors are an outstanding feature of leaner language. Teachers can get valuable information from thinking about why learners make errors. Second, it is useful for teachers to know what errors learners make. Third, making errors may help learners themselves to learn an L2 better when they self-correct the errors they make.

Besides the above pedagogical significance, the study of errors can produce even greater theoretical value. Ever since the publication of S. Pit Corder's（1967）article on

"The significance of learners' errors", learner errors were no longer regarded as "bad habits" which should be eradicated, but as sources of insight into the process of learning an L2. According to Corder, errors enable us to "see" the system of language a learner is using at any particular point in the course of L2 development and the strategies the learner is using in his "discovery of the language". In other words, errors are windows through which we can peep into the learner's mind. In this approach, learner language is seen as a target of analysis which is independent of L1 or L2, and the state of learner knowledge is viewed as transitional competence on the path of SLA. Further, it was claimed that making errors is significant because it is part of the learning process. As Corder said, it is "a way the learner has of testing his hypothesis about the nature of the language he is learning". By making errors, the learner is exploring the new system of language rather than just experiencing "interference" from old habits.

3.2.2.2　The procedure of error analysis

(1) Collecting samples.

Learner language samples can be gained from both written data and oral data from learners who are responding to the same kind of task or test. Samples can also be collected from a few subjects who are studied over a period of weeks, months, or even years in order to determine patterns of change in error occurrence with increasing L2 exposure and proficiency. While collecting a sample of learner language, researchers should consider some factors. Many studies paid little attention to these factors, with the result that they are difficult to interpret and almost impossible to replicate. A further problem is that the majority of EAs have been cross-sectional rather than longitudinal, thus making it difficult to determine accurately the different errors that learners produce at different stages of their development. Table 3.2 lists some of the factors that need to be taken into account in learner language sample collection.

Table 3.2 Factors to Consider when Collecting Sample of Learner Language（Ellis，2013：47）

Factors	Variables	Description
Learner	Proficiency level	Elementary，intermediate，or advanced
	Other languages	The learner's L1；other L2s
	Language learning experience	This may be classroom or naturalistic or a mixture of the two.
Language sample	Medium	Learner production can be oral or written.
	Genre	Learner production may take the form of a conversation，a lecture，an essay，a letter，etc.
	Content	The topic the learner is communicating about.
Production	Unplanned	The discourse is produced spontaneously.
	Planned	The discourse is produced under conditions that allow for careful online planning.

（2）Identifying errors.

To identify errors is to determine the elements in the sample of learner language which are wrong in some way compared with the normal or "correct" target language. For example, in the sentence "*A man and a little boy was watching him.*"（Ellis，2000），we find the error "was" since the correct form should be "were". However，things are not always as easy as expected，since the definition of "error" is problematic. We should be aware of the difficulty which centers around a number of issues. The first is whether grammaticality or acceptability should serve as the criterion. An utterance that is grammatically correct may not be pragmatically acceptable. For example，the utterance "I want to use your glasses" addressed to a stranger is grammatical but pragmatically unacceptable. What's more，whether an utterance is grammatical or not is not always easy to determine.

The second issue concerns whether a difference should be made between errors and mistakes. An error is caused by a lack of competence while mistakes are performance phenomena and are the result of processing failures caused by memory limitations，lack of automaticity，and so on. Corder argued that EA should be restricted to the study of errors. Mistakes should be eliminated from the analysis.

The third issue to be concerned is whether the error is overt or covert. An overt error is easy to identify because there is a clear deviation in form as in the sentence "He comed late." A covert error occurs in an utterance that is superficially well formed but which does not mean what the learner intended it to mean. For example, the utterance "It was stopped" is grammatical until it becomes clear that "it" refers to "the wind".

The final issue is whether inappropriate uses of the L2 should be considered erroneous. Often, a learner may produce a form that is grammatical but may not be the form preferred by native speakers. For example, in the sentence "One day an Indian gentleman, a snake charmer, arrived in England, and he was coming from Bombay.", the use of "was coming" is erroneous, because the preferred form is probably "had come".

（3）Describing errors.

After deciding what is erroneous in the learner language, it is time to classify the errors, which enables us to discover the rule-governed system in learners' mind. For example, the above misuse of "was" belongs to subject-verb agreement error. Errors can be classified according to general linguistic category such as auxiliary system, passive sentences or negative construction. Also, they can be classified according to specific linguistic elements such as articles, prepositions and verb forms.

The difference between an error and a mistake should be reemphasized here. Mistakes are akin to slips of tongue. They are only one-time events. The learner who makes a mistake is able to recognize it as a mistake and correct it if necessary. But an error is systematic. It may occur repeatedly and not be recognized by the learner as an error. The learner has incorporated an erroneous form into his own linguistic system. In this way, errors are only errors from a teacher's perspective, not from the learner's.

In Corder's （1974）framework for describing errors, he distinguishes three kinds of errors according to their systematicity: pre-systematic errors, systematic errors, and post-systematic errors. Pre-systematic errors are random, and occur when the learner is unaware of the existence of a particular rule in the target language, and thus cannot explain why a particular form is chosen. In contrast, systematic errors occur when the learner has discovered a rule but it is a wrong one. The learner is unable to correct these errors, but he can explain the mistaken, self-discovered rule. Post-systematic errors occur when the learner knows, and can explain, the correct target language rule but uses it inconsistently.

（4）Explaining errors.

Explaining why an error was made is the most important step in trying to understand the process of SLA. The job of explanation is related to establishing the source of the error, or accounting for why an error is made. The error source may be psycholinguistic, sociolinguistic, epistemic, or may reside in the discourse structure (Taylor, 1986). Sociolinguistic sources relate to the learners' ability to adjust their language according to the social context. Epistemic sources concern learners' lack of world knowledge. Discourse sources involve problems in the organization of information into a coherent "text". Here, we will focus on the first type—psycholinguistic sources, for EA's main aim is to provide a psychological explanation. Researchers have identified some different sources or causes of psycholinguistic errors.

Two most likely causes of L2 errors are interlingual factors and intralingual factors. The interlingual errors, also called transfer errors, are the result of negative transfer or interference from L1, while intralingual errors cannot be traced to cross-linguistic influence. They are regarded as developmental errors and often represent incomplete learning of L2 rules or overgeneralization of them. Look at two examples from a Chinese-speaking learner of English:

Sample 1: interlingual error

Soldier should love country.

The speaker did not add determiners before the two nouns, "soldier" and "country". Obviously, his English is influenced by his mother tongue, in which nouns do not usually take articles or other determiners. They say "士兵应该热爱祖国" instead of "一个士兵应该热爱他的祖国". However, in English, nouns, especially singular countable nouns, often take determiners: *A soldier should love his country.* Therefore, this is an interlingual error, since the error is the result of L1 interference.

Sample 2: intralingual error

He standed beside me.

The same speaker, using "standed" instead of "stood", has learned a rule that the past tense verb takes an *-ed* suffix, and forgotten that irregular verbs have special past tense forms. He has obviously over-generalized the rule. This error, which is not influenced by the L1, shows that the learner is constructing his own rule for an L2.

Many researches has focused on determining what proportion of errors are transfer as opposed to intralingual. This is related to the competing claims of a behaviorist, habit-formation account of L2 acquisition and a mentalist, creative construction account. According to behaviorist accounts, errors were viewed as the result of the negative transfer of L1 habits. According to mentalist accounts, errors were predicted to be similar to those found in L1 acquisition because learners actively construct the grammar of an L2 as they progress. This issue dominated early work in SLA. It must be pointed out that subsequently researchers have come to recognize that the correlation between behaviorist learning theory and mentalist learning theory is simplistic and misleading, and transfer is now treated as a mental process in its own right (Ellis, 2013: 54).

(5) Evaluating errors.

While the above four steps have examined errors from the point of view of the learner who makes them, this step of error analysis will touch upon what effect the error has on the listener or the reader. That is, how serious is the error? Or to what extent does it affect intelligibility or social acceptability? This effect can be determined either in terms of the addressee's comprehension of the learner's meaning or in terms of the addressee's affective response to the errors. A sentence may have one or two grammatical errors, but it may not affect communication, such as the above two examples produced by Chinese-speaking learners of English. This is called a local error. A local error only affects a single constituent in a sentence, such as a verb, and does not create any processing problem. Hence, no misunderstanding results. However, a global error is different because it violates the overall structure of a sentence. For this reason, it may bring more problems in understanding the meaning of the sentence produced by a speaker. For example:

That computer you want to use now is impossible.

The error in this sentence is global, since there is something wrong in the structure. It is confusing in meaning and difficult to understand. It may be that *The computer is impossible*, which does not really make any sense; it may also be that *It's impossible for you to use the computer*, but the speaker does not seem to mean that. A close study of the erroneous sentence suggests the effect of mother tongue interference: it is a sheer transfer from the L1 "那台计算机你想现在用是不可能的".

Error evaluation research calls for three decisions: who will be the addressees (i. e. the judges), what error will they be asked to judge, and how will they be asked to judge them. The judges can be native speakers (NSs), or non-native speakers (NNSs). They can be "experts" (i. e. language teachers) or "non-experts". The errors to be judged may cover semantic or lexical aspects of the target language, different grammatical features, and spelling. The instruments used to elicit judgements, in most cases, consist of decontextualized sentences containing one or several errors. These sentences are usually taken from actual samples of learner language (mainly written compositions) but they are sometimes contrived. In some studies, the sentences are contextualized. The errors can be presented orally and more often in writing. The judges may be asked to evaluate the "comprehensibility" of the erroneous sentence, the "seriousness" or the "naturalness" of errors, or the degree of "irritation" they arouse. Sometimes they may be asked to correct errors and explain why they judged some errors as especially problematic.

Three main questions have been addressed in error evaluation studies. The first question concerns whether some errors are more problematic than others. Some research findings indicate that NS judges tend to regard lexical errors as more serious than grammatical errors. Global grammatical errors are also judged as more likely to interfere with comprehension than local errors. What's more, NS judges may also be influenced by markedness factors. For example, as is shown in Santor' study (1987), errors involving the substitution of marked forms (such as "an book") for unmarked forms (such as "a book") are judged more severely than errors in which unmarked forms (such as "a apple") replace marked forms (such as "an apple"). NS judges also find it easier to deal with insertion than with omission or wrong choice errors (Tomiyana, 1980).

The second question concerns whether there are differences in the evaluation made by NSs and NNSs. The answer is definitely yes. There are distinct differences in the judgements made by NSs and NNSs. Compared with NSs, NNSs are much more severe and their judges seem to be especially hard on morphological and functor errors. However, they tend to evaluate lexical and global errors less severely than NS judges.

The third question concerns what criteria judges use in evaluating learners' errors. Judges appear to use different criteria in evaluating errors. The three general criteria identified by Khalil (1985) are: intelligibility, acceptability and irritation. Intelligibility concerns the extent to which sentences containing different kinds of error can be comprehended. Acceptability is a rather vague criterion, involving judgements of the seriousness of an error. Irritation concerns the emotional response of an addressee but is also related to the frequency of errors. NS and NNS judges differ in the criteria they use. NS judges seem to be more concerned with the effect that an error has on their comprehension. NNS judges, however, are more influenced by their ideas of what constitute the 'basic' rules of the target language. Transfer errors are often viewed leniently, but grammatical errors will be seen as more serious by NNS judges.

3.2.2.3 Shortcomings of EA

EA is a useful procedure for the study of SLA. However, it has encountered some criticisms. One problem of EA is that it totally focuses on errors to the exclusion of correct forms. It is argued that one should also consider non-errors as well as errors to get the entire picture of learners' linguistic behaviour. Perhaps the most serious attempt at showing the inadequacies of EA comes from Schachter's study.

Schachter collected 50 compositions from each of the four groups of learners of English: native speakers of Persian, Arabic, Chinese, and Japanese. Her research focused on the use of English restrictive relative clauses (RCs) by each of these four groups. The findings in terms of errors are: Persian group made 43 errors; Arabic group made 31 errors; Chinese group made 9 errors; Japanese group made 5 errors. As a contrast, American group made no errors. If judging from the error number, we would have concluded that the Japanese and Chinese speakers have a good control over the formation of English restrictive relative clauses and that the Persian and Arabic speakers do not. However, Schachter's analysis went beyond the errors to look at the total production of RCs, including error-free RCs, as shown in Table 3.3.

Table 3.3   Relative Clause Production (Gass and Selinker, 2008: 105)

NL Speakers	Correct	Error	Total	% errors
Persian	131	43	174	25
Arabic	123	31	154	20
Chinese	67	9	76	12

(To be continued)

NL Speakers	Correct	Error	Total	% errors
Japanese	58	5	63	8
American	173	0	173	

Although it is true that the Persian and Arabic speakers had a greater percentage of errors than did the Chinese and Japanese speakers, it is also the case that the Chinese and Japanese produced roughly half as the many relative clauses as did the Persian and Arabic groups. Why is it so? And how shall we account for this discrepancy? The fact is that Chinese and Japanese languages form relative clauses in a different way, that is, by placing the modifier (the relative clause) before the noun it modifies. However, Persian and Arabic relative clauses are similar to English in that the RC is placed after the noun it modifies. It is because of this great difference that Chinese and Japanese learners of English do not use the RC with great frequency. When they do use it, they use it cautiously and with a high degree of accuracy. The Persian and Arabic learners, however, use RCs more frequently and thus produce more errors, because their NL structure resembles the TL structure.

A second problem with EA is that it is difficult to determine the type of error. Let's look at the following examples from Chinese learners of English.

There are so many Taiwan people live around the lake.
There were lots of events happen in my country.
There is a mountain separate two lakes.
There are so many tourist visit there.

(Gass and Selinker, 2008: 106)

Superficially, these sentences look like relative clauses without relative pronouns (*that*, *who*, *which*) . Another explanation is that they are constructions that are similar to topic-comment constructions in Chinese language. That is, these learners are following a Chinese pattern of establishing a topic and then making a comment about it, as shown in Table 3. 4.

Table 3.4   Topic and Comment

Topic	Comment
Taiwan people	They live around the lake.
Lots of events	They happen in my country.
Mountain	It separates two lakes.
Tourist (s)	They live there.

Such sentences produced by Chinese learners of English are very commonplace in both speaking and writing. Partially because they have not yet mastered English relative clauses, they tend to produce two simple sentences such as *You see that boy? He just broke the window* instead of *Did you see the boy who just broke the window?* Therefore, there can be a difference between what a researcher determines to be the TL structure and what the learner is attempting to produce.

Another problem of EA is that we tend to believe that a learner has formed the correct rule because he has temporarily produced correct forms. But actually, the absence of errors does not mean correct rule formation. For example, when a learner produces correct sentences like *I asked him to come*, and *I enjoyed reading the book*, we might say that the learner knows which verb takes which kind of complements. But the error in *I saw him to cross the street* clearly suggests that the learner has not mastered the correct rule.

3.2.3   The Monitor Model

Another early approach to SLA is the Monitor Model, which was proposed by Stephen Krashen (1978). The Monitor Model adopts the notion of language acquisition device (LAD), a metaphor used by N. Chomsky for children's innate knowledge of language. Krashen's Monitor Model has enjoyed considerable prominence in SLA research. It is probably the most comprehensive of existing theories. This model consists of five central hypotheses which present claims and assumptions about how an L2 is acquired. The five hypotheses are listed below:

3.2.3.1   The acquisition-learning hypothesis

According to this hypothesis, acquisition is different from learning. The distinction lies at the heart of Krashen's theory. Acquisition occurs subconsciously as a result of participating in natural communication where the focus is on meaning. Learning, however, takes place as a result of conscious study of the formal properties of the language. Acquisition often occurs in natural contexts while learning usually takes place in classroom contexts. Krashen (1982: 10) has the following definition for acquisition and learning:

Acquisition [is] a process similar, if not identical, to the way children develop ability in their first language…Language acquirers are not usually aware of the fact that they are acquiring language, but are only aware of the fact that they are using the language for communication. The result of language acquisition, acquired competence, is also subconscious. We are generally not consciously aware of the rules of language we have acquired. Instead, we have a "feel" for correctness. Grammatical sentences "sound" right, or "feel" right, and errors feel wrong, even if we do not know what rule was violated.

The second way to develop competence in an L2 is by learning.

We will use the term "learning" to refer to conscious knowledge of a second language, knowing the rules, being aware of them, and being able to talk about them. In nontechnical terms, learning is "knowing about" a language, known to most people as "grammar" or "rules". Some synonyms include formal knowledge of a language or explicit learning.

As can be seen, L2 development takes place in different ways. In Krashen's view, learners also use the language developed through these two means for different purposes. What's more, learned knowledge cannot be converted into acquired knowledge. This position has become known as non-interface position. These two separate systems of knowledge are like the two pockets in a person's jacket. You can put things into one, but you can never take them out from the other. The acquired system is used to produce language. When learners generate utterances they focus on meaning, not the form. The learned system serves as an "inspector" of the acquired system. It checks to make sure that the utterance is correct against the knowledge in the learned system.

3. 2. 3. 2　The natural order hypothesis

The natural order hypothesis draws on the SLA research literature that indicates that learners may follow a more or less invariant order in the acquisition of formal grammatical features. This hypothesis suggests that learners acquire the rules of a language in a predictable order. The order is the same regardless of whether instruction is involved or not. This order is like the order of acquisition we discussed in the first two chapters. When the learner is engaged in natural communication tasks, he will manifest the standard order. But when he is engaged in tasks that require or permit the use of metalinguistic knowledge, a different order will emerge (Ellis, 1999: 262).

3. 2. 3. 3　The monitor hypothesis

According to Krashen, the learned rules are only used as a monitor, for the purpose of editing or making changes in what is produced through the acquired system. However, the monitor can not be used at all times. There are three conditions that must be met to activate the monitor. The first condition is *time*. That is, a learner needs time to think about and use the rules in their learned system. The second condition is *focus on form*. A learner must also pay attention to how we are saying something in addition to what we are saying. The third is *know the rule*. That is, a learner has to know a rule in order to use it. In other words, they must have a learned system in order to apply it. Therefore, the monitor is intended to connect the acquired system and the learned system in language use, as can be shown in Figure 3. 1.

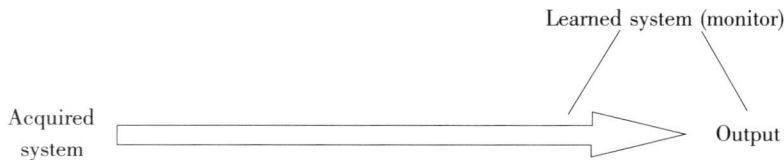

Learned system (monitor)

Acquired system ⟶ Output

Figure 3. 1　The Monitor Function of Learned System

3. 2. 3. 4　The input hypothesis

According to Krashen (1985: 2), language acquisition takes place because there is comprehensible input. If input is understood, and if there is enough of it, grammar can be picked up automatically. As Krashen says, second languages are acquired "by understanding messages or by receiving comprehensible input".

Defined by Krashen, comprehensible input is the language that is heard or read and that is slightly ahead of a learner's current state of grammatical knowledge. If the input contains structures a learner already knows, it serves no purpose in acquisition. Similarly, input containing structures far beyond a learner's current knowledge is not useful either. Krashen described a learner's current state of knowledge as i and the next stage as $i + 1$. Thus, the input a learner receives must be at the $i + 1$ level so that it can be acquired. "We move from i, our current level to $i + 1$, the next level along the natural order, by understanding input containing $i + 1$" said Krashen (1985: 2). According to Krashen, a teacher's main role in a classroom setting is to provide students with comprehensible input.

3.2.3.5 The affective filter hypothesis

One explanation of why some are less successful in learning an L2 is, in Krashen's view, "inappropriate affect". Affect includes factors such as motivation, attitude, self-confidence, and anxiety. Krashen proposed the existence of an affective filter. When the filter is up, input is prevented from passing through; if input is stopped, acquisition does not occur. In contrast, if the filter is down or low, and the input is comprehensible, it will reach the acquisition device and acquisition will take place. One reason why children can successfully acquire their mother tongue may be that affective filter does not exist or is very low.

According to Krashen, acquisition can be explained by two of the above five hypotheses, the input hypothesis and the affective filter hypothesis, besides the LAD. Relevant claims are as follows: ① Learners progress along the natural order by understanding input that contains structures a little bit beyond their current level of competence ($i + 1$). ②Although comprehensible input is necessary for acquisition to take place, it is not sufficient, as learners also need to be affectively disposed to "let in" the input they comprehend. ③Input becomes comprehensible as a result of simplification and with the help of contextual and extralinguistic clues. ④Speaking is the result of acquisition, not its cause. Learner production does not contribute directly to acquisition.

Although the Monitor Model was severely criticized by researchers, it has had a significant influence on language teaching in the USA in 1980s and 1990s, which was

conducted by avoiding explicit teaching of grammar in the classroom settings. Since then, the pendulum began to swing back in the opposite direction: formal grammar teaching was introduced for adult L2 learners, who benefit from an explicit explanation of grammatical structure.

Above we have discussed three early linguistic approaches to the study of SLA, CAH, EA, and the Monitor Model. Although there exists a heated debate among proponents of different approaches, there was widespread agreement on some important points. First, the L2 learner is acquiring a "rule-governed" language system. Second, L2 acquisition involves creative mental processes. Third, age is a primary factor in explaining why some are more (or less) successful in L2 acquisition (Saville-Troike, 2008: 45 – 46). During 1980s, new ideas in Chomskyan theoretical linguistics had a major influence on SLA. Universal grammar became the dominant approach focusing on internal factors.

3.3　Universal Grammar（UG）

3.3.1　Introduction

As for the source of language knowledge, there are two views which have confronted each other for over 2000 years. One view represented by Plato is that language knowledge comes from universal truths, and the other (which is not discussed here) represented by Aristotle is that language knowledge comes from convention. Today, some linguists still stand in Plato's camp, but the names of the camps have changed. They are now called the nativists or mentalists, and they still believe that human beings do have an inborn knowledge of language which must be universally correct and acceptable. The location of such innate knowledge is just in our genes. Since all animals have some qualities genetically inherited from generation to generation, such as spiders inheriting skills of spinning webs, bees inheriting skills of collecting nectar and producing honey, why can't human beings inherit a certain universal logic of language to facilitate their language acquisition?

The UG approach to SLA begins from the perspective of learnability. The assumption of innate universal language properties is motivated by the need to explain why children are universally successful in acquiring their L1 despite insufficient input. As noted by Chomsky (1995: 167): The theory of a particular language is its grammar. The theory of languages and the expressions they generate is universal grammar. UG is a theory of the initial state of the relevant component of the language faculty. Chomsky believed that there is a biological, physiological entity inside our brain which decides what we speak, and this entity is named universal grammar (UG). He has the following concepts about the knowledge of language:

(1) Every human being has language competence, because he has an inborn UG which other species lack.

(2) UG is the initial state of the human language faculty which alone cannot enable a human baby to speak. A baby needs to be exposed to the environment of a certain language and accumulate experience.

(3) Due to the effect of later experience, the baby's mind develops from the initial state into the steady state, which corresponds to the competence of speaking a specific human language.

It was assumed by UG that language acquisition task involves children's induction of rules from the input they receive. How this could happen remains quite mysterious: Linguistic input goes into a "black box" in the mind, something happens, and the grammatical system of a particular language comes out. A major change in thinking about the acquisition process occurred with Chomsky's reconceptualization of UG in the Principles and Parameters framework (also called the Government and Binding model), and with his subsequent introduction of the Minimalist Program.

3.3.2 Principles and parameters

According to UG theory, every speaker is endowed with a set of principles which apply to all languages and a set of parameters that can change from one language to another within certain limits. To have a better understanding of the two concepts, Cook made an interesting analogy between driving a car and principles and parameters. The principle is compared to the universal traffic rule in every country that every vehicle must run on one side of the road, and the parameter to the specific rule in a specific country in which cars may be only allowed to go on the right side while in another on the left:

Overall there is a principle that drivers have to keep consistently to one side of the road, which is taken for granted by all drivers in all countries... The principle does not, however, say which side of the road people should drive on. A parameter of driving allows the side to be the left in England and Japan, and the right in the USA and France. The parameter has two values or "settings" —left and right. Once a country has opted for one side or the other, it sticks to its choice: a change of setting is a massively complex operation, whether it happens for a whole country, as in Sweden, or for the individual travelling from England to France. So, a universal principle and a variable parameter together sum up the essence of driving. The principle states the universal requirement on driving; the parameter specifies the variation between countries (Cook, 1997: 250 – 251).

An example in language is that all human languages have subject, verb, and object, which may be decided by one of the universal principles. However, these three components are in different orders in the sentences of different languages. In Chinese and English, the dominant order is SVO; in Japanese, it is SOV; in Arabic, we can find VSO. These differences are regarded as different values of the parameter of word order. For example, in Chinese we say "约翰踢球"; in English, we also say *John kicked the ball*. But the Japanese version is: *John-wa booru-wo ketta*. (John ball kicked). Therefore, it can be said that acquiring a language means applying the principles of UG to a particular language, and learning which value is appropriate for each parameter.

A second example is co-reference. A general principle of language is that it permits co-reference by means of some form of reflexive. Let us look at the English sentence: *Tom blamed himself*. In this sentence, the subject, *Tom*, is co-referential with the reflexive, *himself*. Both words refer to the same person. However, in another sentence *Tom knew Gary blamed himself*, the reflective *himself* must be understood as referring to *Gary*, not *Tom*, because English only permits "local binding". "Long distance binding", in which the reflexive co-refers to a subject in another clause, is prohibited. However, some other languages permit long-distance as well as local binding. For example, the Japanese version of the above sentence is ambiguous; the reflexive "himself" may refer to either "Tom" or "Gary".

Other principles and parameter settings accounting for variations between languages include those that determine whether or not agreement between subject and verb must be explicitly expressed, and whether or not a subject must be overtly present. Compare the following three sentences with the same meaning in three different languages:

English: *It is raining.*

Chinese: *Xia yu* (down rain)

Spanish: *Está lloviendo* (is raining)

(Saville – Troike, 2008: 48 –49)

The English speakers say *It is raining*, with a meaningless subject it, while the subject is omitted in the Chinese *Xia yu* and Spanish *Está lloviendo*.

There is no complete listing of principles and parameters, and there will never be one, since proposals concerning their identity keep changing as the theory evolves. Anyway, the specification of universal principles and parameters is related to theoretical developments and understandings and may have practical value in second language teaching and learning. It must be pointed out that children never use such a list, nor could they understand it if one were available. Principles and parameters are not, cannot, and need not be learned in the acquisition of any L1, because they are assumed to be built into the LAD we are born with. This may partially be true for adult L2 learners, though an awareness of parameter settings in an L2 may help learners focus perception on input and thus facilitate learning.

3.3.3   UG and SLA

We know that UG is the initial state of the human language faculty, and the reason why children can successfully pick up their mother tongue is that UG exists in their minds. What we are concerned about here and now is the relationship between UG and L2 acquisition. Does UG work for SLA? We now focus on three key issues: the initial state in SLA, the nature and development of interlanguage, and the final state in SLA.

3.3.3.1   Initial state in SLA

An essential question to be considered is what the nature of the linguistic knowledge is with which learners begin the L2 acquisition process. When L2 acquisition begins, the learners already have the knowledge of L1. Guided by UG, they have made all the parametric choices that are appropriate for their L1. It is a normal phenomenon for some L1 knowledge to be transferred into L2. When L1 and L2 parameter settings for the same principle are the same, positive transfer is likely to take place. On the contrary, when L1 and L2 parameter settings are different, negative transfer or interference may occur. For example, an L1 Chinese learner of English might say *kick the ball* as a result of positive transfer of a parameter setting from Chinese to English; however, a Japanese beginning learner of English might say *ball kick*, which is clearly caused by negative transfer of parameter setting from Japanese into English.

As for access to UG in L2 acquisition, there are a number different views: ① The complete access view L2 learners have full access to UG principles. It is assumed that there is no critical period blocking L2 acquisition and L2 learners will be able to attain full linguistic competence. ② The no access view. This position is also called the fundamental difference hypothesis. It is assumed that adults fail to achieve full linguistic competence. ③ The partial access view. Learners may have access to linguistic principles but not to the full range of parametric variation. ④ The dual access view. Adult learners have access to UG but also make use of general learning strategies. The use of the latter can "block" the operation of UG, causing learners to produce "impossible" errors and fail to achieve full competence. It can be clearly seen from the above contradictory positions that the role of UG in SLA is still uncertain.

3.3.3.2 Nature and development of interlanguage

From an UG perspective, interlanguage (IL) can be defined as intermediate states of L2 development containing IL1, IL2, IL3, etc. If L2 learners retain some access to UG, the process of IL development is, in large part, one of resetting parameters based on the input of the new language. For example, a Japanese speaker learning English needs to reset the word order parameter from SOV to SVO. Learners change the parameter setting because the L2 input they receive does not match the L1 settings they have. If UG is still available, then that will limit their choices, and their IL grammars will not deviate from structures that are allowed by UG. **Positive evidence**, which is the input gained from experiencing L2 in natural use or formal instruction, will provide sufficient information for the learners to set necessary parameters. **Negative evidence**, which includes explicit correction, is often also provided to L2 learners, and this may play a role in parameter resetting for adult L2 learners.

From a constructionist perspective, an approach to SLA formulated within Chomsky's Minimalist Program, IL development is considered as the progressive mastery of L2 vocabulary along with the morphological features (which specify word form) that are part of lexical knowledge. While the general principles and parameters do not need to be learned, "morphological paradigms must gradually be added to the lexicon, just like words" (White, 2003: 194). There are stages and variations in IL development because these morphological features in learners' competence are not specified completely. In L1 acquisition, parameter setting and mastery of morphological features are linked; but for adult L2 learners, they are not necessarily linked. Therefore, failure to reach a state of full feature specification in the lexicon is seen as the main reason that many L2 learners fossilize at an intermediate level of development without gaining near-native competence.

In an UG approach, lexical acquisition plays an important role in providing information for parameter (re) setting and other aspects of grammar. This is quite different from the structuralists and behaviorists' view in that all the basic grammatical structures of L2 can be learned in conjunction with minimal vocabulary. If learners no longer have access to UG, IL development would need to be explained as a fundamentally different learning process than that taking place for L1.

3. 3. 3. 3　Final state in SLA

The question of why some L2 learners are more successful than others is highly relevant for the second language acquisition, though it is not relevant for first language acquisition since all children achieve a native final state. The following are a few possibilities, summarized by Saville-Troike (2008: 52), within the UG framework that can account for the great variability found in the ultimate level of achievement made by L2 learners:

(1) All learners may not have the same degree of access to UG.

(2) Different relationships between various L1s and L2s may result in differential transfer or interference.

(3) Some learners may receive qualitatively different L2 input from others.

(4) Some learners may be more perceptive than others of mismatches between L2 input and existing L1 parameter settings.

(5) Different degrees of specification for lexical features may be achieved by different learners.

It should be noted that SLA researchers have been careful to point out that UG is very

strictly defined, covering only part of the total phenomena which a comprehensive theory of L2 acquisition will need to account for. As a strictly defined theory of L2 acquisition, UG, in contrast to many cognitive theories, affords very precise hypotheses about the nature of interlanguage grammars. Nevertheless, there are other issues in SLA that are not addressed, or are not addressed satisfactorily, by a narrow UG approach, with its strictly internal focus on the mental organization for the learner. In the coming section, we move from the internal to the external analysis of linguistic universals and look at L2 acquisition from the perspective of typological universals.

3.4　Typological Universals and SLA

3.4.1　The concept of markedness

A typological approach to linguistic analysis involves a crosslinguistic comparison of specific features such as articles, word order, or relative clause construction. Its purpose is to identify commonalities across languages. Three types of universals have been identified. The first type are absolute universals. They refer to those features present in all the world's languages. For example, all languages have nouns and verbs and vowels and consonants. The second type are frequency universals. That is, a specific feature may be found in a large number of languages, but be missing from some. For example, there is a universal tendency for the negator to have a definite position relative to the finite element. There is also a definite preference for the negator to take a pre-verbal rather than a post – verbal position. The third type of commonalities are implicational universals. These universals take the form of "if/ then" statements. For example, "If a language has a noun before a demonstrative, then it has a noun before a relative clause". Or "If a language is SOV, then if the adjective precedes the noun, then the genitive precedes the noun."

A fundamental concept underlying much grammatical work in typology is markedness. Traditional view of markedness viewed features as either unmarked or marked (for example, in the pair of indefinite articles "a" and "an", "a" is unmarked while "an" is marked). Language typology sees markedness primarily as a relative phenomenon (that is, one feature is more marked than another). But how can we tell which feature is marked and which is unmarked? Three main types of evidence have been identified by Croft for determining markedness:

(1) Structure. This concerns the presence or absence of a feature. For example, plural can be considered more marked than singular because it typically involves the addition of a morpheme.

(2) Behavior. This is concerned with whether an element is grammatically more "versatile" than another. The more versatile it is, the more unmarked it is. Versatility is evident in both the number of inflections a grammatical category has and in the number of syntactic contexts in which a specific element can occur. In the former case, for example, singular third person has 3 forms in English (he, she, and it), whereas plural third person has only one. In the latter, for example, more constructions occur with the active voice than with the passive voice.

(3) Frequency. The unmarked value is likely to occur with greater frequency than the marked value.

A considerable number of SLA studies have examined phonological features and grammatical features. Given the extent of SLA research based on typological universals, we only examine in this section two major issues related to L2 acquisition: ① whether markedness can account for learning difficulty; ②whether typological universals can explain the order of acquisition of grammatical features. In order to answer the questions, quite a few grammatical areas have been examined. Below we focus on the relative clauses since they have attracted the attention of a number of SLA researchers.

3.4.2　The study of relative clauses

Typological studies of relative clauses focus on a few features. The first feature is the position of the relative clause. Languages differ according to whether modification is prenominal or postnominal. English and French are examples of languages where the relative pronoun follows the head noun while Japanese and Chinese are languages that position the relative clause before the noun they are modifying.

The second feature is relativization. The noun phrase accessibility hypothesis (NPAH) provides a universal hierarchy of relativized functions. In English language, for example, the relative pronoun has 6 functions: ①as the subject of the relative clause ("The woman who

saw the burglar called the police"); ②as the direct object ("The woman whom the burglar saw called the police"); ③as the indirect object ("The woman to whom the burglar gave the money called the police"); ④as the object of a preposition ("The woman about whom the children told a story called the police"); ⑤ as the genitive ("The woman whose daughter was a burglar called the police"); ⑥as the object of the comparative ("The woman whom the burglar is richer than called the place"). According to research, languages differ in the noun phrases that were "accessible" to relativization. The following hierarchy was proposed, as shown in Table 3.5.

Table 3.5 Accessibility Hierarchy for Relative Clauses

SU > DO > IO > OPREP > GEN > OCOMP
SU = subject
DO = direct object
IO = indirect object
OPREP = object of preposition
GEN = genitive
OCOPM = object of comparative

According to this hierarchy, if a language has a relative clause of type X, then it will also have any relative clause type higher on the hierarchy, that is, to the left of the type X. For example, if a language has OPREP (object of preposition) relatives (*That's the woman about whom I told you*), then it has the first three types, SU, DO and IO clauses. Thus, the most marked relativized position is OCOMP.

The third feature is related to resumptive pronouns. Languages also vary according to whether they permit resumptive pronouns (pronoun copy) in relative clauses. English does not. Thus, the sentence "*The boy who I gave the puppy to him was delighted*" is ungrammatical. Typologically, languages with resumptive pronouns are more common than those without resumptive pronouns. Therefore, the presence of resumptive pronouns is seen as unmarked and their absence marked. However, languages that do permit resumptive pronouns do not necessarily do so in all relative clauses. A pronominal copy was most likely to occur with relative pronouns lower down the hierarchy (for example, IO) than with those higher up (for example, SU). In other words, if a language manifested resumptive pronouns in an unmarked type of relative clause it would also allow them in more marked clauses but not vice versa.

The fourth feature is the role of the head noun and the relative pronoun. The roles of the head noun and the relative pronoun can be matching as in the sentence *"The man who saw the rabbit caught the fox"* where both the head noun ("the man") and the pronoun ("who") function as subjects of their clauses, or non-matching as in *"The man saw the fox that caught the rabbit"* where the head noun ("the fox") functions as direct object in the main clause while the relative pronoun ("that") functions as subject of the relative clause. It is predicted that learners do better when the head noun and the relative pronoun are matching than when they are non-matching.

The fifth feature is the matrix positions. Relativization is not the only problem learners face in acquiring relative clauses. Another question is where the relative clause occurs in the matrix sentence. A relative clause can function as part of the direct object of the sentence as in *"Than man saw the fox that caught the rabbit"* in which the relative clause is joined onto the main clause, or it can function as part of the subject of the sentence as in *"The man who saw the fox caught a rabbit"* in which the relative clause is embedded in the main clause. Whether the relative clause is joined onto or embedded in the main clause can affect L2 acquisition.

The sixth feature is the depth of embedding. Relativization can vary in terms of the structural distance between the relative pronoun and the noun phrase that it replaces and that figures as a "gap" or a "trace" in the relative clause. Thus, in the case of sentences with a relativized subject, the distance is minimal (for example, *"I bought the puppy that* [__] *made me laugh"*). However, in a sentence where the relativized noun phrase is extracted from a prepositional phrase, the distance is much greater (for example, *"The kennel in which I put the puppy* [__] *was expensive"*). There are crosslinguistic differences relating to extraction. For example, languages vary in terms of whether the pronoun filler appears before or after the gap. They also vary in terms of whether the "gap" is filled with a resumptive pronoun. It is suggested that these differences affect the ease with which different relative clauses can be processed.

3. 4. 3　Relevant hypotheses

Presented above are typological accounts of relative clauses, based on which SLA researchers have proposed a number of hypotheses. The following four assumptions serve as a basis for investigating how L2 learners handle relative clauses and the sequence in which they are acquired.

(1) The Noun Phrase Accessibility Hierarchy (NPAH) Hypothesis. NPAH reflects the relative ease of relativization. That is, learners will find it easier to process the relative clauses that appear higher up the hierarchy than those appearing low down. For example, the SU function is easier to acquire than the DO function, and IO function than OP function. A further assumption concerns resumptive pronouns. Learners will be more likely to insert a resumptive pronoun in clauses where the relativization is marked than in clauses where it is unmarked.

(2) The Perceptual Difficulty Hypothesis (PDH). Based on differences relating to the position of the relative clause in its matrix sentence, PDH claims that center-embedded relative clauses will be more difficult to process and acquire than right-conjoined and left-conjoined clauses.

(3) The Structural Distance Hypothesis (SDH). SDH is based on depth of embedding. It is predicted that the relative difficulty of subject and object relative clause is determined by the distance between the gapped noun phrase and the head noun phrase. In other words, the shorter the distance, the greater the ease of processing.

(4) The SO Hierarchy Hypothesis (SOHH). This hypothesis claims that the ease/difficulty of processing/acquiring relative clauses depends on both the matrix position of the relative clause and the depth of embedding involved. SOHH predicts the order of difficulty in clauses involving subject and object functions: OS > OO/SS > SO. The first letter in each term refers to whether the relative clause modifies the subject or object of the matrix clause; the second letter refers to the function of the relative pronoun in the relative clause. Thus, the order of ease/difficulty can be illustrated by the following examples:

OS: The man saw *the fox* (O) that (S) caught the rabbit. (Easiest to learn)

↓

OO: The man saw the *fox* (O) *that* (O) the hunter talked about.

SS: *The man* (S) *who* (S) saw the fox caught the rabbit.

$$\downarrow$$

SO: *The fox* (S) *that* (O) man saw caught the rabbit. (Most difficult to learn)

3. 4. 4　SLA research on relative studies

The central issue in SLA research is concerned with the effect of markedness on learning difficulty and that of typological universals on the order of acquisition. Many research results have important implications for L2 learning and teaching. According to the early studies, there is some evidence to show that linguistic markedness may have an effect on the extent to which learners avoid relative clauses, the order in which they acquire relative pronoun functions, and the extent to which learners make resumptive errors. The general finding is that acquisition is easier in the unmarked, higher positions and more difficult in the marked, lower positions of the hierarchy.

Later studies attempted to investigate the claims of different hypotheses presented above. For example, Izumi (2003) set out to test the predictions of three hypotheses: NPAH, PDH, and SOHH. A variety of instruments were used to measure learners' ability to produce relative clauses, process them receptively, and judge their correctness. The results supported the NPAH hypothesis with data collected from the sentence combination test and partially with data collected from the grammaticality judgement test, but not from data collected by means of the interpretation test. In contrast, the data from all three instruments lent support to the PDH and partial support for the SOHH. It was concluded that the NPAH and the PDH are complementary rather than competing hypotheses and that the results indicated some obvious task effects. He suggested that the ability to produce relative clauses is more susceptible to processing difficulties based on predictions regarding typological markedness and the ability to comprehend them.

The well-known NPAH is not without limitations. One interesting criticism is that it is a mistake to include genitive in the hierarchy, as it has a separate and complete hierarchy of its own. For example, it was argued that there are in fact two hierarchies: one for − Genitive and the other for + Genitive (as shown in Table 3. 6) . Another criticism is that OCOMP is problematic in English—a language that is supposed to manifest this function—because some native speakers do not accept that sentences with this function are grammatical.

The NPAH serves as an example of how SLA and linguistics can assist each

other. Linguistic facts can be used to explain and even predict acquisition. In addition, the results of empirical studies of L2 acquisition can be used to refine our understanding of linguistic facts.

Table 3.6   The Accessibility Hierarchy for − Genitive and + Genitive

Function	− Genitive	+ Genitive
Su	The man who came…	The man whose wife came…
DO	The man (whom) I saw…	The man whose wife I saw…
IO	The man (whom) I gave the book to…	The man whose wife I gave the book to…
OPREP	The man (whom) I looked at…	The man whose wife I looked at…
OCOMP	The man (whom) I am bigger than	The man whose wife I am bigger than…

3.5   Functional Approaches

Unlike UG, which is a linguistic approach with an internal focus on language acquisition, functional approaches take an external focus on language learning. Functional models are different from structuralist and generative model in that they emphasize the information content of utterances and consider language primarily as a system of communication rather than a set of rules. The term "function" includes both structural function and pragmatic function. The former is concerned with the role a structural element plays as a subject or object, or an actor or goal, while the latter concerns what the use of language can accomplish, such as convey information, control others' behaviour, or express emotion. The scope of concern in functional approaches goes beyond the sentence to include discourse structure and how language is used in interaction, and to include aspects of communication beyond language. In this part, we will first introduce the functional tendency in the study of language. Then we will review systemic linguistics and functional typology.

3.5.1 Functional tendency in recent research of language

From the recent constructivist perspective on the study of language, we have seen a shift in patterns of research. The shift has not been far away from the generative/cognitive side of the continuum, but rather move more deeply into the essence of language (Brown, 2021: 32). Language began to be seen as just one manifestation of the cognitive and affective ability to deal with the world, with others, and with the self. The generative rules that were proposed under the nativist framework were abstract, formal, explicit, and quite logical, but they dealt with the forms of language (such as morphemes, words, sentences, and the rules that govern them) and not with the deeper functional levels of meaning constructed from social interaction. Functions differ from forms in that they are the meaningful, interactive purposes within a social context which we accomplish with the forms.

Evidence can be found in the explanations of children's telegraphic utterances (which we mentioned in chapter one). The nativists described the telegraphic utterance "Mommy sock" as a sentence consisting of a pivot word and an open word. Bloom (1971) criticized the pivot grammar, pointing out that the relationships in which words occur in telegraphic utterances are only superficially similar. She found that there are at least three possible underlying relations in "Mommy sock": ①agent-action (Mommy is putting the sock on); ②agent-object (Mommy sees the sock); ③possessor-possessed (Mommy's sock). Bloom analyzed data in real contexts and concluded that children learn underlying structures, and not superficial word order. Therefore, depending on the social context, "Mommy sock" could mean a number of different things to a child.

Bloom's study paved the way for a new way of child language research, centering on the relationship of cognitive development to L1 acquisition (Brown, 2021: 32). It was argued, by Piaget for example, the overall development is the result of children's interaction with their environment. According to Piaget, what children learn about language is determined by what they already know about the world. Gleitman and Wanner (1982: 13) noted that children appear to approach language learning equipped with conceptual interpretive abilities for categorizing the world. Slobin (1997), who found seven types of function in children's telegraphic speech (as we discussed in chapter one), demonstrated that in all languages, semantic learning depends on cognitive development and that sequences of development are determined more by semantic complexity than by structural complexity. Bloom also noted that what children know will determine what they learn about the code for both speaking and understanding messages. In a word, researchers attended to children's acquisition of the functions of language, and the relationships of the language forms to those functions.

A clear tendency in recent years is that language development is interwoven not only with cognition and memory but also with social and functional acquisition. Attention has fallen on the interaction between children's language acquisition and the learning of how social systems operate in human behavior. There are also studies investigating one of the most problematic areas—interactive, communicative functions of language. Researchers show great interest in such questions as what children learn about talking with others, about connected pieces of discourse (relations between sentences), about the hearer-speaker interaction, and about conversational cues. Within such a perspective, researchers are tackling the very heart of language—its communicative and pragmatic function.

3. 5. 2   Systemic linguistics

Systemic linguistics, developed by M. A, K. Halliday in late 1950s, is a model for analyzing language in terms of the inter-related systems of choices that are available for expressing meaning. There is a basic notion that language structures cannot be studied without considering the circumstances of their use, including the extralinguistic social context. Halliday has the following functional view of language acquisition:

Language acquisition…needs to be seen as the mastery of linguistic functions. Learning one's mother tongue is learning the uses of language, and the meanings, or rather the meaning potential, associated with them. The structures, the words and the sounds are the realization of this meaning potential. Learning language is learning how to mean.

(Halliday 1973: 345)

What do language learners essentially acquire? In Halliday's view, it is not a system of rules but the "meaning potential", that is, what the learner can; not what he knows. The process of acquiring a language is "mastering certain basic functions of language and developing a meaning potential for each" (Halliday, 1975: 33) . Halliday (1975) describes the evolution of the following pragmatic functions in early child L1 acquisition (what he called the "functions of language as a whole"), which are universal for children, as shown in Table 3. 7.

Table 3.7 Universal Functions of Language

Function	Description
Instrumental	Language used as a means of getting things done (one of the first to be evolved) : the "I want" function
Regulatory	Language used to regulate the behavior of others : the "do as I tell you" function
Interactional	Language used in interaction between self and others : the "me and you" function
Personal	Awareness of language as a form of one's own identity : the "here I come" function
Heuristic	Language as a way of learning about things : the "tell me why" function
Imagination	Creation through language of a world of one's own making : the "let's pretend" function
Representational	Means of expressing propositions, or communicating about something (one of the last to appear) : the "I've got something to tell you" function

The functional view of the study of SLA is that L2 learning is a process of adding multilingual meaning potential to what has been achieved in L1. In other words, "SLA is largely a matter of learning new linguistic forms to fulfill the same functions within a different social milieu" (Saville-Troike, 2008 : 54) . Saville-Troike himself once observed children's linguistic performance who had just arrived in USA from different countries, and found that all of them could accomplish a wide range of communicative functions even they had limited English means at their disposal. The following are the different functions performed by different means, including both nonlinguistic and linguistic strategies :

Table 3.8 Functions Fulfilled by Different Forms

	Regulatory	Interactional	Heuristic
Nonlinguistic	(hitting another child who is annoying)	Unh? (uttered as a greeting)	(pointing at an object with a question look to request the English item for it)

（To be continued）

	Regulatory	**Interactional**	**Heuristic**
L2 formula or memorized routine	Don't do that.	Hi!	What's it?
Single L2 word	He! (pointing at another child's offending behavior to a teacher)	Me? (an invitation to play)	What? (asking for an English term for an object)
L2 phrase or clause	That bad!	You me play?	What name this?
Complex L2 construction	The teacher say that wrong!	I no like to play now.	What is name we call this?

3.5.3 Functional typology

Functional typology is based on the comparative study of a wide range of the world's languages. This approach of functional study involves the classification of languages and their features into types. Its purpose is to describe patterns of similarities and differences among them, and to decide which types occur more frequently or are universal in distribution. The reason why this approach is called "functional" is that the analysis takes into consideration not only language structure, but also its meaning and use.

Functional typology has been applied to the study of SLA most fruitfully in accounting for developmental stages of L2 acquisition, for why some L2 forms are more or less difficult than others for learners to learn, and for why some L1 elements transfer to L2 and some do not. An important concept related to these accounts is "markedness", dealing with whether a specific feature of a language is "marked" or "unmarked". An unmarked feature is more frequently used, and more "normal" than a marked one, while a marked feature is more complex in light of structure and concept. For example, in phonology, the most common syllable structure CV (consonant + vowel, such as in *me*, *tea* and *banana*) is "unmarked", while the less common type, such as a sequence of consonants (*str* in streets) is "marked". In vocabulary, the preposition *in* signifies location while *into* is more complex, indicating both location and direction. Thus, *into* is "marked" in contrast with *in*. In syntax, the basic word order SVO is unmarked while SOV is relatively marked. Even in discourse, there are marked and unmarked expressions. An "unmarked" response to the English greeting *How are you*? is *Fine*. However, a response giving information about one's health or other personal conditions is "marked" because such a response is not expected in the normal routine exchange.

The degrees of markedness will correspond to degrees of difficulty. The marked features are predicted to cause difficulty. The Markedness Differential Hypothesis (MDH) (also known as markedness theory), proposed by Eckman (1977), can be used to explain why there seems to be a certain order of acquisition of morphemes in English. Relevant studies showed that unmarked elements are likely to be acquired before marked ones in children's L1, and to be easier for a learner to master in L2. In phonology, for example, the babbling and first words of a child in L1 are likely to have an unmarked CV syllabic structure (no matter what the NL) and marked CC sequences appear only at a later stage of development. It is also likely that L2 learners will find marked CC sequences more difficult to produce, especially if they do not occur at all in the speakers' L1. The MDH predicts that unmarked features in L1 are more likely to transfer, and that marked features in L2 will be harder to learn, as is shown in Table 3.9.

Table 3.9 Markedness and Predictions in L2 Learning

Feature in L1	Feature in L2	Prediction
Unmarked	Marked	L1 feature will transfer to L2
Marked	Unmarked	L2 feature will be easy to learn L1 feature will not transfer to L2

To have a better understanding, we will look at an example of pronunciation in English and Spanish. The pronunciation of consonant sequence /sk/ in English is marked (as in *school*). This is difficult for Spanish people to learn because Spanish phonological system is simpler, and it does not allow two voiceless consonants to occur together. So, beginning Spanish ESL learners tend to break the /sk/ combination apart into two syllables and pronounce the word *school* in the Spanish way /es-kul/, thus avoiding the marked structure. Just in opposition, those who learn Spanish will have no difficulty in pronouncing the Spanish word *escuela* (school), since it doesn't contain any consonant cluster in any syllable.

It seems that functional typology resembles contrastive analysis in comparing elements of different languages in order to predict or explain transfer from L1 to L2. However, it goes beyond the surface-level structural contrasts of CA to more abstract patterns, principles, and constraints. The Markedness Differential Hypothesis is also an advance over the traditional CA approach: "Eckman's work suggests that transfer is not always a bidirectional process, as might be inferred from a strict contrastive analysis approach. Instead, this work on linguistic universals indicates that the reason why some first-language structures are transferred and others are not relates to the degree of markedness of the structures in the various languages." (McLaughlin, 1987: 90)

An important implication we might draw from MDH is that some aspects of some languages are more difficult to learn than others, despite the traditional claim within linguistics that all languages are equally complex. Another issue to speculate about is why some types and patterns of features are more or less frequent than others in both L1s and L2s. Functional explanations tend to refer to extralinguistic factors. Certain factors having been suggested are: perceptual salience, ease of cognitive processing, physical constraints (for example, the shape of the human vocal tract), and communicative needs.

Assignment

1. Questions for self-study.

(1) What are the common characteristics of human language?

(2) What are the main criticisms against the CAH? Give examples to illustrate.

(3) Why is the study of learner errors beneficial to both the teaching and learning of a second language?

(4) What is the procedure of error analysis? What are the main shortcomings of EA?

(5) While collecting samples, what factors and variables should be considered?

(6) How do you distinguish an interlingual error from an intralingual error? Give examples to illustrate.

(7) What is the difference between a local error and a global error? Give examples to illustrate.

(8) What are the five assumptions of the Monitor Model?

(9) What is the difference between acquisition and learning according to Krashen?

（10）What is the relationship between a principle and a parameter in language? Give examples to illustrate.

（11）Is there a general agreement that L2 learners have access to UG in the initial state of SLA? What are the different opinions on it?

（12）What is accessibility hierarchy? What is the basic principle of accessibility hierarchy?

（13）What is the functional view of language acquisition? What is the primary purpose of language according to a functionalist perspective?

（14）What is the definition of "markedness"? How does "markedness" affect L2 learning?

2. Match the following theories with their central figures.

（1）Contrastive Analysis （CA）　　　　a. Krashen

（2）Error Analysis （EA）　　　　　　b. Chomsky

（3）Interlanguage　　　　　　　　　　c. Lado

（4）Monitor Model　　　　　　　　　　d. Halliday

（5）Universal Grammar （UG）　　　　e. Corder

（6）Systemic linguistics　　　　　　　f. Selinker

3. Fill in the blanks in the following passage.

According to Krashen, second language learners have two independent means of developing knowledge of a second language—one way is through _____ and the other is through _____ . There are two different knowledge types. The _____ system is used to produce language, while the _____ system is used as an "inspector" of the acquired system. It checks to make sure that the utterance is correct against the knowledge in the learned system.

According to Halliday, Language acquisition ... needs to be seen as the mastery of linguistic _____ . Learning one's mother tongue is learning the _____ of language, and the _____ , or rather the meaning potential, associated with them. The structures, the words and the sounds are the _____ of this meaning potential. Learning language is learning how to mean.

4. Open discussion for pair or group work.

（1）Read the following scenarios and decide which aspect of language is mentioned in each instance. You can choose from lexicon, morphology, phonology, and syntax.

a. The English word "talk" has near synonyms like "speak", "say", "express", "shout", "yell" and "whisper".

b. The English word "talk" can be pronounced differently depending on the geographical locations of the speakers.

c. In English, the appropriate word order is SVO, like saying "The man was talking to the child". In Japanese, the word order is SOV, so one would say "The man the child to was talking."

d. If we say the word "talks" alone, outside of any context, we could consider it to be composed of the root "talk" and a plural -s to make a noun （more than one talk/discussion/ address）, or we could consider it to be made up of the root "talk" and a third person -s to make a conjugated verb （like "he talks," "she talks," or "it talks"）.

（2）Krashen's Input Hypothesis is crucially dependent upon the concept of i + 1 and comprehensible input. How can you determine whether there is sufficient comprehensible input? If a learner seems to have fossilized, does it mean that there is insufficient input? If a learner has fossilized and you can show that the input is rich with a particular structure, what other explanations can you give for the non-progress?

（3）Listen to someone who learns and speaks your language non-natively. Write down some ungrammatical sentences they have spoken. Use principles of CA and the procedures of EA in this chapter and try to classify the errors into different types. Finally, explain why the learner makes such errors.

（4）The following data are from the written compositions of some Chinese ESL junior school students. Study them carefully. First identify the errors. Then describe the errors by categorizing them into different types. Finally, explain why these errors occurred.

1）My brother only 5 years old.

2）She have bread and milk for breakfast.

3）Alice's brother is a Canada boy.

4）The students in her class all like she.

5）There are pencils and a ruler are in my schoolbag.

6) Teacher don't like me.

7) His students are all very like him.

8) No thank you.

9) He standed beside me.

10) He like fruit.

11) They are five people in my family, there are my grandparents, my parents, and me.

12) Why does he tall?

13) He has two basketball and four volleyball.

14) She cooks food are very delicious.

15) There are six peoples in Betty's family.

16) He comed late.

17) His room is clean because he likes tidy.

18) Anne is university student.

19) Saran likes play volleyball.

20) She name is Smith Ella.

Chapter Four　Psychological Aspects of SLA

In the previous chapter we discussed SLA from the perspective of linguistics, concerning linguistic rules, linguistic principles, and linguistic universals. In this chapter, we will examine psychological accounts of SLA which adopt a broadly cognitive perspective— seeing language acquisition as involving mental processes that explain how L2 knowledge is represented and acquired. We will first examine the relationship between language and brain, and review briefly the behaviorist way of L2 learning. Then, we will focus on the cognitive perspective of language learning, introducing some related L2 learning theories such as information processing, connectionist/emergentist models, the competition model (CM), skill-acquisition theories, Bialystok's theory of L2 learning, Gass's integrative model of SLA, and usage-based model. Finally, we will discuss some individual learner differences which affect both the process of L2 learning and the learning outcomes.

4.1　Language and the Brain

In this section, we will look at briefly how the brain handles language and its acquisition from the neurological perspective. We begin by understanding how certain parts of the human brain relate to L2 acquisition. An interesting area of inquiry in SLA is the study of the function of the brain in the process of acquisition. Early in the 19th century, there were notions that certain parts of the brain may be specialized for language functions. For example, French surgeon Paul Broca (1861, 1865) observed that an area (later called "Broca's area") in the left frontal lobe seemed to be responsible for the ability to speak. An injury to this part of the brain will lead to extreme difficulty in producing speech. Such a patient has to make great efforts to produce a sentence. He uses distorted articulation, and most typically, fails to use functional morphemes. If the impairment is very serious, he may forget word sequence. For example, a patient with this disease once described the breakfast he had by saying *I eggs and eat and drink coffee breakfast.*

A German doctor, Carl Wernicke (1874) further identified a nearby area (named Wernicke's area), which is central to language processing. If one suffers from a language disorder called Wernicke's aphasia, his semantic and pragmatic ability will be robbed. Any large destruction in this area results in the loss of understanding and the ability to make meaningful speech. For example, some patients of Wernicke's aphasia speak fluently, but their words are difficult to understand, with general terms conveying little meaning, such as *I don't know what's happened to that, but it's taken that out. That is mm there without doing it, the thing that are being done.* Although some exceptions have been found, language is represented primarily in the left hemisphere of the brain including both Broca's area and Wernicke's area.

Specialization of the two halves of the brain is called lateralization. As a child's brain matures, different functions became lateralized to the left or right hemisphere. For example, the left hemisphere is associated with logical, analytical thought, with mathematical and linear processing of information. The right hemisphere, however, is related to the perception and memory of visual, tactile, and auditory images, and is more efficient in the processing of holistic, integrative, and emotional information. The characteristics of each hemisphere are listed in Table 4.1:

Table 4.1   Left and Right Brain Characteristics (Brown, 2021: 118)

Left-brain Dominance	Right-brain Dominance
Relies strongly on the intellect	Uses intuitive processes
Remembers names	Remembers faces
Responds to verbal instructions and explanations	Responds to demonstrated, illustrated or symbolic instructions
Experiments systematically and with control	Experiments randomly and with less restraint
Makes objective judgments	Makes subjective judgments
Planned and structured	Fluid and spontaneous
Prefers established, certain information	Prefers elusive, uncertain information

（To be continued）

Left-brain Dominance	Right-brain Dominance
Reads analytically	Reads with synthesis
Relies on language in thinking and remembering	Relies on images in thinking and remembering
Is stronger in talking, writing, and verbal communication	Is stronger in drawing, images, and manipulating objects
Prefers multiple-choice tests	Prefers open-ended questions
Controls feelings	More free with feelings
Deciphers linguistic cues, lexical, and grammatical subtleties	Interprets body language, attends to facial, nonverbal communication
Uses empirical description	Uses metaphors and verbal imagery
Favors logical problem solving	Favors intuitive problem solving

The specialization increases as the brain matures and becomes less plastic. That is, if one area of the brain is damaged, it becomes less able to perform the functions of another. An interesting question is when lateralization takes place and whether or not that lateralization process affects language acquisition. As suggested by Lenneberg （1967）, lateralization is a slow process that begins around the age of 2 and is completed around puberty （though there are disagreements on this issue from other scholars who posited a much earlier age of completion）. During this time the child is neurologically assigning functions little by little to one side of the brain or the other. Language is one of these functions. And it was found that children up to the age of puberty who suffer injury to the left hemisphere are able to re-localize language functions to the right hemisphere, to "relearn" their first language with relatively little impairment.

Another interesting question we are concerned with here is: what do these arguments and findings say about the relationship between lateralization and language acquisition? Scovel （1969） suggested that the plasticity of the brain prior to puberty enables children to acquire not only their first language but also a second language, and that possibly it is the very accomplishment of lateralization that makes it difficult for people to easily acquire fluent control of a second language. This is associated with a "critical period", also called sensitive period for language acquisition: a biologically determined period of life when language can be acquired more easily and beyond which time language is increasingly difficult to acquire. The so-called Critical Period Hypothesis will be discussed below in relation to the influence of age on the second language acquisition.

However, another branch of neurolinguistic research focused on the role of the right hemisphere in the acquisition of an L2. For example, Obler (1981: 58) noted that in L2 learning, there is significant right hemisphere participation and that "this participation is particularly active during the early stages of learning the second language". Obler cited the strategy of guessing at meanings, and of using formulaic utterances, as examples of right hemisphere activity. Learners, in informal contexts, use greater right hemisphere processing than left. It was argued that the right hemisphere is crucially involved in the processing of pragmatic aspects of language use. Such findings seem to suggest that L2 learners, particular adults, might benefit from more encouragement of right-brain activity in the classroom context (Brown, 2021: 57).

As discussed above, the left-brain and right-brain dominance is a potentially significant issue in developing an SLA theory. It also has some significant implications for L2 learning and teaching. According to Krashen, left-brain dominant L2 learners preferred a deductive way of teaching, while right-brain dominant L2 learners were more successful in inductive approach to teaching. A good summary made by Stevick (1982) was that left-brain dominant L2 learners are better at producing separate words, gathering the specifics of language, carrying out sequences of operations, and dealing with abstraction, classification, labeling, and reorganization; right-brain dominant type of learning appears to deal better with whole images, with generalizations, with metaphors, and with emotional reactions and artistic expressions.

4.2   Behaviorist Way of Learning

Behaviorism played a very important role in psychology during the first half of the 20th century. The typical behaviourist position is that language is speech rather than writing. Within the behaviourist framework, speaking is composed of mimicking and analogizing. When we say or hear something, we analogize from it. Basic to this view is the stimulus-response relationship. Bloomfield (1933: 22 – 23) illustrated such a relationship with the following situation:

Suppose that Jack and Jill are walking down a lane. Jill is hungry. She sees an apple in a tree. She makes a sound with her larynx, tongue and lips. Jack vaults the fence, climbs the tree, takes the apple, brings it to Jill and places it in her hand. Jill eats the apple.

Bloomfield divides such a situation into three parts: ①practical events before the act of speech, e. g., the hungry feeling, sight of apple; ② speech event, e. g., producing sound with larynx, tongue, and lips, and ③hearer's response, e. g., Jack's jumping over the fence, fetching the apple, giving it to Jill. In this situation, the events of feeling hungry and seeing an apple constitute stimulus; making a sound (practical reaction) is the response, which is a new stimulus causing Jack's response of climbing the tree and getting the apple for Jill.

One of the earliest attempts to construct a behavioral model of language acquisition was made by Skinner in his *Verbal Behavior* (1957). Skinner was commonly known for his experiments with animal behavior. He also gained recognition for his contributions to education through teaching machines and programmed learning. His theory of verbal behavior was an extension of his general theory of learning by operant conditioning, which refers to conditioning in which a human being gives out a response, or operant (a sentence or utterance), without necessarily observable stimuli; that operant is maintained (learned) by reinforcement (for example, a positive verbal or nonverbal response from another person). If a child says "Want milk" and a parent gives the child some milk, the operant is reinforced and, over repeated instances, is conditioned. Verbal behavior, according to Skinner, is just like other behavior and is controlled by its consequences. When consequences are rewarding, behavior is maintained and is increased in strength and perhaps frequency. When consequences are punishing, or there is a lack of reinforcement, the behavior is weakened and eventually extinguished.

Behaviourism also had an influence on L2 learning and teaching. As illustrated above, Behaviorism was based on the view that all learning—including language learning—takes place through a process of imitation, practice, reinforcement, and habit formation. According to behaviorism, environment plays a crucial role in language learning. First, it provides the source of language stimuli that learners need to form associations between the words they hear and the objects or events they represent. Second, environment provides feedback on learners' performance. It is claimed that when learners correctly produce language that approximates what they are exposed to in the input, and when these efforts receive positive reinforcement, habits are formed. For example, a learner hears the sentence "Give me a pencil", uses it himself, and thereby is rewarded by achieving his communication goal. That is, he is given a pencil by the hearer.

Behaviorist ideas had some impacts on second language development. One notion was the L1 interference with L2. That is, the L1 habits learners have already established would interfere with the formation of new habits in the L2. And this poses difficulty in second language learning, as was described by Fries (1957): Learning a second language, therefore, constitutes a very different task from learning the first language. The basic problems arise not out of any essential difficulty in the features of the new language themselves but primarily out of the special "set" created by the first language habits.

It should be pointed out that behaviorist accounts of L2 acquisition emphasize only what can be directly observed (the input to the learner and the output), and ignores what goes on in the learner's mind. If we want to see the picture clearer, we have to probe into the learner's mind to observe the learner's cognitive process.

4.3   Cognitive Perspective of Learning

What differs between a cognitive account and a behaviourist one is that the former is trying to explain L2 acquisition in terms of mental processing. As is known, a popular metaphor is that human brain is like a computer. The "black box" incorporates a device that extracts information from the "input", works on it, stores it, and subsequently uses it in "output". Here we will discuss some cognitive models of language learning and their implications for L2 learning.

4.3.1   Information processing (IP)

Since the late 1980s, there existed a revival of interest in psychological theories of language learning. Cognitive psychologists hypothesized that SLA requires the learner's attention and effort—whether or not the learner is aware of what is being attended to. Some information processing theories suggested that language is first acquired through intentional learning of "declarative knowledge" and that, through practice, the declarative knowledge can become "procedural knowledge". Other theories make a similar contrast between "controlled" and "automatic" processing. Controlled processing occurs when a learner is accessing information that is new or rare or complex. It requires mental effort and takes attention away from other controlled processes. For example, a language learner who appears relatively proficient in a social conversation may struggle to understand complex information because the controlled processing involved in interpreting the language itself interferes with the controlled processing that would be needed to interpret the content. Automatic processing, however, occurs quickly and with minimal attention and effort. Indeed, it is argued that we cannot prevent automatic processing and have little knowledge of its occurrence.

Information processing approach is concerned with the mental processes involved in language learning and use. There are three layers of mental processes including ①perception and the input of new information; ②the formation, organization and regulation of internal representations; and ③retrieval and output strategies. The IP approach makes a number of assumptions on second language acquisition (McLaughlin, 1987):

(1) Second language learning is the acquisition of a complex cognitive skill. In this respect language learning is like the acquisition of other complex skills.

(2) Complex skill can be reduced to sets of simpler component skills, which are hierarchically organized. Lower-order component skills are prerequisite to learning of higher-order skills.

(3) Learning of a skill initially demands learners' attention, and thus involves controlled processing.

(4) Controlled processing requires considerable mental "space" or attentional effort.

(5) Humans are limited-capacity processors. They can attend to a limited number of controlled processing demands at one time.

(6) Learners go from controlled to automatic processing with practice. Automatic processing requires less mental "space" and attentional effort.

(7) Learning essentially involves development from controlled to automatic processing of component skills, freeing learners' controlled processing capacity for new information and higher-order skills.

(8) Along with development from controlled to automatic processing, learning also essentially involves restructuring or reorganization of mental representations.

(9) Reorganizing mental representations as part of learning makes structures more coordinated, integrated, and efficient, including a faster response time when they are activated.

(10) In second language acquisition, restructuring of internal L2 representations, along with larger stores in memory, accounts for increasing levels of L2 proficiency.

Information processing has three stages (as shown in Table 4.2): input, central processing and output (Skehan, 1998).

Input for SLA refers to whatever sample of L2 the learner is exposed to. But it is not available for processing unless learners notice it. Then it can become intake. At this point of perception of input, priorities are determined, and attentional resources are channeled. This concept can be applied to foreign language teaching: in order for intake to occur, teachers should heighten learners' awareness of input and arouse their attention.

Table 4.2 Stages of Information Processing

Input	Central Processing	Output
Perception	Controlled-automatic processing Declarative-procedural knowledge Restructuring	Production

Central processing is the essential part of this model. It is here that a learner goes from controlled to automatic processing, and where restructuring of knowledge takes place. According to Anderson (1976), development from declarative to procedural stages of knowledge is parallel to development from controlled to automatic processing in many ways. The declarative stage involves acquisition of separated facts and rules, and the processing is relatively slow and often under attentional control. The procedural stage involves processing of longer associated units and increasing automatization, which frees attentional resources for high-level skills.

Output is the language produced by the learner, in speech or writing. Swain (1995) has expounded the importance of output for successful L2 learning: ①enhancing fluency by furthering development of automaticity through practice; ② noticing gaps in their own knowledge as they are forced to move from semantic to syntactic processing, which may lead learners to give more attention to relevant information; ③ testing hypotheses based on developing interlanguage, allowing for monitoring and revision; ④talking about language, including eliciting relevant input and solving problems.

As for the implications on second language learning, IP has emphasized the importance of repeated practice, restructuring and noticing. First, according to the IP model, it is the repeated practice that helps the controlled knowledge become automatic. Learning starts with a controlled process. At this stage of process, the learner makes a one-off attempt to handle new information by allotting it maximum attention. This is gradually transformed into an automatic process when the learner gets more used to handling the process by means of practice.

Second, it is also hypothesized that "restructuring" may occur in the learner's interlanguage systems. Restructuring is a cognitive process in which previously acquired information that has been somehow stored in separate categories is integrated and this integration expands the learner's competence (McLaughlin and Heredia, 1996). It should be pointed out that sometimes restructuring can lead learners to make errors that had not previously been present. For example, when a learner comes to understand that English question forms require inversion, there might be a period of time in which embedded questions such as *Do you know what the children are doing* would be produced with inversion as well *Do you know what are the children doing.*

Third, some researchers on IP models of SLA have argued that nothing can be learned without "noticing". That is, at least for some features of language, it is not enough for the learner to be exposed to it through comprehensible input. The learner must actually notice what it is in the input that makes the meaning.

4. 3. 2　Connectionist/emergentist models

According to emergentist accounts of language acquisition, knowledge is not seen as rules, nor is there any distinction between declarative and procedural knowledge. Probably the most influential emergentist model in SLA is connectionism. The connectionist models of L2 learning have much in common with IP perspectives. However, connectionism focuses on the increasing strength of associations between stimuli and responses rather than on the inferred abstraction of "rules" or restructuring. Connectionism originated in the relatively well-established concept in psychology of "parallel processing". Here we are concerned about how such a connectionist model explains second language learning.

Language is exemplar-based rather than rule-based. It was argued that language is governed by an "idiom principle" and that the data that learners obtain from input are "chunks" that are stored as "memories". As N. Ellis (2002: 166) stated, the knowledge underlying fluent language is not grammar in the sense of abstract rules or structure but a huge collection of memories of previous experienced utterances. In other words, learning consists of sequences of sounds (letters), words, phrases and entails item-learning rather than rule-learning. The learning process involves the building of associations between phonological or orthographic elements.

Learning a language involves learning "constructions". Constructions are recurrent patterns of linguistic elements that serve some well-defined linguistic functions (N. Ellis, 2003: 66). Constructions can be at sentence level or below. They are formulaic in nature since many of them are based on particular lexical items which can be single words or whole sentences. Constructions can also be abstract expressions such as the ditranstive pattern with verbs like "give" (for example, "I gave him my cellphone number"). These abstract patterns cater to creativity of language. Speakers are allowed to construct unique utterances such as "Pat sneezed the napkin off the table". More discussions about construction will be presented in the usage-based model in this chapter.

Learning is a process of gradually strengthening associations between elements. In other words, learning takes place as the network is able to make associations, and the associations come through exposure to repeated patterns. The more often an association is made, the stronger that association becomes. New associations are formed and new links are made between larger and larger units until complexes of networks are formed. There is a growing interest in this explanation for second language acquisition. Related to this model is the observation that much of the language consists of chunks or strings of language that have a high probability of occurring together. It is proposed that language is represented in the mind as a very large number of linguistic units with varying degrees of likelihood of co-occurrence, rather than as a set of linguistic rules for producing novel sentences.

Language learning is frequency-driven. The emphasis of this connectionist approach to language acquisition is on usage. Learning does not rely on an innate module, but it rather takes place based on the extraction of patterns from the input. As these patterns are used over and over again, they are strengthened. This is because "humans are sensitive to the frequencies of events in their experience" (N. Ellis, 2002). For instance, when a learner produces *I run* and *he runs*, the latter does not reflect an underlying knowledge of a rule that the third person singular verb takes an "s". Rather, the connection between *he* and *runs* is thought to be established through high-frequency exposure to these co-occurring structures in the linguistic input. The pronoun *he* activates *runs* and the pronoun *I* triggers *go* since the learner has heard these forms in combination many times.

4.3.3 The competition model

The competition model (CM) is another psychological approach on the general question of how languages are learned. The competition model is different from UG in that UG separates the form of language from its function, while the competition model proposes that the form and function can not be separated. According to MacWhinney, Bates, and Kliegl (1984), "the forms of natural languages are created, governed, constrained, acquired and used in the service of communicative functions". Any one form may realize a number of functions and conversely, any one function can be realized through a number of forms. Learning a language means is to discover the particular form-function mappings that characterize the target language. It is important to understand that the CM is concerned with how language is used in real context instead of how it is structured linguistically. The main concept of CM is that speakers must have a way to determine relationships among elements in a sentence.

Language processing concerns competition among various cues. Each of the cues contributes to a different resolution in sentence interpretation. Here we introduce four popular cues: word order, agreement, case and animacy. For example, in the sentence *Mary kissed John*, *Mary* is the agent, since the word order cue proposes that the first noun in a clause is likely to function as the agent. Agreement cue suggests that the noun phrase which functions as agent may agree in number with the verb. So in the sentence *She likes chocolates*, *she* takes a singular verb form; similarly, in *They like chocolates*, *they* agrees in number with the verb *like*. Both *she* and *they* are agents, and the objects of the sentences have no effect on the verb form. According to the case cue, the noun phrase functioning as agent may be morphologically marked in some way. For example, in *She kissed him*, the agent, *she*, is signaled in nominative case, while *him* is signaled in accusative case. According to animacy cue, the agents are normally animate, and the patients are normally inanimate. For example, in the sentence *This story Tom likes best*, it is *Tom*, not *this story*, that is the agent.

Any one language is likely to utilize several devices for signaling the "agent" of a sentence. For example, English uses all four, as illustrated in the sentences: *Mary kissed John* (word order); *Money they like* (agreement); *She kissed him* (case); *This book Mary likes a lot* (animacy). Languages are different from each other in that they use different cues to interpret a sentence. English uses word order and agreement as primary determinants while Russian uses case marking and Japanese animacy.

The CM takes its name from the "competition" that arises from the different cues that signal a particular function. For example, in the sentence *This speaker we like a lot*, there is competition between *speaker*, *we* and *lot* for the role of agent of the verb. *Lot* rapidly loses out because it is inanimate, and because it comes after, rather than before the verb. *Speaker*, though at the beginning of the sentence and is animate, is weaker than *we* because *we* is animate, nominative in case and because it agrees in number with the verb. So *we* finally wins the title of agent in the competition.

The task facing the L2 learner is to discover ①which forms are used to realize which functions in the L2, and ②what weights to attach to the use of individual forms in the performance of specific functions. This is what is meant by "form-function" mapping. There has been some attempt to specify how learners use the information available from "cues" to construct their language systems. The most basic determinant of cue strength is the raw frequency of the basic task. Feedback also plays a role. According to a learning-on-error model (proposed by McDonald, 1986), the weights attached to specific form-function mappings are changed when the learner interprets an input cue incorrectly and subsequently provided with feedback. This may account for the developmental shift noted in L1 acquisition from an initial dependence on cue reliability/availability to dependence on conflict validity. For example, children first respond to those cues which are salient and easily detectable (such as word order), but once these have been established they turn their attention to sentences containing conflicting cues. For example, in the sentence "That person we all love", there is conflict between the word order and agreement cues. Ultimately, it is these sentences that help them to establish the dominance patterns of the cues.

MacWhinney (2007) outlined a development of the CM, which he called the Unified Model because it sought to provide an account of both L1 and L2 learning. According to this model, forms are stored in associative maps for syllables, lexical items, constructions, and mental models. For example, in lexical maps, words are viewed as associations between forms and functions. Construction maps consist of patterns that show how a predicate (verb, adjective, preposition) can combine with its argument. The idea of self-organizing associative maps is derived from computer modelling of language learning. These show learning involving 3 phases. In the first phase, all units in the model are activated by the input with each unit computing its current activation. In the second phase, units compete with the best matching unit emerging as the winner. In the third phase, the weights of the responding unit are adjusted to increase the precision of function activation.

Within these associative maps, learning is self-organized, modulated by a number of processes—buffering, chunking, and resonance. Buffering serves as a mechanism for preserving competing information in short-term storage to enable selection of the final form/interpretation. Chunking (the process of storing formulaic sequences) provides a data base from which grammar can emerge through analogic processing. Resonance is the process by which robust connections within neural structure of the brain are formed. It is achieved through careful timing of practice to stimulate "resonant activation" of the relevant neurons.

The main weakness of the CM is its over-reliance on rather artificial interpretation tasks, a problem that is worsened by the unnatural sentences that figure in such tasks. Nevertheless, the CM is a powerful theory in that it affords very precise predictions about L2 acquisition which have received uniform support in related studies.

4.3.4 Skill-acquisition theories

Skill-acquisition theories are based on the view that language learning is just like other kinds of skill and is characterized by a progression from an initial declarative knowledge stage involving controlled processing, to a final procedural knowledge stage where knowledge is automatic. Practice plays a very important role in acquiring skills and needs to be skill-related as well. Thus the development of skill in listening requires practice in processing input while the development of speaking requires practice in oral production. According to this view, procedural knowledge is unidirectional. That is, automatization of one skill (such as listening) does not directly assist automatization of a different skill (such as speaking).

However, automatization of one skill may have an indirect effect on a different skill by improving and strengthening declarative knowledge which is bi-directional (that is, it can be used in the development of other skills).

The basic concept of skill-acquisition theories is that proceduralization can be achieved by extensive practicing in using the L2. But what does it mean by "practice" in L2 learning? The traditional view is that practice involves the process of repeatedly and deliberately attempting to produce some particular target feature. This view led to the use of mechanical drills in the audiolingual and oral-situational methods of language teaching. The problem existing in this view is that practice is often not effective in enabling learners to use new structures automatically. Practice, in this situation, does not make perfect as is often expected.

Why is practice ineffective? This is because practicing a structure in a mechanical way reifies the structure by decontextualizing it and thus does not affect long-term memory or cause any change in behavior. To change behavior, or develop automatic processes, it is necessary to provide practice of the actual behavior itself. In the case of language learning, "behavior" must entail attempts to communicate. Thus, in order for practice to develop the speaking skill, it must involve learners producing the target structure in the context of communicative activity. In this new light, then, communicative practice serves as a device for proceduralizing knowledge of linguistic structures that have been first presented declaratively. Instructional intervention with such practice can be helpful in proceduralizing declarative knowledge, as is shown below:

…proceduralization is achieved by engaging in the target behavior—or procedure—while temporarily learning on declarative crutches … Repeated behaviors of this kind allow the restructuring of declarative knowledge in ways that make it easier to proceduralize and allow the combination of co-occurring elements into larger chunks that reduce the working memory load (DeKeyser, 1998: 49).

Feedback is also important in the learning process. Johnson (1996) suggested that instructional sequence should be one of "learn→perform→learn" rather than the traditional sequence of "learn→perform". During or after the "perform" stage, learners must have the opportunity to receive feedback, which should consist of "mistake correction". For feedback to be effective, learners need to see for themselves what has gone wrong in the operating conditions under which they went wrong. Johnson also suggested that this can probably be best achieved by means of extrinsic feedback that shows the learner what is wrong by modelling the correct form while they are attempting to communicate. Skill acquisition theories produce implications for grammar instruction. For example, a sequence of practice activities were designed to lead a learner from "accuracy" to "fluency". "Accuracy" refers to the performance based on declarative knowledge, while "fluency" the performance based on procedural knowledge. This sequence involves "controlled drills", "meaningful drills", "guided meaningful practice", "structure-based free sentence composition", "structure-based discourse composition" and "free discourse".

Although language learning does involve skill-learning in the sense that practice aids the process by which L2 knowledge is automatized, the skill-acquisition theories are problematic in two related respects. First, they provide no explanation for the orders and sequences of acquisition. Second, it is difficult to accept that the acquisition of all L2 features begins with declarative knowledge. This implies a role for metalinguistic awareness in L2 acquisition that far exceeds that outlined in this section.

4.3.5 Bialystok's theory of L2 learning

In contrast to Krashen's non-interface view between explicit and implicit knowledge (as we discussed in chapter three), Bialystok's theory of L2 learning allows for an interface between the two types of knowledge. According to the theory, implicit knowledge is developed through exposure to communicative language use and facilitated by the strategy of "functioning practicing". That is, learners make attempts to maximize exposure to language through communication. But how does explicit knowledge develop? Explicit L2 knowledge occurs when learners focus on the language code, and is facilitated by "formal practicing". Formal practicing refers to either conscious study of the second language or the attempts to automatize the already learnt explicit L2 knowledge. What makes Bialystok's theory different from Krashen's monitor model is that it considers an interaction between explicit and implicit knowledge. In Bialystok's theory of L2 learning, explicit L2 knowledge can become implicit L2 knowledge through formal practice. Also, explicit knowledge can be derived from implicit knowledge by inferencing. This model distinguishes two kinds of output: Type I and Type II. Type I is spontaneous and immediate, while Type II is deliberate and occurs after a delay (Bialystok, 1978: 74). As can be seen, Type I output depends completely on implicit knowledge, while Type Ⅱ output relies on both implicit and explicit knowledge. Both types of output constitute a feedback loop, which allows for continual modification of a response. Bialystok's theory of L2 learning is illustrated in Figure 4. 1:

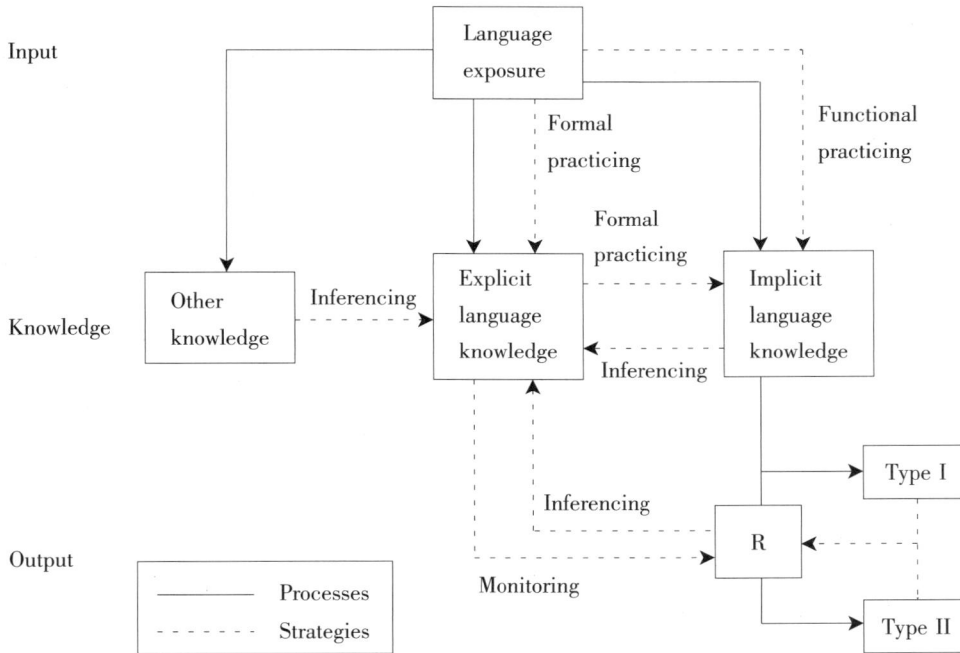

Figure 4. 1　Bialystok's Model of Second Language Learning（Revised）

It must be pointed out that Bialystok's model has been considerably revised later. What most concerns us here is the reconceptualization of L2 knowledge. In the early model, the knowledge was either explicit or implicit. But later, it is represented in terms of two intersecting continua, which reflects the extent to which rules and items are "controlled" or "analyzed". The definition of "control" has shifted somewhat. It used to concern the ease and rapidity with which knowledge can be accessed in different types of language use. Later, it refers to three different functions: the selection of items of knowledge, their co-ordination, and the extent to which selection and co-ordination can be carried out automatically. By "analysis", it refers to the extent to which the learner has abstracted an account of some linguistic phenomenon. As defined by Bialystok (1991: 65), "Analysis of knowledge is the process by which mental representations of this knowledge are built up, structured, and made explicit for the learner."

It may be assumed that analyzed knowledge, in a sense, corresponds to explicit knowledge, and unanalyzed knowledge to implicit knowledge. Bialystok, in fact, did equate analysis with the development of an explicit representation of knowledge, but she emphasized that analyzed knowledge does not need to involve consciousness because "a criterion of consciousness seriously underestimate the level of analysis with which linguistic knowledge is represented."

In explaining how analyzed knowledge is developed, Bialystok outlined a 3-stage model (based on the work of Karmiloff-Smith's three phases of skill development) of Implicit→ Explicit 1 → Explicit 2. In the first phase (Implicit), knowledge of a linguistic item is closely associated with procedures for using it in communication and is not represented independently. For example, the learner may supply linguistic determiners with a variety of nouns and yet not have organized them into a system of determiners. In the second phase (Explicit 1), learners examine, analyze, and organize their performances in order to construct explicit and independent representations of linguistic knowledge. In the third phase (Explicit 2), linguistic knowledge is available for conscious consideration. It should be noted that this model was intended to account for language development in children, and thus progress is reflected in movement from Implicit to Explicit 1 and finally to Explicit 2. It is not clear how, or whether, this model can be applied to L2 acquisition. Bialystok did not consider this in her later work.

The problems with Bislystok's theory of L2 learning are evident. In particular, the claim that language must begin with unanalyzed knowledge seems unwarranted in the case of L2 acquisition. The fact is that many instructed L2 learners begin with explicit knowledge.

4.3.6　Gass's integrative model of SLA

So far, we have discussed different approaches to second language acquisition, which are crucial in dealing with a part of what occurs in learning a second language. However, none of them alone is powerful enough to account for the total picture. To this end, Susan Gass has developed an integrative model, which will explain where the various factors fit and how each relates to a larger picture of L2 acquisition. This integrative model considers what a learner must do to convert input to output. The model has five main parts: apperceived input, comprehended input, intake, integration, and output.

Actually, the whole model has a cognitive nature, because most components of the model, apart from input and output, deal with the internal processing. Apperceived input and comprehended input are two crucial processing steps inside the mind; in addition, intake and integration are further key processes a learner goes through before he produces speech. The whole model can be illustrated in Figure 4. 2. Let us look at the components inside the square, the processes that take place inside the learner's mind: apperceived input, comprehended input, intake and integration.

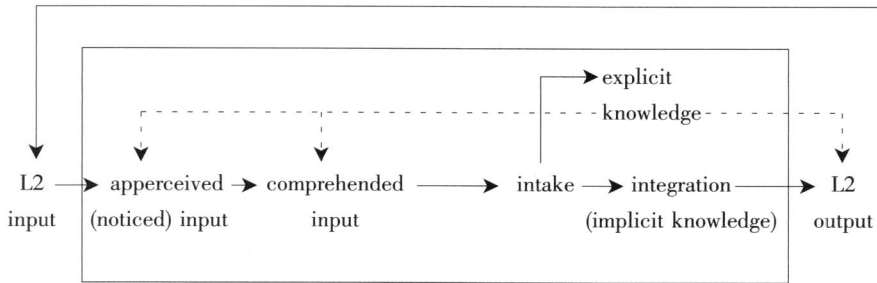

Figure 4. 2   An Integrative Model of L2 Learning

4. 3. 6. 1   Apperceived input

In order to have a better understanding of apperception, we need to take into consideration another important term, noticing. A well-established fact about SLA is that not everything the learner hears or reads is used in formulating L2 grammars. Some language input is never noticed; only those that are noticed by the learner enter the learner's mind and interact with other already learnt knowledge, waiting to be further processed. This noticed input is called apperceived input. Apperception is an internal cognitive act, which identifies a linguistic form as being related to some prior knowledge. Therefore, apperceived input is that bit of language that is noticed in some way by the learner because of some particular features. There are quite a few factors, i. e. , those input filters, which determine whether input can be noticed or not.

The first factor is frequency, which is probably at both extremes. That is, something that is very frequent in the input is likely to be noticed. Also, something that is unusual because of its infrequency is often noticed, but this occurs particularly at advanced stages of learning.

The second factor influencing apperception is affect, which includes such factors as social distance, status, motivation, and attitude. If a learner has a feeling of psychological and social distance from the target language community, the language input will not be available to the learner, let alone for him to notice.

The third factor is the learner's schematic knowledge. That refers to a learner's prior knowledge, as in Gass's model. Learning takes place when new knowledge integrates with the prior (already learnt) knowledge. The latter serves as some sort of anchor on which new knowledge is grounded. The schematic knowledge is one of the factors that determine whether the input is meaningful. Schematic knowledge includes language universals, knowledge of the native language, knowledge of other languages, existing knowledge of the L2 being learned, and even general world knowledge. All these different kinds of schematic knowledge play a role in a learner's success or lack of success in interpreting the input, and particularly in noticing and perceiving the input.

The fourth factor is attention. This is concerned with whether a learner attends to the input. Attention is important because it allows a learner to notice a mismatch between what he knows about the second language and what is produced by native speakers of the second language. If a learner is going to modify his grammar, he must recognize that changes need to be made. The perception of a mismatch is the prerequisite for the re-adjustment of one's grammar.

4.3.6.2 Comprehended input

Let us first distinguish comprehended input from the comprehensible input in Krashen's model. First, comprehensible input is controlled by the person providing input. However, comprehended input is learner-controlled. That is, the learner is doing the "work" to understand. This distinction is essential in relationship to the subsequent intake, because it is the learner who ultimately controls that intake. Second, in Krashen's view, comprehensible input is treated as dichotomous. It is either comprehensible or it is not comprehensible. However, in Gass's model, there is a broader sense of the word "comprehension", which includes comprehension of structure and comprehension of meaning. Comprehension in this sense is a continuum of possibilities ranging from semantics to structural analysis. For example, a learner can comprehend something at the level of meaning. On the other hand, a more analytic understanding may take place. The learner might understand what the component parts of an utterance are and thus gain an understanding of the syntactic or phonological pattern. Recognizing different levels of comprehension is important in relation to the subsequent level of intake, too. Here, it is worth mentioning that an L2 learner has to learn different kinds of knowledge about the L2; not only syntax and phonology, but also discourse, pragmatics and vocabulary.

4.3.6.3 Intake

Intake takes place after apperception and comprehension. It refers to the mental activity that mediates between input and grammars. It is the process of assimilating language material; it is the process of grammar formation. Intake is different from apperception and comprehension in that the latter two do not necessarily result in grammar formation.

What facilitates the occurrence of intake? First, the quality of analysis, i.e., the comprehended input is an important factor. What's more, knowledge of the L1 and the L2 is also important. Second, whether a particular feature is part of UG or is part of a universal typological feature will also relate to eventual intake. Features that are part of universal knowledge and present in the native language are most likely to be candidates for a deep analysis and the candidates for intake.

Intake is the component where psycholinguistic processing takes place. It is in this component that the incoming information is matched up against prior knowledge. Generally, the processing takes place against the background of the existing internalized grammatical rules. It is in this component that generalizations and overgeneralizations might take place. It is in this component that memory traces are formed. It is from this component that fossilization stems. Some of the major processes that take place in the intake component are hypothesis formation, hypothesis testing, hypothesis rejection, hypothesis modification, and hypothesis confirmation.

4.3.6.4 Integration

Integration takes place after, and interacts with, intake, and there are two kinds of integration: development of grammar and storage. How does this relate to input? There are four possibilities for dealing with input:

(1) Hypothesis confirmation or hypothesis rejection. This takes place in the intake component. Input is used for confirming or rejecting a current hypothesis. Whether the hypothesis is confirmed or rejected, it results in integration.

(2) Seeming nonuse. Nonuse seems to happen because the information contained in the input has already been incorporated into the learner's grammar system. But this does not mean that the additional input is useless. Instead, it is used in another way. For example, it might be used for rule strengthening, or hypothesis reconfirmation. An L2 speaker becomes fluent because he can retrieve information automatically from his knowledge base, which is developed through practice or repeated exposure to exemplars. Therefore, the phenomenon, where input seems redundant temporarily, is only a seeming nonuse. It enables the learner to have much easier access to that information.

(3) Storage. Storage takes place in the integration component. This occurs probably because some level of understanding has taken place. However, it is not clear how integration into a learner's grammar can or should take place. Sometimes, a learner just stores a particular feature in his mind without understanding it, and waits for a chance to integrate it later.

(4) Nonuse. In this case, an L2 learner does not make any use of the input at all. This may be caused by his failure in understanding the input for any communicative purpose.

Instead of being a one-off affair, integration involves different levels of analysis and reanalysis from storage of linguistic features into the formation of grammar. It is essential to point out that integration does not function as an independent unit. It is interwoven with the apperceived input, comprehended input, and intake, because SLA is a dynamic and interactive process.

4.3.7 The usage-based model

Coined by Langacker (1988), the term usage-based model focuses on language use in the real world. According to this model, language is regarded as an interconnected, complex, emergent and dynamic system, which can not be simply divided into static grammatical rules and lexicon dichotomously, and language structure emerges from language use. But how does this actually happen?

Just like generative (non usage-based) theories of language, the usage-based model takes the explanation of language acquisition as its goal. The same question is asked: How is it that a child can acquire the grammaticality and facility of a language in such a short time? To explain this phenomenon, generativists hold that there is a language-specific faculty in the mind that accounts for universal structures, i. e., principles and parameters that determine the grammaticality of a given language. However, usage-based theories generally believe that language builds up a conventional inventory of units, including units that convey grammatical patterns, which a speaker can draw on and put together for communication. This inventory of units is based on hearing and using the language, and through use the units become entrenched (Langacker, 1987).

Compared with the traditional generative approach, the usage-based model has the following characteristics. First, the usage-based model focuses on naturally occurring language in use, while the generative grammar chiefly concerns formal properties of language, using idealized and invented utterances as the aim of study. Second, the usage-based model emphasizes the external experiences such as frequency of input, context, and interaction. It also focuses on how general human cognitive abilities contribute to language acquisition. Third, different from the generative grammar which takes highly abstract syntactic rules as the core of language, the usage-based model holds that all levels of language involve form and meaning/function pairings. Branches of the usage-based model are highly compatible and have many commonalities. Below are three fundamental principles summarized by Gao (2016: 69 – 79).

(1) Constructions are the basic units of language.

In contrast to generative model, the usage-based model posits no innate rules, and language is not modularized either. In the usage-based model, constructions are considered the basic units of language. Language is a system consisting of symbolic units with form-meaning connections (Tomasello, 2003; Goldberg, 2006) and these form-meaning connections exhibit both general grammatical properties and idiosyncratic features (Diessel, 2004). Knowledge about language consists of systematic collections of constructions gained through input learners hear around them, not derived from general linguistic rules. The term "construction" is defined by Goldberg as follows:

Any linguistic pattern is recognized as a construction as long as some aspect of its form or function is not strictly predictable from its component parts or from other constructions recognized to exist. In addition, patterns are stored as constructions even if they are fully predictable as long as they occur with sufficient frequency.

(Goldberg, 2006: 5)

In actual use, constructions occur at different levels of language such as morphology, lexicon, syntax. The morphemes, words, phrases, clauses, and sentences form a gradation and are described as assemblies of symbolic structures. Thus every linguistic unit is a construction of its own, irrespective of whether the meaning of it is general or specific, or whether its structure is complex or simple (Gao, 2016). Therefore, *un-* is a construction just as the word *unhappy* is; the complex word *touch-me-not* is a construction as the idiom *jog one's memory* is; so is *The more you think about it, the less you understand*; even the double-object structure *She lent me a book* and passive pattern *The doctor was knocked down by a car* are constructions. In traditional grammar, some complex multi-word expressions might have been interpreted as "sentences"; however, they are institutionalized and have been pre-established in a speech community, so speakers and hearers don't have to, or can not, analyze such a "sentence" according to syntactic rules. Take daily greetings for example. When people meet, they might say *Hello*, *How are you*, *How are you doing*, *It's a pleasure to meet you today*, or *Long time no see* etc. as daily routines automatically in specific situations. When uttering or hearing these routines, people never analyze their syntax; instead, they are driven by the context in which a certain utterance frequently occurs as a whole unit. Such a form-function combination is an entrenched pairing as a result of frequent use.

(2) Linguistic experience plays an important role in language acquisition.

Linguistic input was thought to be insufficient for language acquisition according to the Poverty of Stimulus Hypothesis (PSH). However, evidences show that this is not really so. It has been proved that input children receive is not so fragmentary as it was suggested by PSH. For example, Dabrowska and Lieven (2005) studied 2- and 3-year-old children's utterances and found that about 90% of children's utterances could be traced back to the input they had been exposed to. This attests to the fact that learners have enough positive evidence for acquiring constructions and therefore do not require innate grammatical representations beforehand. It is held that children learners are not born with a specific set of communicative behaviors, and during their individual ontogeny, they must learn the set of linguistic conventions used around them which consist of hundreds of thousands of words, expressions, and constructions (Tomasello, 2003).

An assumption for children's successful mastery of language is that language must be learnable from input and general cognitive abilities, which distinguish the usage-based model from other models such as behaviorism and UG. Acquiring a language, therefore, is experiential, exemplar-based and emergent, going through a typical route from formula, through low-scope pattern, to fully abstract constructions (Ellis, 2002). According to Ellis, during the process of learning utterances and abstracting regularities within them, certain facets of linguistic experience, such as cue competition and the effects of type and token frequency, serve as major determinants of pattern productivity. It is necessary for us to have some understanding of token frequency and type frequency before we know their links to construction-based language learning.

First, what are token and type? In linguistics, a distinction is often made between classes of linguistic items (phonemes, words, or utterances) and actual occurrences in speech or writing of examples of such classes. The class of linguistic units is called a "type" and examples or individual members of the class are called "tokens". For example, *hi*, *hello*, *how are you*, *good morning* are four different tokens of the type "Greeting". In some cases, we talk about "token" when we want to know how long a book or an article is, or how fast one reads or speaks in a minute. On the other hand, if we want to know how many different words one knows or uses, we count word "types". In this light, the sentence "To be or not to be, that is the question" has 10 tokens, but only 8 word types; only 8 types because the words *to* and *be* are repeated and only 8 words are used.

By token frequency, we mean "the number of times a given instance is used in a particular construction" (Goldberg, 1995: 134), that is, how often a particular unit appears in the input. For example, if there are 10 occurrences of the word "delay" in a passage, we say the token frequency of "delay" is 10, counting each appearance as one instance of the word. What token frequency contributes to language learning is the "instance entrenchment". If one instance of the construction is of higher token frequency, it will be more entrenched in learners' minds as an independent unit in its own right. The more entrenched an instance is, the easier it will be accessed next time (Bybee, 2007). People tend to respond more quickly to high-frequency words than to low-frequency words.

In contrast to token frequency, type frequency only applies to schematic linguistic patterns. It concerns how many distinct items are represented by a pattern, whether it is a word-level construction for inflection or a syntactic construction specifying the relationship among words (Ellis, 2002). Type frequency may apply to phonotactic sequences, as to how many words start with /sp/ and how many begin with /sf/, for example. It may apply to morphological pattern (e. g. stem + affix). Here we are more concerned about the type frequency of syntactic constructions. For example, the ditransitive pattern *He gives me the change* is used with only a small set of verbs, while *He gives the change to me* is possible with a larger class of verbs (Goldberg, 1995).

(3) General cognitive abilities contribute to language learning.

Different from generativist grammar, usage-based theorists doubt the universal rules that are claimed to be specific to human language. They regard language acquisition as a result of our general conceptual or perceptual apparatus together with experience in the world (Goldberg, 2006). For usage-based theorists, it is not that language users are born with innate universal grammar. They have their own explanations for the existence of linguistic universals. For example, Diessel (2004: 37) believes that nouns and verbs might be universal because all languages need these categories to denote two different types of concepts that are essential to human categorization. Tomasello (2003) claims that the language universals are not universals of particular linguistic symbols, grammatical categories or syntactic constructions, but rather they are universals of communication, cognition and human physiology. Linguistic phenomena are the result of human cognition, communicative needs, and human biological and phylogenetic adaptations. Then, how do human cognitive abilities help us acquire a language? Here we discuss two fundamental skills which play significant roles in language learning:

①**Intention-reading skills.**

As human-unique form of social learning, intention-reading skills emerge near the end of the first year of life, and serve as a prerequisite of language learning. Intention-reading skills exist in three ways: the joint attentional frame, understanding communicative intention, and cultural learning by imitation. The joint attentional frame refers to objects and activities that children and adults know as part of both their attentional focus. This attentional focus creates a common ground of joint engagement in "what we are doing". Only in this frame can children understand adults' communicative intention. This makes language learning possible. Otherwise, linguistic symbols from adults would just be noise. For children, sounds become language "when and only when they understand that the adult is making that sound with the intention that they attend to something" (Tomasello, 2003: 23) . The ability to understand another's communicative intentions in cooperative contexts is a prerequisite to linguistic abilities. When communicating with children, adults devised behavioral means to meet their communicative intentions. Children may attend to those behavioral means and imitate the intentional actions. In this way children learn to produce language. This is possible because in human linguistic communication, the most fundamental unit of intentional action is the utterance as a relatively complete and coherent expression of a communicative intention, and so the most fundamental unit of language learning is stored exemplars of utterances (Tomaselo, 2003: 296) .

②**Pattern-finding skills.**

To simply imitate and memorize heard utterances is not enough. Children must learn to generalize patterns from the utterances so as to understand and produce new utterances. Then, pattern-finding skill is a must. It has been confirmed that even pre-linguistic infants possess the ability to find patterns from input. Children can not only attempt to reproduce what is heard, but they can also analyze the exemplars and break them down into constituents. They use their already existing skills of categorization and statistical learning on the utterances they experience to move down the road of grammatical development (Tomasello, 2003: 41) . Statistical learning of patterns, concrete or abstract, is a prerequisite for language learning, especially for grammar development. Even a one-year-old child could understand linguistic symbols and use pattern-finding skills on the functional side of things. Thus, to form linguistic schemas is to imitatively learn the recurrent concrete structures, concrete functions, and to generate abstract patterns with abstract functions. Such a process is called, by Tomasello (2006) , schematization.

4. 4   Individual Differences

In the previous section, we discussed the process of second language acquisition from a cognitive perspective; that is, how the L2 knowledge is being formed in the learner's mind. Another important question SLA has to answer is why some learners are more successful than others. This can be considered from the psychological perspective. Therefore, we will focus on some internal differences among learners themselves. The differences to be discussed here are language aptitude, age, motivation, cognitive style, personality, and learning strategies.

4. 4. 1   Aptitude

Aptitude refers to one's potential for learning new knowledge or new skills. As for language aptitude, it constitutes a special ability for learning an L2. Language aptitude is typically held to involve a number of distinct abilities including auditory ability, linguistic ability, and memory ability. It has been noted that intelligence and working memory both seem to be implicated in language aptitude, just as in any other kind of learning task. However, research indicates that, in addition to these general abilities, language learning also involves more specific abilities. Language aptitude is best viewed as a composite of both general and specific abilities. Carroll (1965) identified the following four key components of language aptitude:

(1) Phonemic coding ability. This is the ability to code foreign sounds in a way that they can be remembered later. This ability is seen as related to the ability to spell and to handle sound-symbol relationships.

(2) Grammatical sensitivity. This refers to the ability to recognize the grammatical functions of words in sentences.

(3) Inductive language learning ability. This means the ability to identify patterns of correspondence and relationships involving form and meaning.

(4) Rote-learning ability. This is the ability to form and remember associations between stimuli. This ability is hypothesized to be involved in vocabulary learning.

Skehan (1989) suggested that (2) and (3) should be combined into one ability, language analytic ability, because they are both concerned with central processing of the brain to infer structure, identify patterns, make generalizations, recognize grammatical functions and formulate rules. The early research mainly dealt with language aptitude tests or measurements, as well as its relationship with the learning outcomes and achievement. Two main instruments used to measure aptitude—The Modern Language Aptitude (MLAT) and

The Pimsleur Language Aptitude Battery (PLAD) —are the most commonly used in aptitude research and have the great predictive power. According to research, measures of language aptitude have been correlated with measures of language proficiency and achievement, with the aim of establishing to what extent it is possible to predict learning outcomes.

Later research, however, was less concerned with just confirming the relationship between aptitude and proficiency, but focused more on exploring different issues about the role that language aptitude plays in language learning. Ellis (2013: 657 – 658) summarized some important issues: ①Is language aptitude relevant to informal as well as formal language learning? ②Is language aptitude a cumulative aggregation of abilities or as differentiated, affording more than one route to success? ③Is there any relationship between L1 language skills and language aptitude? ④To what extent is language aptitude immutable or responsive to training? ⑤To what extent and in what ways is language aptitude related to the processes of L2 acquisition?

4.4.2 Age

It is commonly believed that children are more successful L2 learners than adults. This is supported by the Critical Period Hypothesis (CPH). According to Birdsong, there is a limited developmental period during which it is possible to acquire a language to normal, nativelike levels. Once the window of opportunity is passed, however, the ability to learn language declines (Birdsong, 1999: 1). Given the relationship between brain and language, there is a critical period for L1 acquisition. Within that period, normal acquisition is possible. Beyond that, physiological changes cause the brain to lose its plasticity. Individuals are deprived of the linguistic input, which is needed to trigger first language acquisition. So, they will never learn any language normally. A best example to support this hypothesis is that of Genie. Genie was an abused girl who was kept isolated from all language input and interaction until she was 13 years old. When discovered, she had no language and could not talk. In spite of years of intensive efforts at language learning, Genie never developed linguistic knowledge and skills for her mother tongue, English.

The question of whether, and how, age affects L2 learning has been a major issue in SLA, on which there are different points of view. Since the beginning of SLA as a field of study, the role that age plays in L2 acquisition has attracted the attention of researchers such as Krashen, Long and Scarcella (1979: 161). They reviewed a number of the earlier studies and came to three conclusions:

(1) Adults proceed through the early stages of syntactic and morphological development faster than children, where time and exposure are held constant.

(2) Older children acquire faster than younger children, again in the early stages of syntactic and morphological development, where time and exposure are held constant.

(3) Acquirers who begin natural exposure to an L2 during childhood achieve higher second language proficiency than those beginning as adults.

These conclusions do not entirely agree with the lay belief that "younger is better" where L2 learning is concerned. While it is true that learners who start learning in childhood often achieve higher levels of ultimate proficiency than learners who start later, research indicates that in the earlier stages of L2 acquisition, older learners do better than younger learners, especially where knowledge of grammar is concerned.

It is supposed by Lenneberg (1967) that the critical period applies to SLA as well as to first language acquisition, and this accounts for why almost all L2 speakers have a "foreign accent" if they do not start learning the language before the cut-off age. Other researchers, such as Seliger and Long, argue that there are multiple periods which place constraints on different aspects of language. That is, different periods relate to the acquisition of phonology versus the acquisition of syntax. These periods do not impose absolute cut-off points. L2 acquisition will more likely be complete if begun in childhood than if it starts at a later age.

Despite the general belief that younger learners achieve higher levels of L2 proficiency, there is evidence showing that adolescents and adults learn faster in initial stages. Therefore, the fact is that both young learners and old learners have advantages in learning an L2. Some of the advantages which have been reported for both younger and older learners are listed in Table 4.3.

Table 4. 3　Age Advantages in SLA（Saville-Troike，2008：82）

Younger Advantage	Older Advantage
Brain plasticity	Learning capacity
Not analytical	Analytic ability
Fewer inhibitions	Pragmatic skills
Weaker group identity	Greater knowledge of L1
Simplified input more likely	Real-world knowledge

4. 4. 3　Motivation

Another factor which is used to explain why some L2 learners are more successful than others is individual motivation. Motivation involves the attitudes and affective states that influence the degree of effort that learners make to learn an L2. Motivation plays an important role in L2 learning. Brown （2021） vividly compared motivation to "a star player in the cast of characters assigned to L2 learning scenarios around the world". Research has shown that motivation is a key factor to learning in general. In the field of SLA，the issue of motivation has gained huge amounts of attention.

Motivation has been defined from various theoretical orientations. From a behavioral perspective，it refers simply to the anticipation of reward. Since learners are driven to acquire positive reinforcement，and by previous experiences of reward，they act to achieve further reinforcement. In cognitive terms，motivation emphasizes the individual's decision. Some cognitive psychologists see underlying needs or drives as the compelling force behind our decisions. A constructive view of motivation，however，places prime emphasis on social context as well as individual personal choices. Our choices to expend effort are always carried out within a cultural and social context. Motivation is derived from both our interactions and our self-determination. Here we look at two pairs of motivation：instrumental and integrative；intrinsic and extrinsic.

Instrumental and integrative motivation. Learners may make efforts to learn an L2 for practical reasons，such as passing an examination，getting a better job，getting a place at university. Learners may also have other purposes—to increase business opportunities，to enhance their prestige or power，or simply to access scientific and technical information. In certain learning contexts，an instrumental motivation seems to be the major force which

decides success in L2 learning. For instance, one who has an educational opportunity in an English-speaking country must have a strong motivation in learning English as a second language. As for integrative motivation, learners may be interested in learning an L2 because of a desire to learn about or associate with the people who use that language, or because of an intention to participate or integrate in the L2 speech community.

Intrinsic and extrinsic motivation. This refers to the learner's personal enjoyment of learning a language. If one is intrinsically motivated, he expends effort for which there is no apparent reward except the activity itself, and not because it leads to an extrinsic reward. Intrinsically motivated learners are driven by internally rewarding consequences, such as feelings of competence and self-determination. The motivation involves the arousal and maintenance of curiosity, and it can ebb and flow as a result of such factors as learners' particular interests and the extent to which they feel personally involved in learning activities. Extrinsic motivation, however, is fueled by the anticipation of a reward from outside and beyond the self. Typical extrinsic rewards are money, prizes, grades, and even certain forms of positive feedback. Behaviors initiated solely to avoid punishment are also extrinsically motivated.

Motivation is a complex phenomenon. Each of the above two pairs of motivation should be seen as complementary rather than oppositional. A person may be both instrumentally and integratively motivated at the same time. Motivation may result from learning as well as being the cause of it. In addition, motivation is dynamic in nature. Motivation is not what one has or does not have; it varies from one moment to the next depending on the learning context or task.

4.4.4 Cognitive/learning style

Style refers to consistent and rather enduring tendencies or preferences within an individual person. Cognitive style refers to a person's preferred way of perceiving, conceptualizing, organizing and recalling information. Whatever the relation of cognitive style and success of L2 learning is, it involves a complex interaction with specific L2 social and learning contexts. A person's cognitive style is also closely related to, and interacts with, his personality and learning strategy. Here we will discuss a number of cognitive styles: field dependence/independence, visual/auditory/kinesthetic styles, and reflectivity/impulsivity.

4. 4. 4. 1　Field independence/dependence（FI/FD）

You might remember such a special test. One holds before you a coloring book with a picture of a forest scene with exotic trees and flowers, and asks you to find the hidden monkeys in the trees. If you look carefully, you may soon detect them. Such an ability to find those hidden monkeys is related to your field independent cognitive style. It refers to the perception of a particular, relevant item or factor in a "field" of distracting items. In general psychological terms, that field may be perceptual, or it may be more abstract, pertaining to a set of thoughts, ideas, or feelings within which you must distinguish specific relevant subsets. Field dependence, on the other hand, is the tendency to be "dependent" on the total field so that the parts embedded within the field are not easily perceived, though the total is perceived more clearly as a whole. Field dependence is synonymous with field sensitivity, a term that carries a more positive connotation.

A field independent style enables one to distinguish parts from a whole, to concentrate on something, like reading a book in a noisy background. However, too much FI may produce negative effect: seeing only the parts and not their relationship to the whole. Seen in this light, developing a field dependence style has positive effects: perceiving the whole picture, the larger view, the general configuration of a problem or idea or event. It is clear, then, that both FI and FD are necessary for most of the cognitive and affective problems we face（Brown, 2021: 116）.

As for the relationship to L2 learning, there are two conflicting hypotheses. First, some studies show that FI is closely related to classroom learning that involves analysis, attention to details, and mastering of exercises, drills, and other focused activities. Similar findings from other studies indicate FI's success in paper-and-pencil tests, in deductive lessons, and in pronunciation accuracy. In terms of an information processing model of learning, field independent learners may have better attentional capabilities（Skehan, 1998）. The second hypothesis proposed that an FD style, owing to its association with empathy, social outreach, and perception of other people, yields successful acquisition of the communicative aspects of an L2. However, the learner has difficulty in studying a particular item when it occurs within a "field" of other items.

Can the two learning styles equally important? They deal with two different kinds of language learning. One type of learning implies natural, face-to-face communication, the kind of communication that occurs too rarely in the average language classroom. The other type involves familiar classroom activities: drills, exercises, and texts. It is most likely that "natural" language learning in the "field", beyond the constraints of the classroom, is aided by an FD style, and classroom learning, on the contrary, by an FI style. Obviously, both styles are facilitative within appropriate contexts.

4.4.4.2　Visual/auditory/kinesthetic styles

Learning takes place in different ways and each learner has his/her own preference. It is commonly held that some individuals are visual learners and some are oral learners. How do learners best take information in? Through listening to a passage? Through a teacher writing on the blackboard? Most successful learners use a variety of modalities in learning, and in this way they can accommodate to the various modes in which incoming information is processed.

Visual learners are those who take in information visually. In this respect, reading is preferred to listening. Blackboard use or PowerPoint presentations are preferred to straight lectures. Such learners like reading and studying charts, drawings, and other graphic information. Auditory learners are those who prefer to take in information auditorily. They prefer listening to reading. Lectures are often an effective means of absorbing knowledge. They prefer to talk through material and even to have text read out aloud.

Kinesthetic, or even tactile, learners will show a preference for demonstrations and physical activity involving bodily movement. They perform better when the whole body is involved or when objects can be manipulated, such as in lab work. For kinesthetic learners, movement is a key issue and frequent breaks are necessary, as is moving while repeating or memorizing information important. Of course, most successful learners use both visual and auditory input, but slight preferences one way or the other may distinguish one learner from another, which is an important factor in examining individual differences in L2 learning.

4.4.4.3　Reflectivity/impulsivity

It is common for us to demonstrate our own personal tendencies toward reflectivity sometimes, and at other times, impulsivity. When one is reflective, he tends to weigh all the considerations in a problem, work out all the loopholes, then, after extensive reflection, carefully makes a decision; when one is impulsive, he tends to make a quick or gambling guess at an answer to a problem.

It has been found that children who are reflective tend to make fewer errors in reading than impulsive children. Yet, impulsive persons are usually fast readers, and eventually master the "psycholinguistic guessing game" of reading so that their impulsive style of reading may not necessarily deter comprehension. As for the implications on SLA, it was found that reflective adults were slower but more accurate than impulsive students in reading (Doron, 1973). Another study by Abraham (1981) showed that reflection was weakly related to performance on a proofreading task.

Reflectivity/impulsivity has some important considerations for classroom second language learning and instruction. Teachers tend to judge mistakes too harshly, especially in the case of a learner with an impulsive style who may be more willing (than a reflective student) to gamble at a correct answer. On the other hand, a reflective student may require patience from the teacher, who must allow more time for the student to struggle with responses. It is also possible that those students with an impulsive style may go through a number of rapid transitions of semi-grammatical stages of interlanguage, while reflective ones tend to remain longer at a particular stage with "larger" leaps from stage to stage (Brown, 2002: 113).

4.4.5 Personality

Personality was defined as those characteristics of a person that account for their consistent patterns for feeling, thinking, and behaving. It is composed of a series of traits. For many language teachers, the personality of their students constitutes a major factor affecting success or failure in language learning. Personality research is related to learning style, and has a long tradition in psychology. The Swiss psychologist Jung has discussed the types of personality, saying that an individual has preferences for "functioning" in fundamental ways that are characteristic, or "typical", of that particular individual. There are even discussions of personality in Aristotle.

Personality is typically measured by means of some kind of self-report questionnaire. A number of language-specific questionnaires have been developed by SLA researchers. Two widely used personality questionnaires were Eysenck Personality Inventory (Eysenck and Eysenck, 1964) and the "Myers-Briggs Type Indicator" (Myers and Briggs, 1976), commonly referred to as the "Myers-Briggs test". Actually, there is no theoretical limit to the number of personality types. Any psychologist could provide a new test to describe new types at any time. The following factors are included in the study of SLA, and are often considered endpoints on the continua (shown in Table 4. 4) with most of the learners being somewhere between the extremes.

Table 4. 4   Personality Traits Affecting L2 Learning (Saville – Troike, 2008: 89)

anxious	—	self-confident
risk-avoiding	—	risk-taking
shy	—	adventuresome
introverted	—	extroverted
inner-directed	—	other-directed
reflective	—	impulsive
imaginative	—	un-inquisitive
creative	—	uncreative
empathetic	—	insensitive to others
tolerant of ambiguity	—	closure-oriented

Among these personality factors, some, such as *self-confident*, *risk-taking*, *adventuresome*, *imaginative*, *empathetic*, and *tolerant of ambiguity*, are positively correlated with success in L2 learning. Here we focus on a number of them.

4. 4. 5. 1   Extroversion and introversion

Extroversion/introversion represents a continuum; that is, individual learners can be more or less extroverted. However, it is also possible to identify idealized types. For example, Eysenck and Chan (1982: 154) gave a clear definition of what idealized extroverts and introverts are: extroverts are sociable, like parties, have many friends and need excitement; they are sensation-seekers and risk-takers, like practical jokes and are lively and active. Conversely, introverts are quiet, prefer reading to meeting people, have few but close friends and usually avoid excitement. Research has also been conducted on the relationship between being introvert/extrovert and achievements in L2 learning. It is generally believed that introverts do better in school and extroverts talk more. Some researchers in SLA have assumed that extroverts would be more successful in language learning, but there is no clear support for the advantage of either of the personality factors.

There are two major hypotheses regarding the relationship between extraversion/ introversion and L2 learning. The first is that extroverted learners will do better in acquiring basic interpersonal communication skills. The logic foundation for this hypothesis is that sociability, an essential feature of extraversion, will result in more opportunities to practice, more input, and more success in communicating in the L2. The second hypothesis is that introverted learners will do better at developing cognitive academic language proficiency. Its logical foundation comes from studies which show that introverted learners enjoy more academic success, perhaps because they spend more time reading and writing.

Much research provides support for the first hypothesis. That is, extroversion or similar traits such as sociability, empathy, outgoingness, and popularity, was an advantage for developing "natural communicative language" ability (Strong, 1983). However, not all studies have shown that extraversion is positively related to learners' oral language. For example, after reviewing 30 studies of personality, Dewaele and Furnham (1999) concluded, "Extroverts were found to be generally more fluent than introverts in both L1 and L2. They were not, however, necessarily more accurate in their L2, which reinforced the view that fluency and accuracy are separate dimensions in second language proficiency."

4.4.5.2 Ambiguity tolerance/ambiguity intolerance

Tolerance of ambiguity is concerned with how willing one is to tolerate ideas and propositions that are against their own belief system or structure of knowledge. Those who are ambiguity tolerant (AT) are relatively open-minded in at least considering ideologies, beliefs, and events that contradict their own views. On the contrary, those who are ambiguity intolerant (more closed-minded and dogmatic) tend to reject items that are contradictory with their views. In their ambiguity intolerance (AI), they wish to see every proposition fit into an acceptable place in their cognitive organization, and if they do not, they are rejected (Brown, 2021: 119).

AT has both advantages and disadvantages. In second language learning, a learner may encounter a great amount of contradictory information. For example, words differ from the L1; grammatical rules not only differ but are internally inconsistent because of certain exceptions; foreign culture is distinct from that of the native culture. Tolerance of such ambiguities is, of course, necessary for successful language learning. However, too much AT can have a harmful effect, if a person accepts everything before them without a critical mind. Learning a new language, in this case, may become a burden. This may prevent them from subsuming necessary facts into their cognitive system. Some grammatical rules and word definitions, for example, eventually need to be discarded, or pruned, in favor of more encompassing linguistic conceptualizations.

AI is also double-edged. On the one hand, if intolerance is optimally maintained, it will enable learners to guard against the wishy-washiness mentioned above, by closing off avenues of hopeless possibilities, rejecting contradictory material, and dealing with the reality of the system that one has built. On the other hand, AI also has its disadvantages. For example, if ambiguity is thought of as a threat, AI may close the mind too soon. Thus, it is likely to result in a rigid, dogmatic, brittle mind that is too narrow to be creative. In this respect AI may be particularly harmful in L2 learning. In a word, either too much or too little AI will bring about detrimental effects.

4.4.5.3 Anxiety

In the research of SLA, anxiety has received the most attention, along with lack of anxiety as an important component of self-confidence. Anxiety is associated with feelings of uneasiness, frustration, self-doubt, apprehension, or worry. The research on anxiety suggests that there exist different levels of anxiety, i. e., trait anxiety and state anxiety. The former is a more permanent predisposition to be anxious, while the latter, at a more momentary or situational level, is experienced in relation to some particular event or act. Trait anxiety has not proved to be useful in predicting L2 achievement, because of its global and somewhat ambiguously defined nature.

However, recent research on language anxiety focuses more specifically on the situational nature of state anxiety. To break down the construct into researchable issues, researchers (for example, Horwitz, 2010) have identified three components of foreign language anxiety: ①Communication apprehension, which arises from learners' inability to convey mature thoughts and ideas; ②Fear of negative social evaluation, which arises from a learner's need to make a positive social impression on others; ③ Test anxiety, or apprehension over academic evaluation.

These and other inspired studies conclude that foreign language anxiety can be distinguished from other types of anxiety and that it can have a negative effect on the language learning process. Another important insight to be applied to our understanding of anxiety is the distinction between debilitative and facilitative anxiety. Debilitative anxiety tends to weaken the learner's confidence while facilitative anxiety tends to maintain and even improve his confidence. Anxiety is often assumed to be a negative factor, something to be avoided at all costs. However, according to the notion of facilitative anxiety, a certain amount of anxiety over a task to be accomplished is a positive factor. Facilitative tension keeps one poised, alert, and just slightly unbalanced to the point that one cannot relax entirely. For example, before giving a public speech, the "butterflies in one's stomach" could be a sign of facilitative anxiety, a symptom of just enough tension to get the job done.

Research has shown the benefit of facilitative anxiety in L2 learning. For example, in Bailey's (1983) diary study of competitiveness and anxiety in L2 learning, it was found that facilitative anxiety was one of the keys to success, and was closely related to her inner competitiveness. Bailey found in her self-analysis that while competitiveness sometimes hindered her progress, at other times, it motivated her to study harder. Obviously, she explained the positive effects of competitiveness by means of facilitative anxiety. Research on language anxiety also has a by-product: a debate on whether anxiety is the cause of poor L2 performance, or the result of unsatisfactory performance. Some argued that foreign language anxiety is a consequence of foreign language learning difficulties while others maintained that foreign language anxiety could be the cause of poor language performance.

Ongoing research has enriched our understanding of foreign language anxiety. For example, anxiety was correlated with low perceived self-worth, competence, and intelligence; anxiety is linked with perfectionism, and those who set unrealistically high standards for themselves are likely to develop greater anxiety; anxiety varied depending on whether students talked with other students or with teachers; anxious learners make more errors, overestimate the number of their errors, and corrected themselves more than less anxious learners. In more recent studies, it was found that "willingness to communicate" (WTC) and foreign language anxiety were negatively correlated in university students in China (Liu and Jackson, 2008). Other studies show that students who were younger when starting to learn an L2 have lower levels of foreign language anxiety. These findings reinforce the claim that self-efficacy and attribution are keys to anxiety and that pedagogical attention to foreign language anxiety is of the greatest importance.

As for the implications for foreign language teaching and learning, thus, it can not be simply concluded that anxiety is totally a bad thing, which is only negatively correlated with failure in L2 learning. It is generally accepted that higher anxiety is likely to bring lower levels of success in L2 learning. When a teacher finds his students are anxious, he should first ask himself if that anxiety is truly debilitative. It might well be that a little nervous tension in the learning process is a good thing. Again, as Table 4.4 suggests, any personality trait, including anxiety, has an optimal point along its continuum; it must be pointed out that too much and too little anxiety may impede the process of successful L2 learning.

4.4.6 Learning strategies

A common phenomenon is that not only do some learners perform better than others in language learning, but also that good language learners do different things than poorer learners. Such differences are somewhat underlined by strategies used by learners. Broadly speaking, strategies are those specific actions that people take in order to solve a given problem. They are most often conscious and goal driven, thus facilitating a learning task. In particular, learners' strategies are governed by self-efficacy beliefs, as quite naturally they opt for an approach they feel comfortable with and able to implement and avoid actions that they consider exceed their ability to perform. The actions that learners perform in order to learn a language have been variously labelled: behaviors, tactics, techniques, and strategies. The term most commonly used is "learning strategies" (Ellis, 2013: 703).

The term "learning strategies" has various definitions. Oxford (1989) defined it as "behaviors or actions which learners use to make language learning more successful, self-directed and enjoyable". Great effort has gone to the job of classifying the learning strategies. Two commonly cited taxonomies are from O'Malley and Chamot (1990) and Oxford (2011). Here we focus on Oxford's typology to describe the current state of the art. Oxford (2011) identified three broad categories: cognitive, affective, and sociocultural-interactive strategies.

Cognitive strategies, according to Oxford, help the learner "construct, transform, and apply L2 knowledge". Included in this category are a number of subcategories, each of which includes specific tactics. Tactics are those "specific manifestations of a strategy used by a particular learner in a given setting for a certain purpose". Listed in Table 4.5 are some of the cognitive strategies and their corresponding tactics synthesized by Brown from O'Malley et al. , and Oxford.

Table 4. 5 Cognitive Strategies and Tactics (Brown, 2021: 127 – 128)

Cognitive Strategies	Examples of Tactics
Planning	Previewing, reviewing, setting schedules, deciding to attend to a specific aspect of language input, planning for and rehearsing linguistic components necessary to carry out an upcoming language task, deciding to postpone speaking
Organizing	Deciding to attend to specific aspects of language input or situational details that will cue the retention of language input, reordering, classifying, labelling items in the language
Monitoring	Correcting one's speech for accuracy in pronunciation, grammar, vocabulary, imitating a language model, including silent rehearsal, and self-checking
Evaluating	Checking the outcomes of one's own language learning against an internal measure of completeness and accuracy
Using senses	Creating visualizations and pictures to remember, noticing phonological sounds, acting out a word or sentence
Activating knowledge	Using L1 for comparison/contrast to remember words and forms, applying rules by deduction, using translation to remember a new word
Contextualization	Placing a word or phrase in a meaningful language sequence, relating new information to other concepts in memory
Going beyond the data	Guessing meanings of new items, predicting words or forms from the context

The second category of Oxford's learning strategies is a set of affective strategies that help the learner to employ beneficial emotional energy, from positive attitudes toward the learning process, and generate and maintain motivation. Listed in Table 4. 6 are the affective strategies and tactics:

Table 4. 6　Affective Strategies and Tactics（Brown，2021：128）

Affective Strategies	Examples of Tactics
Activating supportive emotions	Encouraging oneself, making positive statements, making lists of one's abilities, rewarding oneself for accomplishments, noticing what one has accomplished to build self-confidence, writing a language learning diary
Minimizing negative emotions	Using relaxation to lower fear or anxiety, using positive self-talk to lower self-doubt, generating interesting charts, images, or dialogues to lower boredom, making a list of "to do" items to avoid feeling overwhelmed
Generating emotions	Learning about the culture of a language, setting personal goals and monitoring their accomplishment, listing specific accomplishments, turning attention away from tests and toward what one can do with the language
Building positive attitudes	Using relaxation to lower fear or anxiety, generating interesting activities to lower boredom, empathizing with others to develop cultural understanding

The third category is the sociocultural-interactive strategies. They are called communication strategies by Dörnyei (1995) and socio-affective strategies by O'Malley et al. (1985). These strategies refer to the learners' tactics for generating and maintaining interactive communication within a cultural context. According to Oxford (2011), sociocultural-interactive strategies help learners interact and communicate, despite knowledge gaps, and deal effectively with culture. The following (Table 4. 7) are some sociocultural-interactive strategies and tactics:

Table 4. 7　Sociocultural-interactive Strategies and Tactics（Brown，2021：129）

Sociocultural-interactive Strategies	Examples of Tactics
Interacting to learn	Cooperating with one or more peers to obtain feedback, pool information, or model a language activity

(To be continued)

Sociocultural-interactive Strategies	Examples of Tactics
Overcoming knowledge gaps	Asking a teacher or other native speaker for repetition, paraphrasing, explanation, and/or examples, questioning for classification, using memorized chunks of language to initiate or maintain communication
Guessing intelligently	Using linguistic clues in lexicon, grammar, or phonology to predict, using discourse markers to comprehend
Generating conversation	Initiating conversation with known discourse gambits, maintaining conversation with affirmations, verbal and nonverbal attention signals, asking questions
Activating sociocultural schemata	Asking questions about culture, customs, etc., reading about culture (customs, history, music, art)

Some pedagogically useful studies separate strategies for acquiring the four language skills of listening, speaking, reading, and writing (Brown, 2021: 132). Two types have been identified: learning (input) strategies and communication (output) strategies. The former refers to learning receptive skills of listening and reading while the latter refers to productive skills of speaking and writing. O'Malley et al. (1989) found that L2 learners developed effective listening skills through monitoring, elaboration, and inferencing. Strategies such as selective attention to keywords, inferring from context, prediction, using a worksheet, and taking notes were shown to be teachable. Reading strategies such as bottom-up and top-down processing, predicting, guessing from context, brainstorming, and summarizing have been shown to be effective. Communication strategies have another research focus. Current studies (for example, Oxford, 2011) take a positive view of communication strategies as elements of an overall strategic competence in which learners bring to bear all the possible facets of their growing competence in order to send clear messages in the second language. Such strategies can be consciously self-regulatory as well as subconscious or implicit.

But how do we know what strategies learners use in L2 learning? It must be admitted that the measurement of strategy use is a controversial issue. One of the most widely used

instruments for learners to identify strategies is Oxford's (1990) Strategy Inventory for Language Learning (SILL). It is a questionnaire that has been tested in many countries and translated into several languages (Brown, 2021: 133). There are 50 items in the SILL. They are divided into 6 categories, each presenting a possible strategy, which responders must indicate on a 5-point scale of "never true of me" to "always true of me". Once style preferences have been identified, a learner can presumably proceed to take action through strategies.

Some researchers use the method of self-reporting in strategy-discovery research. Self-reporting can be carried out in three ways. First, it can be conducted with interviews and questionnaires about what learners have done while learning an L2. This is termed retrospective report. Second, it can be conducted with think-aloud activities, in which learners are required to talk about what they are doing while performing an L2 learning task. This is termed concurrent report. The third way is to ask learners to keep journals or diaries and to record what they are conscious of doing in their effort to learn an L2. There are other ways of discovering learning strategies. For example, learners who are working at L2 tasks can be videotaped, then interviewed in their L1 about the strategies they were using along with replaying the videotape to them. Recording a learner's speech is also a useful data collection method.

But there are problems in these methods. For example, how adequate are self-reports for identifying strategy use? And is frequency of use (as implied in questionnaires) an appropriate gauge of a learner's ability to select strategies appropriate for many different contexts? When self-report questionnaire is used, it may best be taken with a grain of salt. That is, the answers given by responders may not be totally true. Learners may not actually understand the strategy being named; they may incorrectly claim to use strategies; they could possibly fail to remember strategies they have used.

Learning strategy can be affected by many factors such as age and sex. For example, children tend to use repetition in language learning while adults use analysis more. Similarly, female learners make use of more sociocultural-interactive strategies than male learners. In addition, there is a traditional conceptual distinction between good language learners and poorer language learners. A popular hypothesis is that if we can find out what good language learners have done, we can teach those strategies to poorer language learners so that they can improve. A list of findings have shown that "good learners" have a few common qualities: ①a concern for language form; ②a concern for communication; ③an active task approach; ④an awareness of the learning process; ⑤a capacity to use strategies flexibly in accordance with task requirements (Ellis, 2013: 708).

There have been comparative studies of successful and unsuccessful learners of English in Chinese universities. For example, Gan et al. (2004) noted clear differences in the ways in which they went about learning vocabulary. Whereas the unsuccessful students relied on rote-memorization, the successful students supplemented rote-learning with strategies for reinforcing what they had learned (for example, doing vocabulary exercises or reading). The successful students also reported having a systematic plan for mastering a particular set of new words. This reflected another major difference. The successful students set objectives for themselves and identified systematic ways of achieving these. The unsuccessful learners, however, did not appear to have a clear agenda and experienced difficulty in identifying their learning problems. Halbach (2000) found that the weaker students demonstrated a lack of critical self-awareness. That is, they made little use of the monitoring and self – evaluation strategies. She suggested that weaker learners experience a vicious circle; they are weak because they lack the strategies needed to advance, while they also lack the proficiency needed to employ effective strategies.

There are problems in the studying of learning strategies. A rational question is: Does the teaching of learning strategies that work for good language learners help those poorer ones? Not always so. This is because learning is also affected by many other elements. Strategies which help one learner do not necessarily work for another. A further problem with some of the early examples of strategy research is that not all behavior can be accepted as strategies. Some researchers such as Rubin (1975) held that good learners are "willing and accurate guessers". Actually, "guess" may be a strategy, but "be willing to guess" can not be a real strategy. In addition, "guess accurately" cannot be called a strategy; it is a goal. Another problem is whether learning strategies are considered conscious or unconscious. Some researchers refer to them as "deliberate actions", while others regard them as unconscious. Next, there is also a debate as to whether learning strategies have direct or indirect effects on interlanguage development. Finally, opinions are different about what motivates the use of learning strategies. It is argued that learning strategies are used in order to learn something about the L2. It is also argued that learning strategies have an affective purpose, that is, to increase enjoyment.

Assignment

1. Questions for self-study.

(1) What does lateralization mean? How does it influence second language learning?

(2) How does behaviorism affect second language acquisition?

(3) What are the three stages of information processing?

(4) What is the importance of output in successful L2 learning?

(5) How does learning take place according to connectionist/emergentist model?

(6) What's your understanding of the competition model?

(7) What's Bialystok's view on the relationship between implicit knowledge and explicit knowledge?

(8) What's the difference between Krashen's comprehensible input and Gass's comprehended input?

(9) What is the difference between generative approach and the usage-based model?

(10) Why are "constructions" important in language learning?

(11) What is the difference between "type" and "token"?

(12) What is the difference between "type frequency" and "token frequency"?

(13) What is the difference between field-independence cognitive style and field-dependence cognitive style?

(14) What cognitive abilities do children have in language learning?

(15) How does age affect the second language acquisition?

(16) What is the difference between trait anxiety and state anxiety?

2. Fill in the blanks in the following sentences.

(1) When a learner may make efforts to learn an L2 for practical reasons, we say he has an _____ motivation.

(2) When a learners may be interested in learning an L2 because of a desire to learn about or associate with the people who use that language, or because of an intention to participate or integrate in the L2 speech community, we say that he has an _____

motivation.

(3) If you are able to perceive a particular, relevant item in a "field" of distracting items, we say that you have a _____ cognitive style.

(4) If you tend to be "dependent" on the total field so that the parts embedded within the field are not easily perceived, you have a _____ cognitive style.

(5) _____ processing begins with a rule and then applies it to language learning. _____ processing, in contrast, starts from using the language and then discovers the rule from particular instances.

(6) _____ strategies are those strategies that help the learner construct, transform, and apply L2 knowledge. _____ strategies are those that help the learner to employ beneficial emotional energy, from positive attitudes toward the learning process, and generate and maintain motivation. _____ strategies are those strategies that help learners interact and communicate, and deal effectively with culture.

3. Open discussion for pair or group work.

(1) You have learned English for quite a few years. At what age did you start to learn it? Are you more successful now in the English language than at an early age? Based on your personal experience, what do you think of the Critical Period Hypothesis? Do you know others whose experiences would support or refute it?

(2) We have discussed in this part that good language learners do different things than poorer learners. If we know what the characteristics are of a good language learner, and if we know what strategies good language learners use, does it follow that teaching poor language learners to use these strategies will result in their successful language learning? Why or why not?

(3) It is assumed that younger learners are probably more successful in informal and naturalistic learning contexts, and older learners are more successful in formal instructional settings. Do you agree or disagree? Use your own experience, together with theoretical support from this chapter to make your own argument.

(4) Integrative and instrumental motivation can both play a role in the desire to learn an L2. How have these two kinds of motivation influenced your L2 learning? If you have learned more than one L2 (like French or Japanese), is it different depending on the L2 in question? Ask other L2 learners about what kinds of factors motivated them to learn, and

compare them to your own.

(5) In your L2 learning, have you experienced a quest for perfection or fear of negative evaluation? Or have you identified other sources that could account for anxiety? If your anxieties are debilitative, what approaches and activities can help to alleviate them? If you are a teacher, how would you embrace a degree of facilitative anxiety in your students?

Chapter Five   Socio-cultural Aspects of SLA

In chapter 4 we considered the psychological aspects of second language acquisition. We discussed the relationship between language and brain, reviewed briefly the behaviorist way of language learning, focused mainly on some popular cognitive models of second language learning, and touched upon individual differences. In this chapter we move from the internal to the external factors of L2 learning, but adopt a broader perspective by examining questions such as how social and cultural factors influence second language learning and how learners participate in the construction of social contexts of acquisition. When we discuss what is acquired in SLA, it is insufficient to discuss the language itself. We should also include social and cultural knowledge embedded in the language being learned, which is needed for appropriate language use. Effective L2 communication not only requires knowledge involving different ways of categorizing objects and events and expressing experiences, but also involves learners understanding their own and others' social roles. We mainly discuss two types of context affecting L2 learning, which are termed microsocial and macrosocial factors by Saville-Troike (2008).

5. 1   Microsocial Factors and L2 Acquisition

By microsocial factors, we mean those factors that deal with the potential effects of different immediate surrounding circumstances. In this section we mainly consider input and interaction and their relation to the second language acquisition. We also include some sociocultural accounts of interaction and L2 acquisition. It must be pointed out that in this chapter, input, interaction, and intake will be used with specific meanings and in particular contexts. *Input* is used to refer to the language addressed to the L2 learner either by a native speaker or by another L2 learner. *Interaction* consists of the discourse which is jointly constructed by the learner and his interlocutors. *Input*, therefore, is the result of interaction. It is a fact that not all the available input is processed by the learner, either because some of it is not understood or because some of it is not attended to. That part of input that is processed or "let in" will be referred to as intake. The microsocial factors to be discussed in this section can also be called external factors in L2 learning.

5.1.1 Three views on input in second language acquisition

Input can be non-interactive in the form of texts that learners hear or read. It can also be interactive especially when learners participate in conversations. In second language learning, the importance of language input and interaction can never be overemphasized. A lot of research has been conducted on whether and how input and interaction affect second language acquisition. Although all theories of L2 acquisition acknowledge a role for input, there are a number of different theoretical positions on it.

According to the behaviorist theories, language learning is environmentally determined; there is a direct relationship between input and output. The learner is viewed as "a language producing machine". In this model of learning, input is the language made available to the learner in the form of stimuli and feedback. As for stimuli, the learner's interlocutor models specific forms and patterns imitated and then internalized by the learner. Thus the availability of suitable stimuli is an important determining factor in L2 acquisition. Therefore, it is necessary to regulate the stimuli by grading the input into a series of steps, so that each step constitutes the right degree of difficulty for the level that the learner has reached. Feedback serves two purposes. First, when L2 learners produce correct utterances, it reinforces them. Second, when L2 utterances are ill-formed, it corrects them. Therefore, L2 learning is shaped by the regulation of the stimuli and the provision of feedback.

Mentalist theories view input as only a "trigger" that sets off the internal language processing. It is assumed that learners are equipped with innate knowledge of possible forms that any language can take. They arrive at the forms that apply to the L2 they are trying to learn on the basis of the information supplied by the input. A common assertion of mentalist theories is that the input is insufficient to enable learners to arrive at the rules of the target language. Thus, whereas a behaviourist view of language acquisition seeks to explain progress purely in terms of what happens outside the learner, the mentalist view emphasizes the learner's internal factors.

Interactionist theories on input view verbal interaction as being essential for language learning in a number of ways. Interaction provides learners with input which contains the data they need for acquisition. It also creates opportunities for learners to receive feedback, thereby making the L2 features salient. Interactionist view of L2 learning underlines the importance of both input and internal processing mechanism. It is held that learning is caused by a complex interaction between language environment and learners' internal mechanisms. Learners' processing mechanisms both determine and are determined by the nature of input. Similarly, the quality of input affects and is affected by the nature of the internal mechanisms. According to the interactionists' view of language acquisition, the important data are not just the utterances produced by the learner, but the discourse which is jointly constructed by both the learner and their interlocutors, either a native speaker, a caretaker or another learner.

5. 1. 2 Input modification: Foreigner talk

It is a widespread phenomenon that when mothers or caretakers speak to babies learning their L1, they modify their speech to facilitate comprehension. Similarly, when native speakers (NSs) talk to L2 learners, they also change their way of speaking. Such a modified speech is called foreigner talk (FT), which is quite different from native speaker speech. The term foreigner talk was first introduced by Ferguson (1971). By foreigner talk, he meant the speech variety used by native speakers (NSs) when addressing non-native speakers (NNSs). There have been a number of explanations as to the origin of FT. For example, Ferguson likens FT to baby talk and suggests that it comes about because it is the way NSs believe NNSs speak, just as adults believe babies speak in the case of baby talk. Some behaviorist theorists claim that FT is an NS's contemptuous imitation of a NNS's attempt at speaking a target language. In this view, the purpose of using FT is to make oneself understood to an NNS. Yet, disagreement comes from Whinnom (1971), who views FT as a stereotyped version of a learner's use of the target language, and the motivation is to achieve a comic effect rather than a simple imitation. Meisel (1980) argues that FT cannot be explained on the basis of imitation, and makes the interesting suggestion that the type of simplification found in FT is the result of the same cognitive processes that are used by NNSs in the acquisition of an L2.

Many researchers have investigated the features of foreigner talk. For example, Hatch (1983) has summarized foreigner talk features from the perspectives of phonology, vocabulary, syntax, and discourse:

Table 5. 1 Summary of Foreigner Talk Features

SLOW RATE (**clearer articulation**)	Final stops are released Fewer reduced vowels Fewer contractions Longer pauses
VOCABULARY	High frequency vocabulary Less slang Fewer idioms Fewer pronoun forms Definitions Overtly marked (e. g. , *This means X*) Semantic feature information (e. g. , *a cathedral usually means a church*, *that's a very high ceiling*) Contextual information (e. g. , *if you go for a job in a factory*, *they talk about a wage scale*) Gestures and pictures
SYNTAX	Short and simple sentences Movement of topics to front of sentence Repetition and restatement New information at the end of the sentence NS grammatically repeats / modifies learners' incorrect utterances NS fills in the blank for learners' incomplete utterances
DISCOURSE	NS gives reply within a question NS uses tag questions NS offers correction

Similarly, Long (1966) also listed some common characteristics of the foreigner talk:

Simple vocabulary, using high-frequency words and phrases

Long pauses

Slow rate of speech

Careful articulation

Loud volume

Stress on key words

Simplified grammatical structures

Topicalization (topic at the beginning followed by comment)

More syntactic regularity

Retention of full forms (less contraction, fewer pronouns)

The foreigner talk used by native speakers (NSs) when communicating with non-native speakers (NNSs) displays many of the characteristics of caretaker talk. There are also some differences when the NNSs are adults. Freed (1981) compared the speech of 15 mothers with that of NSs of American English to 11 adult NNSs. She found no differences in the degree of well-formedness and syntactic complexity, but she did find some differences in the distribution of sentence types and the interpersonal functions they encoded. In particular, declaratives were much more common in the FT, and yes/no questions and imperatives less common. According to Freed, this reflects a general difference in purpose. The main function of caretaker talk is to direct the child's behavior, but the functional intent of FT is the exchange of information. It should be noted, however, that when FT is used to young children, it appears to resemble caretaker talk fairly closely.

Foreigner talk is a universal phenomenon, and the majority of studies have shown that NSs modify their speech when addressing NNSs. A detailed study of FT necessitates a consideration of a number of issues: ①the extent to which FT occurs in NS-NNS interaction, ②ungrammatical input modifications, ③grammatical input modifications, ④interactional modifications, ⑤the discourse structure of FT, and⑥the functions served by FT (Ellis, 2003: 213). Below we discuss two main types of FT. As we will see in this section, FT is important because it constitutes a source of input that can facilitate L2 acquisition.

Foreigner talk falls into two kinds: ungrammatical and grammatical. In the ungrammatical foreigner talk, the speaker often omits certain grammatical features such as the auxiliary verb *do*, copula *be*, modal verbs *can* and *must* and articles. In one of the earliest discussions of FT, Ferguson (1971) noted that in languages where native speakers use a copula in equational clauses in normal communication (for example, "Mary is a doctor"), they often omit it in talk directed at foreigners. This is because, as Ferguson suggested, the absence of the copula is considered simpler than its presence. Besides, the base form of the verb is often used instead of the past tense form; special constructions such as "no + verb" also appear in FT. Look at the following utterances used by a native English-speaking teacher to L2 children in an art activity (Saville-Troike, 2008: 106):

Mommy look at your work? (*does* is omitted)
You have Indians in Korea? (*do* is omitted)
Would you give us pencil? (*a* is omitted)
See, Siti's made mouth real scary. (*the* is deleted)
Babysitter take care of baby. (*-s* is omitted)

A number of factors appear to induce ungrammatical FT. Long (1983) suggested that four factors may be involved: ① The L2 learner's level of proficiency. That is, ungrammatical FT is more likely when the learner's proficiency is low. ②The status of the NS. Ungrammatical FT is more likely when the NS thinks he/she is of higher status. ③The NS has prior experience of using FT but only of the limited kind used to address NNSs of low proficiency. ④The extent to which the conversation is spontaneous. Ungrammatical FT is less likely in planned, formal discourse or in experimental situations.

Factors other than those listed above are at work as well. For example, ungrammatical FT can occur both with interlocutors who are familiars and with strangers. It is not yet possible to identify the exact conditions resulting in ungrammatical FT, probably because NNSs vary both culturally and individually in the kind of FT they prefer to use.

Compared with ungrammatical FT, which is highly marked, grammatical foreigner talk, however, is the normal pattern. There are different types of modification of the baseline talk (the kind of speech native speakers address to other native speakers). First, grammatical FT is made at a slower rate. Second, the input is often simplified. Generally, shorter sentences are preferred, subordinate clauses are avoided, and complex grammatical forms are omitted. Third, grammatical FT sometimes contains regular sentences. Regularization entails the selection of forms that are in some way as "basic" and "explicit". Examples include: fewer false starts; a preference for full forms over contracted forms; a preference for canonical word order; the use of explicit markers of grammatical relations (for example, "He asked if he could go" rather than "He asked to go"); movement of topics to the front of sentences (for example, "John, I like him"); avoidance of forms associated with a formal style; and avoidance of idiomatic expressions and use of lexical items with a wide coverage (for example, "flower" rather than "rose") (Ellis, 2013: 218). Fourth, FT sometimes contains elaborated language, such as lengthened phrases or sentences in order to make the meaning clearer. In the following example of foreigner talk, "when you are coming home" is an example of elaboration, which has the same meaning as "on your way home". Compare the following baseline talk with the FT:

Baseline talk: *You won't forget to buy the ice-cream on your way home, will you?*
Foreigner talk: *The ice-cream—You will not forget to buy it on your way home—Get it when you are coming home. Right?*

Not only is modification made in spoken language, but it is also applied in written language input. Modification of written input for L2 learners also includes controlled vocabulary and shorter, simpler sentences. Table 5.2 illustrates both simplification and elaboration in examples of written text modifications.

Table 5.2 Simplification and Elaboration of a Written Text (Long and Ross, 1993)

Type of Speech	Example
Baseline (speech addressed to NSs)	Catfish have gills for use under water and lungs for use on land, where they can breathe for twelve hours or more. The hot daytime sun would dry them out, but they can slip out of their ponds at night and still stay cool while they hunt for food.

（To be continued）

Type of Speech	Example
Simplified FT	Catfish have both gills and lungs. The gills are used for breathing under water. The lungs for use on land. The fish can breathe on land for twelve hours or more. At night these fish can slip out of ponds. They move at night so they can stay cool. The hot sun would dry them out. They hunt at night too.
Elaborated FT	Catfish have two systems for breathing: gills, like other fish, for use under water, and lungs, like people, for use on land, where they can breathe for twelve hours or more. Catfish would dry out and die from the heat of the sun, so they stay in water during the daytime. At night, on the other hand, they can slip out of their ponds and stay cool while they hunt for food.

In written academic texts, modifications which are intended to help L2 learners understand what they read are the same as those which are used in the textbooks for native speakers of English. These modifications include the following (Saville-Troike, 2008: 108):

Frequent organization markers such as headings and linking devices

Clear topic statements

Highlighting of key terms and inclusion of synonyms and paraphrase

Bulleted or numbered lists of main points

Elaboration of sections which require culture-specific background knowledge

Visual aids, such as illustrations and graphs

Explicit summations at regular intervals

Questions used for comprehension checks

5.1.3 Input modification: Interlanguage talk

Many of the formal characteristics of FT are very similar to those found in other simplified registers such as learner language, caretaker talk, teacher talk, and pidgins. This suggests that it reflects universal processes of simplification, knowledge of which constitutes part of a speaker's linguistic competence. Different from FT, which is the language used by NSs when speaking with NNSs, interlanguage talk (ILT) consists of the language that learners receive as input when addressed by other learners. A key issue we are concerned about is the extent to which ILT provides learners with adequate access to the grammatical properties of the target language. It is not surprising that ILT has been found to be less grammatical overall than FT or teacher talk.

In a detailed study of the ILT produced by intermediate and advanced L2 learners in pair work and comparable FT, Porter (1986) found that whereas only 6% of FT was "faulty", 20% of ILT proved to be so. Porter also found that ILT is socio-linguistically deficient. By observing a number of speech acts expressing opinions, agreement, and disagreement, she found that the learners failed to use politeness strategies as NSs do. Nor did they, in general, generate the kind of sociocultural input which is needed for language learning. Learners repeated only a very small amount of the faulty input they heard.

Despite the findings mentioned above, interlanguage talk can be considered superior to foreigner talk. When learners talk among themselves in the L2, they are more likely to experience communication problems and more likely to negotiate solutions to these problems. For example, Porter (1986) found that learners prompt each other 5 times more than the NSs prompted NNSs, while repair frequencies were similar. Some researchers such as Mackey, Oliver, and Leeman (2003) compared NS-NNS speech with NNS-NNS speech in terms of the feedback provided and the learners' response to this feedback. They found that feedback from NNSs was more likely to result in the child learners modifying their output than feedback from the NSs although there was no difference in the case of the adult learners. Overall, these studies suggest that the input that learners obtain from other learners may be beneficial.

5.1.4 Interactional modifications

In addition to input, social interaction is also very important for language acquisition. No children can learn their mother tongue by solely listening to the tape recordings, radio news or TV programs. Compared with the modifications of oral input, interactional modifications made by L1 speakers in discourse with L2 learners seem to offer more significant help in second language learning (Saville-Troike, 2008: 108). Increasingly, studies of foreigner talk have switched their attention from linguistic to interactional modifications. This has been motivated in part by the finding that interactional modifications occur even when input modifications do not and also by theoretical claims regarding the importance of this type of modification for comprehension and acquisition (Ellis, 1994: 257).

It is necessary that a distinction be made between interactional modifications involving discourse management and those involving discourse repair. During the course of discourse management, NSs may try to simplify the discourse so as to avoid communication problems. Discourse repair, however, occurs when a communication breakdown has taken place; it may also occur in response to an erroneous learner utterance of some kind, either a factual error, a linguistic one, or an error in discourse.

Discourse management

One of the most effective ways of managing discourse is to enable NNSs to understand the topic of the conversation. Some strategies which NSs use to achieve this goal are: selecting salient topics, treating topics simply and briefly, making new topics salient, and, when necessary, relinquishing topic control (Long, 1983a).

One method used by native speakers to control topic is concerned with the amount and type of information that is communicated. Generally, when addressing to NNSs, NSs tend to reduce the amount of complex information. Also, there is difference in the type of information provided for NNSs. For example, Derwing (1989) found that native speakers adjusted the information they provided about a film they had seen when speaking to low-proficiency L2 learners. The information contained in the speakers' propositions was classified as belonging to one of the three categories: crucial information, non-essential major information, and minor information, which consists of background and irrelevant information. It was found that there was no difference in the amount of crucial information which the NS and NNS addressees received. But there were differences in the relative proportions of major and minor information. The narrator included less major information and more minor information in speech to the learners. So it is clear that often NSs seek to manage discourse with NNSs by regulating the amount and type of information they provide (Ellis, 1994: 259).

A second method NSs use to establish and control topics is to make use of questions. For example, Long (1981b) found that in conversations between native English speakers and elementary level Japanese learners, 96% of the topics were initiated by questions, whereas in NS-NS conversations, only 62% were started by questions. Long explains why questions were preferred: they compel answers; they signal to the NNS that a turn is approaching; they lighten the learner's conversation burden because they encode part (and sometimes all) of the propositional content required to respond. Long also discovered differences in the type of questions used. For example, NSs mostly used yes/no and "or" type questions in conversations with learners. It should be noted that the NSs in the study were adults; child NSs, however, seem less likely to initiate topics through questions.

A third strategy of discourse management is to select topics that can be discussed in a here-and-now context. It is reported that more present-tense verbs are used in NS speech addressed to NNS than in speech addressed to other NSs. The here-and-now orientation allows learners to make use of the immediate context to interpret the meaning of utterances (Ellis, 1994).

Fourth, an NS tries to manage discourse by frequently checking whether the learner has understood his speech. Comprehension checks (such as "You understand?", "Okay?") occur more frequently in NS-NNS conversation than in NS-NS conversation.

Discourse repair

During the course of NS-NNS interaction, when there is an incomplete understanding, discourse repair arises. Repair takes the form of negotiation of meaning, which is the collaborative work speakers undertake to achieve mutual understanding. NSs often use requests for clarification (*Sorry?*, *Huh?*, *I beg your pardon*, to name a few examples) and requests for confirmation, in which, intonation and tag questions are often used. What's more, there are other conversational modifications which help to repair discourse: self-repetitions and other-repetitions. The repetitions can be exact; they can be also paraphrases. They can be complete repetitions; they can also be partial repetitions.

Interactional modifications made by NSs in discourse with non-native L2 learners appear to provide even more significant help than do the modifications of oral input. Listed below are some interactional modifications in English learning contexts (Saville-Troike, 2008: 109).

5.1.4.1   Repetition

This device is used by native speakers to offer the nonnative speakers more time for processing and an opportunity to confirm or correct perception.

NS: *This is your assignment for tomorrow.*
NNS: *What?*
NS: *This is your assignment.*

5.1.4.2 Paraphrase

Paraphrase is not only intended to make the input easy to understand; it may also help the NNS to learn new words or phrases. In the following example, the learner has understood the meaning of the phrase "reading glass" through interaction with the native speaker.

NS: *There's a pair of reading glasses above the plant.*
NNS: *a What?*
NS: *Glasses reading glasses to see the newspaper?*
NNS: *Glassi?*
NS: *You wear them to see with, if you can't see. Reading glasses.*
NNS: *Ahh ahh glasses to read you say reading glasses.*
NS: *Yeah.*

5.1.4.3 Expansion and elaboration

An NS sometimes expands and elaborates the NNS utterance in length or complexity, which goes a bit beyond the learner's ability to produce.

NNS: *Hot.*
NS: *Yes, it is very hot today.*

5.1.4.4 Sentence completion

An incomplete sentence made by the learner may be completed by a native speaker in a conversational interaction. This helps the learner to master words or chunks of language which they can use in the coming turns of talk. In the following interaction, the NNS has learned to use the new word "rings", which in turn serves the continuation of the conversation.

NNS: *To tell how old this tree is, you can count...*
NS: *Rings. Tree rings.*

5. 1. 4. 5　Comprehension check

Comprehension checks are often used by NSs to focus NNS's attention on segments of sentences which are unclear. In the following example (Gass, 2009: 428 – 429), the NS asks the NNS again and again about two key terms in his utterance.

NNS: *There has been a lot of talk lately about additives and preservatives in food. How—*

NS: *—a, a, a lot, a lot of talk about what?*

NNS: *uh. There has been a lot of talk lately about additives and preservatives in food.*

NS: *NOW just a minute. I can hear you—everything except the important words. You say there's been a lot of talk lately about what* [*inaudible*] *.*

NNS: *—additive, additive, and preservative, in food—*

NS: *Could you spell one of these words for me, please.*

NNS: *A D D I T I V E*

NS: *Just a minute. This is strange to me.*

NNS: *h h*

NS: *—uh—*

NNS: *'n other word is P R E S E R V A*

NS: *oh, preserves.*

NNS: *preservative and additive.*

NS: *—preservatives, yes, okay. And what was that—what was that first word I didn't understand?*

NNS: *Okay in—*

NS: *additives?*

NNS: *Okay.*

NS: *—additives and preservatives*

NNS: *yes.*

NS: *ooh right...*

5. 1. 4. 6　Clarification request

In the following example (Gass, 2009: 565 – 566), the NS uses clarification request, usually in a question form, to enable the NNS to make clear expressions, or repair his utterance.

NNS: *A sleeping girl is in front of the house. A big house.*

NS: *The house or the barn?*

NNS: *Barn, I don't—two, big one.*

NS: *OK.*

NNS: *A girl who is roller blade, roller skating is in the top of small house. The big one is next to the house under the tree.*

NS: *OK.*

NNS: *Left side, in the middle, skin head boy is standing. He is putting his hand in his pockets. Red skirts—he's wearing red skirts and blue pant.*

NS: *He's out aguin; where has he been? Where is he again?*

NNS: *In the front of—no, no. Left side of middle, middle. In front of the pond.*

NS: *Oh, OK, by the mushrooms?*

NNS: *Mush? No.*

NS: *No?*

NNS: *The end of the pond, left side.*

NS: *Where?*

NNS: *A curly haired girl, or maybe girl, who is holding an apple is sitting in front of that pond. It's near skin head boy. Near.*

5.1.4.7 Vertical construction

Vertical construction is a strategy used by native speakers to allow non-native speakers to construct discourse sequences beyond their current independent means. In other words, by vertical construction, the native speaker provides a scaffolding for the non-native learner. The following example (Saville-Troike, 2008: 109) will illustrate.

NNS: *Taki.* (name of another student)

NS: *What did Taki do?*

NNS: *Pencil.*

NS: *What did Taki do with the pencil?*

NNS: *Throw.* (makes throwing motion)

NS: *Taki, don't throw pencils.*

The above are some important means in the negotiation of meaning between NSs and NNSs, which help preventing or repairing breakdowns in mutual communications. An important question we are concerned about is how these input and interactional modifications contribute to second language acquisition. The related empirical evidence that these modifications do facilitate interlanguage development is still limited; however, arguments have been proposed that suggest that they do (Ellis, 2000: 47).

5.1.5 Feedback

Feedback is a type of interaction which can enhance second language acquisition and which makes NNSs aware that their utterance is not acceptable in some way; besides, it provides a correct expression. Unlike children who rarely receive negative evidence in L1, second language adult learners need correct feedback in order to achieve their language competence. Negative feedback, also known as corrective feedback and error correction, has been defined as information provided to learners about the ill-formedness of their L2 production. Feedback may occur in response to learners' oral or written production. The oral feedback usually occurs immediately during interaction, while written feedback is often provided some time after a text has been produced. Here we only consider oral feedback and its role in facilitating L2 learning.

Negative feedback to second language learners may be direct or indirect. Direct correction is explicit; it includes explicit statements such as *This is wrong*; directives involving what "cannot" or "must" be said; and explanations which are related to grammar and usage. Indirect correction is implicit. It includes some of the interactional modifications introduced above. However, their function is different. The purpose of implicit feedback is to indicate that the learner's utterance is incorrect or ill-formed. Compare the following two types of feedback.

Direct feedback:

NNS: *John goed to town yesterday.*

NS: *No, you cannot say "goed", you should say "John went to town yesterday".*

NNS: *John went to town yesterday.*

Indirect feedback:

NNS: *John goed to town yesterday.*

NS：*Yes*，*John went shopping.*

Clearly, the NS's response in the second example is an indirect indication that the NNS's utterance is wrong. What he provides is a paraphrase, which is an alternative way to say the same thing without directly pointing out that an error has been made. This is called recast, which substitutes a correct element for an incorrect one. More examples：

NNS：*Why he is very unhappy?*
NS：*Why is he unhappy?*
NNS：*Yeah why is he unhappy?*

NNS：*I can't assist class.* （meaning *I can't attend class.*）
NS：*You can't what?* （meaning *You've got the wrong word. Try again.*）
NNS：*Sorry，I can't attend class.*

This appears to be a comprehension check or clarification request in social interaction. But it is actually intended to mean that the NNS's utterance is wrong.

NNS：*John goed to town yesterday.*
NS：*John goed to town?* （meaning *The word "goed" is wrong.*）

In this example, the NS uses a rising intonation to indicate that the word "goed" is wrongly used. However, when the NS uses a falling intonation to repeat part or all of a NNS's utterance, it often confirms correctness, as is shown in the following example. The NS stresses the word "is" with a falling intonation to confirm that the usage is correct.
NNS：*This book is hard.*
NS：*This book is hard.*

Disagreement arises as to which type of feedback is better for L2 learning. There is some evidence that direct feedback is more effective in that it evokes the learner's immediate correct use of a structure and ensures the subsequent correct use. But there is also some evidence and strong theoretical reasons to support indirect or implicit feedback. This kind of feedback is like the focus-on-form because it ensures that learners are more likely to stay focused on meaning. As Muranoi (2000) suggests, indirect feedback is probably more effective when it is targeted intensively at a pre-selected form than when it occurs extensively in incidental focus on form. In the latter case, explicit attention to form may be more successful.

Considerable research has investigated the features of negative feedback. In addition to direct and indirect categorization of negative feedback, there are other different ways of taxonomy. Chaudron (1977) developed an extensive taxonomy, including categories such as repetition of the error with or without changes, prompts, and explanations. Lyster and Ranta (1997) refined these categories to six: recast, elicitation, repetition, metalinguistic feedback, explicit correction, and clarification requests. Ellis et al. (2001), in an attempt to move from descriptive categorization of discourse features to a more psycholinguistically-motivated taxonomy, identified three main types of negative feedback: recasts, elicitations, and metalinguistic feedback. Then, Ellis (2008) has reduced the categories to either input-providing feedback or output-promoting feedback. The following are more examples of different types of negative feedback.

Explicit correction:
Student: *He comed here.*
Teacher: *No, you should say "he came here".*

Recast:
Student: *He comed here.*
Teacher: *Yes, he came here.*

Metalinguistic feedback:
Student: *He comed here.*
Teacher: *You need past tense.*
Student: *He came here.*

Elicitation:
Student: *He comed here.*

Teacher：*What did he do*?
Student：*He came here.*

Repetition：
Student：*He comed here.*
Teacher：*He comed here*?
Student：*He came here.*

Clarification request：
Student：*He comed here.*
Teacher：*Pardon*?
Student：*He came here.*

According to whether learners' ill-formed utterances are self-repaired or corrected by others，negative/corrective feedback can be further categorized into two main types：other-repair and self-repair. The former consists of explicit correction and recast，while the latter includes metalinguistic feedback，elicitation，repetition，and clarification request. All the six feedback types are classified along a continuum of explicitness. Recasts are situated at the implicit end of feedback types involving other-repair，whereas clarification requests and repetition of error are located at the implicit end of feedback leading to self-repair，as is shown in Figure 5. 1.

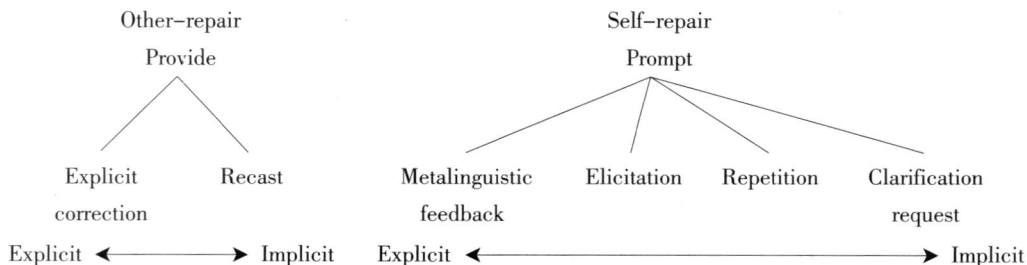

Figure 5. 1　Options for Corrective Feedback（From Loewen and Nabei，2007）

Is feedback effective for L2 learning? This is a contentious issue despite the fact that corrective feedback occurs frequently in the L2 classroom. Communicative language teaching generally rejected negative feedback because it was viewed as hindering learners' attempts to communicate freely as well as being ineffective for developing implicit L2 knowledge. However, research in content-based and immersion instruction contexts revealed that while learners often reached high levels of L2 fluency, they did not achieve correspondingly high levels of grammatical accuracy, even on frequently occurring linguistic structures. Further increasing evidence has shown that negative feedback can be beneficial for learners.

The next question we are concerned about is which features of negative feedback influence its effectiveness. The first issue related to feedback's effectiveness is its salience. It is argued that learners must notice negative feedback in order for it to be effective. The salience of different types of feedback has been the focus of numerous studies, for salience of feedback, to a large extent, invites learners' attention. The most explicit type of feedback is the explicit correction, and while detractors of explicit correction argue that it can be disruptive to communicative interaction, there is some evidence that more explicit feedback may be more effective for L2 learning (Ellis et al. , 2006) .

Another issue in considering the effectiveness of feedback is whether it is effective because it provides positive evidence, negative evidence, or both. On the one hand, negative evidence indicates that a linguistic construction is not possible and therefore serves to be the key component of corrective feedback. On the other hand, positive evidence consists of exemplars of what is possible in a language and also serves as an important component of corrective feedback.

The effectiveness of feedback may also be dependent on the linguistic items targeted by that feedback. Any aspect of language can receive feedback, although grammar, vocabulary, and pronunciation are the most common targets in classroom contexts. Grammatical structures have been the primary focus in quasi-experimental studies. Popular targets of inquiry have included English question formation and past tense, while fewer studies have been conducted in other languages or on other features. Furthermore, almost no research has investigated feedback on pragmatics or discourse features.

Learners' proficiency is also a consideration. Studies suggest that learners need to be developmentally ready to benefit from feedback. In addition, there may be an interaction between proficiency and type of feedback. For example, Ammar and Spada (2006) found that higher proficiency students benefited equally from recasts and prompts, while lower proficiency learners benefited more from prompts than recasts.

The timing of feedback is also important. Generally, feedback occurs immediately after an error, and this immediate correction of incorrect forms is argued to benefit learners. However, delayed feedback is also possible, particularly in computer-mediated communication (CMC) where the nature of synchronous written chat often means that feedback does not follow the error instantly.

A final factor which influences the effect of feedback is the amount of feedback provided to the targeted feature. There is no agreement on the ideal amount of feedback. Li (2010), in his meta-analysis, found that treatments of 50 minutes or less were significantly more effective than were longer treatments. Additionally, Havranek (2002) found no advantage for correcting the same linguistic error multiple times as opposed to correcting it only once. Further investigation into the effects of the intensity of feedback is needed.

5.1.6 The interaction hypothesis

Long's early interaction hypothesis was heavily influenced by Hatch's work on discourse analysis and L2 acquisition and by Krashen's input hypothesis. As Hatch (1978b: 404) claimed: One learns how to do conversations, one learns how to interact verbally, and out of this interaction syntactic structures are developed. According to Krashen's input hypothesis we discussed in chapter 3, second language acquisition takes place when the learner understands the input that contains grammatical forms that are a bit more advanced than the learner's current level. Krashen believes that L2 acquisition depends on comprehensible input. The interaction hypothesis also underlines the importance of comprehensible input.

The early version of the interaction hypothesis encountered a number of criticisms. Ellis (2013: 254) summarized its problems in the following three aspects: First, learners often fake comprehension during the interaction. That is, they frequently pretend that they have understood as a result of negotiating a comprehension problem when they actually have not. There are social constraints that influence the extent to which learners are prepared to negotiate to achieve understanding. Second, the forms used to realize the topic management functions associated with meaning negotiation can also be used to realize entirely different functions. A third problem is that the early version of interaction hypothesis, like the input hypothesis, failed to explain how the comprehensible input resulted in acquisition.

The updated interaction hypothesis addressed the last criticism by emphasizing that the role of negotiation is to facilitate attention to form. It claims that the modifications and collaborative efforts taking place in social interaction promote second language learning because they enable the input to enter the mind for processing: "negotiation for meaning, and especially negotiation work that triggers interactional adjustments by the NS or more competent interlocutor, facilitates acquisition because it connects input, internal learner capacities, particularly selective attention, and output in productive ways." (Long, 1996: 151 – 152)

Contrary to the early version of the interaction hypothesis, which simply assumed an effect for comprehensible input, this revised version sought to explain how interactionally modified input contributes to acquisition by specifying the learner internal mechanisms involved. Interactionally modified input works for acquisition when ① it assists learners to notice linguistic forms in the input, and ②the forms that are noticed lie within the learners' processing capacity.

Interaction may help learners acquire an L2 in two ways. First, the L2 learner often receives negative evidence. Their partners may indicate when they have not understood and, in the course of so doing, may work out the correct target-language forms. This can be seen in the following interaction between two L2 learners:

> Hiroko: *A man is uh drinking c-coffee or tea with uh the saucer of the uh uh coffee set is uh in his uh knee.*
> Izumi: *in him knee.*
> Hiroko: *uh on his knee*
> Izumi: *yeah*
> Hiroko: *on his knee*
> Izumi: *so sorry. On his knee.*
>
> (Gass and Selinker, 2008: 350 – 351)

In this interaction, Hiroko says *in his knee* and Izumi responds with an incorrect form, *in him knee*. Hiroko changes the preposition from *in* to the correct *on*. As a result of reciprocal interaction, both learners mastered the correct form, *on his knee*. This example demonstrates the role of modified output in L2 acquisition emphasized by the new version of interaction hypothesis.

Second, when the L2 learners have the opportunity to clarify something which has been said they are processing the input. This may help them comprehend as well as acquire new second language forms. It can be illustrated by the following example in which negotiation of meaning provides learners with information about semantic and structural properties of the target language. The NS responds to the NNS's trigger by modifying his utterances semantically and formally through the segmentation and movement of input constituents.

NS: *with a small pat of butter on it and above the plate*
NNS: *hm hmm what is buvdaplate?*
NS: *above*
NNS: *above the plate*
NS: *yeah*

(Pica, 1992: 225)

As could be seen from the above evidence, the negotiation of meaning works sometimes, and is useful for some learners in explaining the phenomenon in the second language acquisition. Despite the fact that the interaction hypothesis, with its emphasis on the contributions of negative feedback and modified output as well as comprehensible input, and with its recognition that interaction works by connecting input, internal learner capacities, and output via selective attention, has been updated and accomplished a major advance on the early version, it still has some limitations that we should be aware of. First, a theory of language acquisition based on a single type of interaction or a single interactional strategy, which constitutes only a small part of the total interaction experienced by the learner, would seem to be limited (Ellis, 2013: 257). For example, there are ways of interaction other than negotiation of meaning that may be more facilitative of acquisition.

Another limitation of the interaction hypothesis is that the negotiation may work best with intermediate learners; beginner learners lack the resources to negotiate effectively while advanced learners tend to focus on opinion and interpretation rather than comprehension or linguistic clarity. In addition, negotiation has been shown to center on lexical problems and larger syntactic units and rarely involves inflectional morphology except in experimental studies, which have specifically targeted a morphological feature. Therefore, the interaction hypothesis may not be able to explain how all learners acquire all aspects of linguistic competence. As Gass (2003: 248) stated in her own review of the negotiation research: it is likely that there are limitations to what can and cannot be learnt through the provision of negative evidence provided through conversation.

It should be pointed out that interaction sometimes may overburden the L2 learners with input when one of the speakers presents long paraphrases or definitions of unknown terms. In this light, L2 acquisition may be hindered rather than facilitated. Therefore, the relationship between modified interaction and second language acquisition is rather complex. However, these limitations do not mean that the interaction hypothesis should be dismissed. The hypothesis has generated considerable interest in the field of SLA; it has given rise to numerous studies; it has demonstrated ample explanatory power. No theory of SLA is complete without an account of the role played by interaction. The interaction hypothesis will continue to be one of the most convincing statements of the role to date (Ellis, 2013: 260).

5. 1. 7　Sociocultural theory

As noted in the previous chapters, the research of SLA has focused on linguistic and psycholinguistic aspects. In recent years, however, there has been an increased emphasis on language use, with the interest moving from "inside the mind" to the connection between the mind and the outside social and cultural context. Based on the Russian psychologist Vygotsky's work, Sociocultural theory (S-C theory) has a fundamentally different way of looking at language and language acquisition. Different from most linguistic approaches, S-C theory gives relatively less attention to the structural patterns of the second language being learned, and emphasizes learner activity and involvement over innate and universal mechanisms.

Compared with most psychological approaches, S-C theory has a larger degree of focus on factors outside the learner, rather than on the factors that are purely in the learner's mind. S-C theory denies the claim that the learner is an autonomous processor. S-C theory also differs from other social approaches in regarding interaction as an essential force rather than as only a helpful condition for learning. Although sociocultural theory is rooted in the ontology of the social individual, it does not mean that sociocultural approach is divorced from psychological processes. This is because a sociocultural approach regards language and L2 acquisition as contextually situated and the situated language is related to internal processes.

For Vygotsky, language is seen as a semiotic tool, a means by which humans achieve the goals of social living. In this respect, Vygotsky's views of language are similar to those of Halliday. Halliday and Vygotsky are in agreement in seeing language as a cultural tool that has been developed and refined in the service of social action and interaction (Wells, 1994a: 49). Differences between the two theorists lie in the fact that Vygotsky, as a psychologist, was concerned with the relationship between language and thought and regarded language as the means for mediating higher levels of thinking, whereas, Halliday, as a linguist, was more concerned with how language is used as a tool in communication and how its communicative uses shape language itself.

For Vygotsky it is language at the level of the word that is central, as it is at this level that the child discovers the symbolic function of language and at this level that the close relationship between language and thought develops. For Halliday, however, language is a semiotic system consisting of signs involving phonological, lexical, and grammatical forms encoding the intrapersonal, interpersonal, and textual functions that occur in social behavior (Ellis, 2013: 519). Nevertheless, similarities outweigh the differences, as according to both Vygotsky and Halliday: Language is a particularly powerful semiotic tool because its semantic structure encodes the culture's theory of experience, including the knowledge associated with the use of all other tools, and enables its users to interact with each other in order to coordinate their activity and simultaneously to reflect on and share their interpretations of experience. (Wells, 1994a: 72)

In short, it is the semantic properties of language, not its formal properties, that are at the forefront of a sociocultural view of language. Yet there is no denying that how learners acquire these semantic properties cannot be studied separately from the actual linguistic forms that encode them. Lantolf and Thorne (2006) also emphasized the primacy of the semantic properties of language in sociocultural theory, and presented a sociocultural perspective on language as "communicative activity":

...because S-C theory is a theory of mediated mental development, it is most compatible with theories of language that focus on communication, cognition, and meaning rather than on formalist positions that privilege structure. (p. 4)

They accepted, however, that form "matters" but argued that form cannot be considered in isolation from meaning because "meaning and form are dialectically dependent on one another" (Lantolf and Thorne, 2006: 5). There are a few important concepts in the S-C theory, which are different from more traditional approaches to SLA: mediation, regulation, internalization, and the Zone of Proximal Development. Here we will touch upon each of them and discuss their relationship with L2 learning.

5. 1. 7. 1 Mediation

Mediation is the most important concept in the S-C approach. According to S-C theory, human activities are mediated by symbolic artifacts and material artifacts. The function of these artifacts is to mediate the relationship between humans and the outside social and material world. The symbolic artifacts refer to higher level cultural tools such as language and literacy. The S-C approach claims that learning takes place when simple innate mental activities are transformed into higher order, more complex mental functions. This transformation involves symbolic mediation, which serves as a link between a person's current mental state and higher order functions. Within the S-C theory, man uses symbols as tools to mediate psychological activity and control our psychological processes. A primary tool that man has possessed is language, which allows humans to interact with both physical and social environment in the outside world. It is the language that enables man to have the power to think about and talk about events and objects which are far away both in location and in time.

5. 1. 7. 2 Regulation

Regulation can be regarded as a kind of mediation. While learning a language, children also learn to regulate their activities linguistically. Three stages of development exist on the way to self-regulation. First, objects are used as a way of thinking, as is called object-regulation. For example, parents may use pieces of candy to help kids with the concept of counting. The second stage is termed other-regulation. That is, learning is regulated by others rather than objects. The third stage is self-regulation, which takes place when activities are performed with little or no external support, but by internalization of information. At this stage, addition is no longer carried out with the use of pieces of candy.

5. 1. 7. 3　Internalization

Another central concept in the S-C theory is internalization. This process permits us to move the relationship between an individual and his environment to later performance. Imitation is one of ways by which internalization takes place. Imitation can be immediate; it can be intentional; also, it can be delayed in early child language development. The imitation which is observed by children when they are alone is also known as private speech. Private speech occurs in L2 classroom as well. Those items which are focused on by children in private speech are controlled by the learner; they are not necessarily controlled by the teacher's agenda (Gass and Selinker, 2008: 284).

5. 1. 7. 4　Zone of Proximal Development

Another key concept in the S-C theory is the Zone of Proximal Development (ZPD). So far we have mentioned the interpersonal interaction which occurs between people. An important context for symbolic mediation is such interpersonal interaction between learners and experts. Experts in a learning environment include teachers and more competent learners. Vygotsky defined the term Zone of Proximal Development as: "the distance between the actual developmental level as determined by independent problem solving and the level of potential development as determined through problem solving under adult guidance or in collaboration with more capable peers" (Vygotsky, 1978: 86). It can be clearly seen that learning results from interpersonal activity, which forms the basis for individual functioning. This embodies the social nature of learning and underlines the significance of collaborative learning. The ZPD is an area of potential development, where the learner achieves this potential only with the help of others. According to S-C theory, mental functions that are beyond the learner's current level must be performed in collaboration with other people before they are achieved independently.

Superficially, one might think that the ZPD is analogous to Krashen's i + 1 that we discussed in chapter 3. This notion demonstrates that what learners can acquire is governed by their current interlanguage and what structure comes next in the natural order of acquisition. However, such a comparison was disputed by Dunn and Lantolf (1998) who argued that the two concepts are incompatible. Krashen's i + 1 is rooted in the information-processing model of cognition and the computational metaphor and relates to the acquisition of features of language by autonomous individuals. According to this view, L2 acquisition is something that goes on exclusively inside the learner's mind, driven by the language acquisition device triggered by exposure to input. In contrast, the ZPD belongs to the participation metaphor; a ZPD is constructed dialogically through the mediation of social interaction or private speech. As Lantolf (2005: 337) put it "Krashen's is a model of language acquisition; Vygotsky's is a theory of human development".

An important way in which a learner is assisted in language development within the ZPD is through scaffolding. The metaphor of "scaffolding" refers to the verbal guidance which an expert provides to help a learner perform any specific task, or the verbal collaboration of peers to perform a task which would be too difficult for any one of them individually (Saville-Troike, 2008). That is, scaffolding not only happens between expert and green hand, but also occurs between learning peers who collaborate together in constructing language which exceed the competence of any one of them. Let us look at some examples from Wagner-Gough (Ellis, 1994: 284):

Mark: *Come here.*
Homer: *No come here.*
......
Judy: *Where is Mark?*
Homer: *Where's Mark is school.* (= *Mark is at school.*)

Pay special attention to Homer's utterances. Homer is an Iranian boy, who is having conversations with native English speakers Mark and Judy. Their relationship can be described as learner and expert. Clearly, Homer creates utterances by borrowing a chunk from the preceding utterance and then expanding it by adding an element to the beginning (*no + come here*), or to the end (*Where's Mark + is school*). Obviously, Homer uses the native speakers' utterances as scaffolding to construct more complex syntax. Scaffolding also takes place between two peers:

Joe: *You know what?*
Angel: *You know why?* (ibid.)

In this interactional conversation, Angel uses Joe's utterance as a scaffold, replacing "what" in the previous utterance with "why". This kind of interaction enables learners to practice syntax and pronunciation.

To summarize, the above four key concepts of S-C approach are interwoven together in the interpersonal interaction. For L2 learners, both L1 and L2 can provide helpful mediation. Talk between peer learners collaborating in a task is often conducted in their common L1. The L1 provides an important medium for problem solving, and thus can improve the learning of both L2 and the related academic knowledge learners are learning in a second language. Here language serves as a symbol, thus it is also called symbolic mediation.

When a learner is interacting with an expert or more advanced partner, he is using a scaffold to "climb up" on the way to L2 acquisition. While "climbing up", he forms concepts that are beyond him if he is acting alone; thus, zones of proximal development are created. In this way, a novice comes to solve a problem with the help of an "expert", and then learns to control a concept without others' assistance (internalization of the solution). The whole progressive process can be depicted as moving from other-regulation to self-regulation. Seen in this way, language development is demonstrated in social interaction first and then inside the learner.

5.2   Macrosocial Factors and L2 Acquisition

Unlike microsocial factors, which focus on immediately surrounding circumstances, macrosocial factors relate second language acquisition to broader cultural and social environments. Below we will consider some macrosocial factors in looking at how social contexts influence L2 acquisition. Here we mainly introduce the acculturation model, accommodation theory, the social-educational model, identity, community of practice and investment in L2 learning, ecological approach to SLA, and complex dynamic systems theory.

5.2.1   The acculturation model

Proposed by Schumann, the acculturation model was constructed to explain the acquisition of an L2 by immigrants in majority language settings, excluding learners who receive formal instruction in classrooms. Acculturation means the process of becoming adapted to a new culture, and determines the extent to which a learner performs like a native speaker. According to Schumann (1978: 34), "second language acquisition is just one aspect of acculturation and the degree to which a learner acculturates to the target-language group will control the degree to which he acquires the second language". To put it in another way, if learners acculturate, they will learn; if learners do not acculturate, they will not learn.

This theory was originated from a case study of a 33-year-old Costa Rican, Alberto, who was acquiring English in the United States. Alberto graduated from a Costa Rican high school in which he had learned English for 6 years. Then he moved to Cambridge, Massachusetts at age 33 and lived with another Costa Rican couple. He was the only Spanish speaker at his workplace; other nonnative speakers of English were also employed here. In his daily life, he mainly socialized with other Costa Ricans. Over a period of ten months, Schumann found that Alberto made little progress in linguistic development. In his utterances, Alberto used a reduced and simplified form of English. For example, when expressing negation, he still used the "no + verb" construction. When asking a question, he continued to use declarative word order instead of inversion (*Where you get that?*). Besides, he learned no auxiliary verbs, and he failed to mark regular verbs for past tense, nor did he mark nouns for possession. Then, there were some grammatical features that he seemed to have acquired, but they were actually the result of positive transfer from his mother tongue, Spanish. Therefore, a conclusion can be reached that Alberto appeared to have fossilized. Schumann put it in another way; that is "pidginized" at a very early stage of development. In a word, the young man has stopped making progress in acquiring English as a second language.

Why is it so? Was it because of any cognitive reasons? No. Alberto demonstrated normal intelligence. Age was not a factor as many older learners achieve satisfactory levels of L2 proficiency. Schumann noticed that Alberto's utterance demonstrated similar features to those found in a pidgin (a very simple contact language used among speakers who have no common language). Just as a pidgin has developed in contact situations which require functionally restricted communication, so learners like Alberto seem to fossilize since they also have a limited need to communicate in the L2. In this view, a learner fails to progress beyond the early stage of acquisition because he needs the L2 only for the communicative function of language, not for social identification or for the realization of personal attitudes. Therefore, Schumann proposed that if a learner fails or is unwilling to adapt to the target language culture, this may cause pidginization in second language acquisition.

Then for what reasons does a learner fail to acculturate? Schumann proposed two reasons to account for the failure: social distance and psychological distance. The social distance concerns how well an individual learner fits the target-language group and achieves contact with them. He does well when the social distance is "short". According to Schumann, a learner's learning situation can be "good", or "bad". A good learning situation is one in which①the L2 and target-language groups view each other as socially equal; ②both groups are desirous that the L2 group assimilate (that is, the L2 group give up its own lifestyle and values in favor of those of the TL group); ③there is low enclosure (that is, the L2 group may share the same social facilities); ④the L2 group lacks cohesion (that is, it has more inter-group contact); ⑤the group is small; ⑥both groups display positive attitudes towards each other; ⑦the L2 group envisages staying in the TL area for an extended period (that is, the L2 group may intend to stay in the TL area for a long time). The psychological distance concerns how comfortable a learner feels with the learning task. The social factors are primary; the psychological factors mainly come into play when social distance is indeterminate; that is, when social factors constitute neither a positive nor negative influence on acculturation.

The psychological distance includes a few factors: ①language shock. L2 learners may fear that they will look funny in speaking the L2; ②culture shock. L2 learners may feel anxious and disorientated upon entering a new culture; ③motivation. L2 learners may be integratively or instrumentally motivated to learn the L2; ④ego permeability. L2 learners may be uneasy because they perceive their L1 to have fixed and rigid boundaries. Or they may feel free if they perceive their L1 to have permeable and flexible boundaries.

However, the acculturation model is not without problems. First, the model has nothing to say about how social factors influence the quality of contact that learners experience. Second, it has neglected the fact that learners are not just subject to social conditions, but may become the subject of them as well. Learners may construct the social context of their own learning.

5.2.2 Accommodation theory

Accommodation Theory (AT) derives from the research of Giles and associates into the intergroup uses of language in multilingual communities. Giles operates within a socio-psychological framework, and his primary concern is to investigate how intergroup uses of language reflect basic social and psychological attitudes in inter-ethnic communication. As an offshoot of this, he has also considered SLA from an intergroup stance and it is the resulting view of SLA which has become known as Accommodation Theory. The AT is similar to the Acculturation Model (AM) in some respects, but it also differs from it in a number of ways. Like Schumann, Giles is concerned to account for successful language acquisition, both seeking the answer in the relationships that hold between the learner's social group (called the "ingroup") and the target language community (called the "outgroup").

However, whereas Schumann explains these relationships in terms of variables that create actual social distance, Giles does it in terms of perceived social distance. According to Giles, it is how the ingroup defines itself in relation to the outgroup that is important for L2 acquisition. Also, where AM appears to treat social and psychological distance as absolute phenomena that determine the level of interaction between learners and native speakers, AT sees intergroup relationships as subject to constant negotiation during the course of each interaction. Thus, for Schumann, the social and psychological distance are static, but for Giles the intergroup relationships are dynamic and fluctuate in accordance with the shifting views of identity held by each group in comparison with the other.

Giles and Byrne (1982) identified a number of variables that affect L2 acquisition. They include identification with learners' own ethnic group, inter-ethnic comparison, perception of ethno-linguistic vitality, perception of in-group boundaries, and identification with other social groups. They then discussed the conditions under which subordinate group members—such as immigrants or members of an ethnic minority—are most likely to acquire native like proficiency in the dominant group's language. The favorable conditions they proposed are: ①when in-group identification is weak or the L1 does not function as a salient dimension of ethnic group membership, ② when inter-ethnic comparisons are quiescent, ③when perceived in-group vitality is low, ④when perceived in-group boundaries are soft and open, and ⑤when the learners identify strongly with other groups and so develop adequate group identity and intra-group status. These five conditions are associated with a desire to integrate into the dominant out-group, additive bilingualism, low situational anxiety, and the effective use of informal contexts of L2 acquisition.

In contrast, learners from minority groups will be unlikely to achieve native-speaker proficiency when their ethnolinguistic vitality is high. This occurs under the following unfavorable conditions: ①they identify strongly with their own in-group; ②they see their in-group as inferior to the dominant out-group; ③their perception of their ethnolinguistic vitality is high; ④they perceive in-group boundaries as hard and closed; ⑤they do not identify with other social groups and so have an inadequate group status. Unlike Schumann's model which emphasizes "contact" as the variable mediating between social factors and L2 acquisition, Giles and Byrne see "interaction" as crucial.

According to Gile, the core of the theory is "social accommodation". When humans interact with each other, they have two social purposes: either attempting to make their speech sound similar to that of their partners so as to emphasize their social cohesiveness or to make their speech different in order to underline their social distinctiveness. The former is called convergence while the latter is called divergence. AT theory suggests that second language acquisition involves long-term convergence. That is to say, when L2 learners are motivated to converge on native speakers' normal patterns (trying to speak the way native people do), they may become more proficient learners. In contrast, when the social conditions encourage learners to keep their own social group, they will be less successful in L2 acquisition. As can be seen, social factors influence learners' L2 development through the impact they have on the attitude, which further decide what language learners engage in and how quickly an L2 is learned.

5.2.3 The socio-educational model

Different from the other theories discussed in this section, which account for the role social factors play in natural settings, the socio-educational model was developed to explain L2 learning in classroom settings, especially in the foreign language classroom. Proposed by Gardner (1985), the model seeks to interrelate 4 aspects of L2 learning: ①the social and cultural milieu; ② individual learner differences; ③ the setting, and ④ learning outcomes. According to the socio-educational model, L2 learning—even in classroom setting—is not just a matter of learning new information but of acquiring symbolic elements of a different ethnolinguistic community.

The L2 learners' social and cultural milieu determines their beliefs about language and culture. According to Gardner, individual learner differences are caused by a number of variables, two of them being motivation and language aptitude. The learners' social and cultural milieu determines the extent to which they wish to identify with the target-language culture (the integrative motivation) and also the extent to which they hold positive attitudes towards the learning situation (for example, the teacher and the instructional program). Both contribute to the learner's motivation.

Motivation has a major impact on learning in both formal and informal learning contexts, while aptitude is important only in the former. These two variables determine the learning behaviors seen in different learners in the two contexts, and, thereby, learning outcomes, both linguistic (L2 proficiency) and non-linguistic (attitudes, self-concept, cultural values, and beliefs). When learners are motivated to integrate, they develop both a high level of L2 proficiency and better attitudes. One of the predictions of the socio-educational model is that the relationship between the social/cultural milieu and L2 proficiency and also between learners' attitudes and their proficiency is an indirect one. However, the relationship between integrative motivation and proficiency is more direct.

5. 2. 4   Identity, community of practice and investment in L2 learning

When commenting on the acculturation model, we picked one of its shortcomings that it fails to acknowledge the fact that learners are not only subject to social conditions but also become the subject of the social environment. These notions of "subject to" and "subject of" are important in the view of the relationship between social context and L2 acquisition. In this section, we first introduce the basic concept of identity and its relationship to L2 learning; second we further look at the L2 learning process from the lenses of communities of practice and identity theory; finally, we briefly mention the relationship of L2 learning and investment.

5. 2. 4. 1   The concept of identity

Norton (2013: 4) defined identity as "how a person understands his or her relationship to the world, how that relationship is structured across time and space, and how the person understands possibilities for the future". Social identity was defined as "the relationship between the individual and the larger social world, as mediated through

institutions such as families, schools, workplaces, social services, and law courts"
(Norton, 1997). Perice (1995) points out that language learners have very complex
social identities. They can only be understood in terms of the power relations that shape social
structures. A person's social identity is multiple and contradictory. Language learning is
successful when learners are able to summon up or construct an identity, which allow them
to impose their right to be heard and to be the subject of the discourse. Peirce illustrates this
with an extract from the diary of Eva, an adult immigrant learner of English in Canada:

The girl which (who) is working with me pointed at the man and said:
Girl: *Do you see him?*
Eva: *Yes. Why?*
Girl: *Don't you know him?*
Eva: *No. I don't know him.*
Girl: *How come you don't know him? Don't you watch TV? That's Bart Simpson.*
[It made me feel so bad and I didn't answer her nothing (anything)]

Eva felt embarrassed and humiliated in this conversation since she found herself
positioned as an "outsider", one who did not even know the TV star Bart Simpson. Here she
was subject to a talk that assumed a social identity which she did not have. According to
Perice, Eva could have made herself the subject of the conversation if she had attempted to
reshape the grounds on which the conversation took place. For example, she could have said
that she did not watch the kind of programs of which Bart Simpson was a star. In this way
social identity could have been recreated. However, in this instance Eva did not feel able to
assert such an identity for herself.

Norton's theory is concerned with the relationship between power, identity, and
language learning. Social identity is different from "cultural identity" and "ethnic identity".
Norton preferred to the term "social identity", because she believed that this term best
captures the heterogeneous and dynamic nature of identity in the learners she investigated.

Ellis (2013: 336 – 337) summarized the three general questions the social identity
theory seeks to address: ①under what conditions do language learners speak? ②how can
we encourage learners to become more communicatively competent? ③how can we facilitate
interaction between language learners and target-language speakers? Answers to these

questions are provided by three propositions: first, social identity is multiple, contradictory, and dynamic. Second, L2 learners need to "invest" in a social identity that will create appropriate opportunities for them to learn the L2. They need to be prepared to struggle to establish such an identity. Third, L2 learners need to develop an awareness of the right to speak.

The social identity theory is made concrete through reports of case studies of a number of adult female immigrants to Canada. Norton (2013) reported how their social identities denied them the opportunity to speak and be heard and how they were made uncomfortable. In such a situation, they had a choice: either withdraw from contact with native speakers or fight to establish a preferred social identity that would afford them opportunities to learn English as a second language. Further evidence for the relationship between identity and language learning can be found in McKay and Wong's study (1996) of Chinese immigrant students in junior high schools in California. They reported how these students constantly conduct delicate social negotiations to fashion viable identities. One of the implications of the study is that investment can be highly selective and will result in different kinds of language proficiency. Different learners prioritize different language skills or combinations of skills depending on how they define their social identity.

5.2.4.2 Observing L2 learning from the communities of practice and identity theory

With the incredible development of communications media and heightened global awareness, it became increasingly difficult to understand sociocultural variables in an empirical way. A potentially fruitful model for SLA research appeared in the concept of communities of practice (COP) to examine more accurately issues of identity in L2 learning. The concept of COP was not only applied to any group of people who share a profession or craft, but also to classrooms of learners in educational settings. COP was assumed to have three characteristics: ①mutual engagement: Learners in a classroom build collaborative relationships that bind the learners together as a social entity; ② Joint enterprise: Learners (and teacher) negotiate an understanding of what binds them together as a community; ③Shared repertoire: As part of its practice, the community produces a set of commonly used resources and practices (Brown, 2021: 188).

Imagining classroom learners as communities of practice has opened the doors to SLA teachers and learners to openly recognize the singular contexts of each educational setting. Rather than learning to acquire a real or imagined "second" culture, learners can instead participate in situated learning, which is contextualized to their own particular milieu and individualized to the varying perceptions of identity and culture among the learners.

Like L2 learners (learning an L2 in an L2 culture), foreign language learners (learning an L2 in an L1 culture) are not exempt from construction and negotiation of identity. Kramsch (2009) not only questioned the image of foreign language learners as monolingual, privileged, and secure in their identities, but also argues against the notion that foreign language learning has little effect on identity. Citing L2 learners' subjective accounts of their language learning experiences, she linked emotion to the manner in which learners construct their social realities. Blackledge and Creese (2010) further expanded our knowledge of identity and COP in multilingual students by demonstrating the importance of identity negotiations, and even the development of hybrid identities in learning an L2.

Identity theory presents a marked conceptual shift in SLA research, inspired by Vygotsky's work on sociocultural theory. We use symbolic tools, or signs, to mediate and regulate our relationships with others and with ourselves. Language is the primary symbolic tool through which we construct our identity. Both children and adults acquire new concepts through social or interactional means. Our ultimate autonomous functioning is self-regulation. Identity theory views the L2 learner as situated in a large social world and variable over time and space. The definitions of learners in binary terms (for example, extroverted-introverted) are overgeneralized since learners' traits can vary in contradictory ways and even within a single individual. What's more, identity theory recognizes the investment of learners in pursuing "a community of the imagination, a desired community that offers possibilities for an enhanced range of identity options in the future" (Norton and Toohey, 2011: 415).

Since the advent of COP and identity theory, old models of L2 learning are turned upside down. Those early assumptions, no longer applying in a 21st century world, are removed. SLA is hardly a matter of "second culture learning", since the term implies not only a monolithic community but also that every learner identifies with a "target" culture in the same way. Language is viewed as situated utterances. Speakers struggle to create meanings in dialogue with others. L2 learning is not viewed as a linear path from point A to point B on a map, but rather a multidimensional, individualized, and sometimes meandering journey that never has an end point (Brown, 2021: 189).

5. 2. 4. 3　Investment and L2 learning

Second language learning is compared to a kind of investment. Investment is something that learners will only devote if they trust that their efforts will increase the value of their "cultural capital". That is, these efforts enable them to gain knowledge and modes of thinking, which in turn will enable them to perform successfully in different social contexts. There are different metaphors in the social theory of second language acquisition. The L2 learner participates in a kind of "struggle" and "investment". The learner is not like a computer that processes input data. He is a combatant and fights to assert himself; he is an investor and expects a good return on his efforts. If a learner can reflect critically on how he deals with native speakers, and is prepared to challenge the accepted social order through constructing and creating social identities of his own choice, he will most probably be a successful L2 learner.

The importance of Norton's theory is that it offers a non-deterministic account of how social factors influence L2 acquisition by attributing "agency" to the learner. It explains why some learners are successful and others less successful in a more convincing way than any other preceding theories. However, it must be pointed out that the social identity theory also has some shortcomings and limitations. First, it deals exclusively with learners learning an L2 in a majority setting. Therefore, it is not clear to what extent it can explain L2 learning in foreign language settings. Second, it explains how "learning opportunities" are created but does not address how these opportunities result in acquisition. Indeed, the identity theory is guilty of uncritically equating "learning opportunities" with "learning". The social identity researchers did not provide any evidence to show what the learners they investigated actually learnt as a product of the identities they assumed. Nor did they show that learners who achieved the right to speak learnt more rapidly than those who did not.

There has been a preponderance of recent publications reporting studies of learner identity. Clearly, the learners' social identity serves as a major factor determining success in L2 learning. However, it would be a mistake to overemphasize the role of identity. Purely contextual factors are as important, and perhaps in some contexts, more important than identity (Ellis, 2013: 339).

5. 2. 5　Ecological approach to SLA

As we have discussed in the early sections, the universal grammar emphasized language rules, and classical cognition highlighted logical thought, serial processing, and top-down rule-governed behavior. Such assumptions have been challenged by the ecological approach. Looking at language learning from an ecological-semiotic perspective, van Lier (2011) pointed out that language is not governed by rules, but by interrelated organizational forces; language development is not an accumulation of objects, but a process of transformation, growth, and reorganization. Within the ecological perspective, the socio-cognitive approach sees L2 acquisition as a process in which mind, body, and world function integratively. Human beings are adaptive organisms continually perceiving and adjusting to their environment, and ultimately learning from their dynamic interaction with the environment. Ecology implies a relationship beyond simple cause and effect in a linear relationship. Rather, an interdependent relationship of forces creates viability and balance (Brown, 2021: 301).

Ecological approach to SLA is concerned with situated cognition and agency. Situated cognition features context and the multiplicity of ways the human beings internalize our context, our environment. According to van Lier (2011), context merges along with meanings. Context is an emergent system of those meanings that are assigned relevance by participants in a specific spatio-temporal event. There is no such thing as a context that is separable from meaning, or meaning as separable from context. Operating with situated cognition, humans have a finely tuned mechanism in place that is responsive to the multifaceted and dynamic features of the physical and social environment.

Next, what does agency mean and what's its role in L2 learning? Agency refers to people's ability to make choices, take control, self-regulate, and thereby pursue their goals as individuals leading, potentially, to personal or social transformation (Duff, 2012). It is the socioculturally mediated capacity to act. A sense of agency enables people to imagine, take up, and perform new roles or identities and to take concrete actions in pursuit of their goals. Agency can also enable people to actively resist certain behaviors, practices, or positionings, sometimes leading to oppositional stances and behaviors leading to other identities, such as rebellious, different student. A perceived lack of agency on the part of learners might lead to similar outcomes as they become passive and disengaged from educational pursuits. Agency, power, and social context are therefore linked because those who typically feel the most control over their lives, choices, and circumstances also have the power—the human, social, or cultural capital and ability—they need to succeed. As for agency's role in L2 learning, it is argued that:

Ultimate attainment in second language learning relies on one agency...While the first language and subjectivities are an indisputable given, the new ones are arrived at by choice. Agency is crucial at the point where the individuals must not just start memorizing a dozen new words and expressions but have to decide on whether to initiate a long, painful, inexhaustive and, for some, never – ending process of self-translation.

Pavlenko and Lantolf (2000: 169 – 170)

Agency involves our physical, cognitive, emotional, and social interaction in whatever context we find ourselves. Agency implies our willful ability to be "agents" in our contexts, to create tools for survival on our environment. It means taking initiative, and linguistically, engaging in discourse to promote social relationships that are the foundation stones of survival. According to van Lier (2011), language is activity and process, not object. As a result, it is in the world as well as in the head, and it is happening now, rather than being a finished product that can be described in a grammar book. Both personal and social agency count in L2 learning. It is true that children, displaced people, or students fulfilling language requirements may have relatively little apparent choice or control over their L2 learning. It is also true that reaching advanced levels of L2 proficiency requires concerted effort, sustained and strategic practice—all manifestations of personal and social agency.

An essential matter is how the ecological theory might be applied in educational settings. According to van Lier (2011), "The ecological and semiotic stance on language learning is anchored in agency, as all of life is. Teaching, in its very essence, is promoting agency. Pedagogy is guiding this agency wisely." Then, what does a classroom look like when guided by ecological-semiotic practices? Barbara Rogoff (1995) presented an interesting picture of such a classroom: small groups, pairs, and individual children, along with adults, are busy in various ways, standing, talking, sitting on the floor. Rogoff suggests that such classrooms can be examined using different "lenses": classroom/ institutional, interpersonal, and personal. These three lenses coincide with three participation structures：Apprenticeship, Guided Participation, and Participatory Appropriation. Apprenticeship implies a long time scale of working with a master or a guide; Guided Participation refers to particular patterns of master-apprentice interaction, including modeling, scaffolding, and imitation; Participatory Appropriation refers to the moment-to-moment microgenesis of cognitive understandings resulting from interactional dynamics.

According to Van Lier (2011), ecology refers to ways of being in the world. Students are in the world, but, as language students, they are faced with new and often bewildering worlds, and it is the task of educators to help them construct their identity in it. For this to be possible, the things that happen in the classroom must be meaningfully connected to the things that have happened, that are happening, or that may happen in the life of the students.

5.2.6 Complex dynamic systems theory

As an ecological theory, complex dynamic systems theory (CDST) insists that one cannot understand a system unless one understands how its parts interrelate. As the parts interconnect, new patterns and new complex regimes of order emerge, ones that could not have been anticipated from examining the parts independently (Larsen-Freeman, 2017). Larsen-Freeman outlined the five characteristics of the complex systems, which

(1) are open and dynamic;
(2) manifest disequilibrium;
(3) are adaptive to change within multiple contexts;
(4) have elements that interact with each other in nonlinear patterns, and
(5) exhibit unexpected occurrences.

CDST recognizes that SLA does not take place in static isolation from what is happening in the temporal and spatial environment in which it is situated. Rather, it is emergent from and is dynamically interconnected with the environment. It is not a matter of inputs and outputs, but rather what the environment affords for learners. A characteristic quality of such systems is that they are dynamic, constantly in motion. That is, CDST is a theory of change. Because of this, it is amply suited for dealing with L2 development.

According to Ellis and Larsen-Freeman (2009), language itself is a complex adaptive system. As such, it develops through interaction among its users. Patterns in language emerge from the interaction of its speakers, not from rules being applied from the top down. Language use, change, and development cannot be accommodated within the terms of a fixed language system. Speakers are continuously modifying the system, combining familiar elements in novel ways, and testing existing resources and new environments.

When we view language as a complex adaptive system, we recognize that every meaningful use of language changes the language resources of the learner/user, and the changed resources are then potentially available for the language user and members of the speech community to adapt or appropriate for their own use. CDST no longer sees language development as a process of acquiring abstract rules, but as the emergence of language abilities in real time. SLA is both a cognitive and a social process. But it is not simply one and the other; it is a combination of the two. It is a sociocognitive process. Therefore, CDST unites the cognitive with the social.

CDST enables us to see both L2 learning and L2 teaching in a different way. Since language is a complex adaptive system, learner language is no longer considered an incomplete and deficient version of native speaker language. The developmental change process is never complete, and neither is its learning. Change and dynamic systems are put at the forefront of our investigations of language acquisition/development. Thus, CDST inspires a different way to think about L2 teaching. In language teaching, the implicit process should be accomplished by explicit guidance in focusing students' attention on the learning challenge and participating in the dynamics of language use/learning, especially at the points where the L1 operates differently from the L2.

As for CDST implications for L2 teaching, Larsen-Freeman (2019) proposed some useful ideas: ① Language teaching requires considerable practice. ② Teachers can teach students to take their present system and mold it to a new context for a present purpose. ③Teachers can formatively assess a student by measuring the students' progress in a self-referential way, that is, not looking at what the learner is not doing in light of some idealized distant "target", but rather looking at what the learner is doing over time.

Assignment

1. Questions for self-study.

(1) What are the three different theoretical views (behaviorist, mentalist, and interactionist) on input in second language acquisition?

(2) What is foreigner talk, and what are the characteristics of foreigner talk?

(3) What modifications are made in grammatical foreigner talk?

(4) What strategies or methods are used in discourse management?

(5) What is the importance of feedback in L2 learning? Give examples to illustrate the difference of direct feedback and indirect feedback.

(6) Give examples to demonstrate the difference between the "other repair" and the "self-repair" types of feedback?

(7) What is the Zone of Proximal Development? And how does it help L2 learning?

(8) What reasons does Schumann give to account for a learner's failure to acculturate?

(9) What are the good L2 learning situations according to Schumann's acculturation model?

(10) How did Norton define identity and social identity? What do you think is the relationship between social identity and second language learning?

(11) What are the shortcomings of social identity theory? Do you think it applies to L2 learning in the foreign language settings?

(12) What is the role of agency in L2 learning according to ecological approach to SLA?

(13) Why is language seen as a complex adaptive system? What are CDST's implications for L2 teaching?

2. Fill in the blanks in the following passage.

According to the behaviorists' view, language learning is environmentally determined; it is controlled by the _____ a learner is exposed to and the _____ he receives. However, a mentalist view of language learning emphasizes the importance of the learner's language acquisition _____. It is believed that learners' brain is especially equipped to learn language and what is needed is the minimal exposure to language _____ to trigger acquisition. Interactionist theories of second language learning, however, underline the importance of both input and internal _____ mechanism. It is held that learning is caused by a complex interaction between language _____ and learners' internal mechanisms.

3. Open discussion for pair or group work.

(1) Observe a conversation between an NS and an NNS, taking careful notes on how you think their speech differs from what you would expect in a conversation between two NSs. Pay attention to all aspects of the NS's speech, including his pronunciation, grammar, vocabulary, rate of speech, and so on. Do the features you have noted coincide with what is presented in Table 5.1? Are there any features you noted that are not included in the list?

(2) The following data are from a telephone conversation in which an NNS was conducting an interview about food and nutrition (see Gass and Selinker, 2008: 364). Focus on the language following the NNS's *Pardon me*? How would you describe the difference between that response and the immediately preceding one? What functions do the modifications serve?

Example 1

NNS: *There has been a lot of talk lately about additives and preservations in food. In what ways has this changed your eating habits*?

NS: *Uh, I avoid them, I d-, I don't buy prepackaged foods uh, as much … Uh I don't buy … say … potato chips that have a lot of flavoring on them … and uh, I eat better. I think.*

NNS: *Pardon me*?

NS: *Ummm, pardon me? I, I eat better, I think. I, I don't buy so much food that's prepackaged.*

Example 2

NNS: *How have increasing food costs changed your eating habits*?

NS: *Well, it doesn't. hasn't really.*

NNS: *Pardon me*?

NS: *It hasn't really changed them.*

Example 3

NNS：*How have increasing food costs changed your eating habits?*

NS：*Uh well that would I don't think they've change' em much right now，but the pressure's on.*

NNS：*Pardon me?*

NS：*I don't think they've changed our eating habits much as of now...*

（3）In your L2 learning，what are some examples of the types of feedback described in this chapter? Is one type more effective than another? If so，what causes the effectiveness? Did your teacher help you to respond to feedback? How do they help you? Have you provided uptake to a teacher's feedback? If you are a teacher，how can you maximize uptake in the L2 classroom?

（4）It is known that Krashen's model emphasizes the role of input，how would you rate the possibility of success in a study-abroad situation（say，in the United States）? Suppose you discovered that in a study-abroad situation your fellow students were not members of the host community，but speakers of your native language. As a result the input you received was not standard English but "junky data". Do you think practice with this kind of input would facilitate you acquisition of ESL，because "practice makes perfect"? Or do you think such kind of input would reinforce your interlanguage forms? If the situation were a foreign language classroom，would you answer in the same way?

（5）Considering your own learning，or the learning of someone you know well，do you believe in scaffolding and the zone of proximal development? Describe examples in your own life when you are the learner in need of scaffolding，and when you are the more advanced learner or teacher providing a learner with more opportunity for development.

（6）In your own L2 learning，can you think of examples of the five characteristics of CDST outlined by Larsen-Freeman? How did you experience "disequilibrium"? What were some examples of "unexpected occurrences"? How could a teacher help students to accept and learn from these moments?

Chapter Six Instruction and Second Language Acquisition

In the previous three chapters, we have discussed three main perspectives of studying second language acquisition, namely linguistic, psychological and socio-cultural, and have seen that the three basic questions raised at the beginning of this book—what does the L2 learner come to know, how does the leaner acquire the knowledge and why are some learners more successful than others—have been answered. The three different perspectives all address the basic *what*, *how*, and *why* questions. However, as we have seen, they each focus primarily on one question over the others. The linguistic perspectives of SLA mainly deal with the *what* question, while the psychological perspectives primarily deal with the *how* question, and the social perspectives chiefly offer answers to the *why* question.

Much of the research in the previous sections has involved classroom learners, because the large numbers of learners are more accessible in educational than in naturalistic settings. But the research has not actually been concerned with instructional intervention in L2 acquisition; rather it has used classroom learners to investigate questions of general significance to SLA research. In this chapter, we focus specifically on classroom L2 acquisition, and examine how teaching affects second language acquisition. First we will review the answers to the above mentioned questions in SLA. Then, we will introduce some important theories about instructed L2 acquisition. Finally we will discuss different types and effects of form-focused instruction.

6.1 Response to the Three Fundamental Questions in SLA

Research in SLA has yielded many answers to these fundamental questions. There are remarkable differences of opinion within each perspective and among them, depending on subdiscipline orientations. Still, it is possible to report some answers to the questions. Saville-Troike (2008) integrated findings from the three perspectives, but gave greatest weight to linguistic contributions in answer to *what*, to psychological contributions in answer to *how*, and to social contributions in answer to *why*, as shown in Table 6.1:

Table 6.1 Answers to Key Questions in SLA

Questions	What exactly does the L2 learner come to know?	How does the learner acquire L2 knowledge?	Why are some learners more successful than others?
Answers	—a system of knowledge about a second language —patterns of recurrent elements —how to encode particular concepts in the L2 —pragmatic competence —means of using the L2 in communicative activities —how to select among multiple language systems, and how to switch between languages in specific social contexts and for specific purposes —communicative competence	—innate capability —application of prior knowledge —processing of language input —interaction —restructuring of L2 knowledge system —mapping of relationships or associations between linguistic functions and forms —automatization	—social context —social experience —relationship of L1 and L2 —age —aptitude —motivation —instruction

As for what the L2 learner has learned, there exists a basic disagreement among different linguistic perspectives in considering whether the system of knowledge about an L2 is primarily (a) an abstract system of underlying rules or principles, (b) a system of linguistic patterns and structures, or (c) a means of structuring information and a system of communication. Such a disagreement is caused by different assumptions about the nature of language and language study that arise from different theoretical approaches. It is not likely that the disagreement will be resolved right away, but they complement one another and all are needed for us to gain a full-spectrum picture of the multidimensional nature of SLA.

As for how the learner has acquired L2 knowledge, a fundamental disagreement within both psychological and linguistic perspectives comes in considering language learning as primarily a process of acquiring (a) language-specific systems of rules, (b) very general principles with options to be selected, or (c) increasing strength of associations between linguistic forms and meaning. This disagreement, again, derives from the very differences in theoretical orientations and is not likely to be resolved. However, there is every likelihood that more complex answers to the question of *how* will be accepted with the growing recognition of the complex nature of SLA, and of individual and situational differences.

As for why some learners are more successful than others, disagreement remains in the definition of relative "success" in second language learning. Again, the definition of criteria for "success" depends on theoretical orientation, so it is very difficult to draw general conclusions. Any answer to this question must be considered within the disciplinary framework in which it is posed. Looking to the future, we can anticipate more relativistic criteria for the definition of "success", and even more consideration of the complex interaction of social, psychological, and linguistic criteria in research on L2 learning.

6. 2   Major Theories on Instructed SLA

According to the answers above, we know what an L2 learner has acquired is a system of knowledge about a second language, which goes well beyond what could possibly have been taught. Here comes a natural question: what on earth can instruction do to help second language acquisition? This is what is to be discussed in classroom L2 acquisition, also termed instructed SLA. Before answering this question, it is important to realize what an L2 teacher should know.

First, an L2 teacher should understand how language learning does and does not take place. If one wants to develop language-teaching methodologies, there must be a firm basis for those teaching methods, and this foundation is the understanding of how language learning takes place. The traditional methods have stressed rule memorization and translation. However, studies in SLA have shown that language learning consists of more than rule memorization. What is more important is the need to achieve communicative purposes. Thus, this new concept of language learning results in teaching methodologies that emphasize communication. That is, pedagogical decision-making should reflect the process of learning, which is the domain of second language acquisition.

Second, an L2 teacher should be aware whether learners learn what is taught. Classroom teachers often have expectations of their students. A teacher may spend much time in class drilling students on a specific grammatical structure. It can be assumed that in class the students all produce correct structures and do it in a right context. But after class, in a spontaneous talk, they may not be able to put into practice what is learned in class and produce incorrect forms. What do you think of this? Is the classroom teaching a waste of time? On the contrary, if a student produces the right form, does it necessarily mean that he has acquired the correct rules? The question is not easy to answer, since it concerns the relationship between language form and language use. From the following dialogue between an inspector Wexford and a tourist guide Mr. Sung, we can clearly see that correct forms are hard to put into use. Mr. Sung says "let's go" and the inspector thinks it is an improper form in the context, and takes the chance to provide a correction.

Wexford: *I wish you wouldn't keep saying that. If I may suggest it, you should say, "Shall we go?" or "Are you ready?"*

Sung: *You may suggest. Thank you. I am anxious to speak good. Shall we go? Are you ready?*

Wexford: *Oh, yes, certainly.*

Sung: *Don't reply, please. I practice. Shall we go? Are you ready? Good, I have got it. Come, let's go. Are you ready to go to the site? Reply now, please.*

(Gass and Selinker, 2008: 4)

Obviously, Wexford's instruction does not work: what was taught has not been acquired. This is one of the main issues in language pedagogy called the "code-communication dilemma". There are those researchers who argue while instruction may not be necessary for L2 acquisition, it does help learners to acquire more quickly. Some other scholars maintain that for some aspects of language at least, formal instruction is necessary. As for what roles instructional intervention plays in L2 acquisition, there is a considerable disagreement in the theoretical world. Below we will introduce a few relative theoretical views:

6.2.1 The "zero position"

As the name suggests, the zero position gives up the idea of any intentional instruction of grammatical knowledge in the classroom. It is proposed that classroom language learning will proceed more effectively if language learners are allowed to construct their interlanguages in a natural way. Grammar can be picked up through the process of learning how to communicate. As argued by Prabhu (1987: 1):

...the development of competence in a second language requires not systematization of language inputs or maximization of planned practice, but rather the creation of conditions in which learners engage in an effort to cope with communication.

Prabhu's communicational teaching project sought to demonstrate that language form can best be learnt when the learners' attention is focused on meaning. It must be pointed out that Prabhu did not actually claim that grammar cannot be learnt through formal instruction. Instead, he only claimed that learning grammar through communication is more effective. In contrast, Krashen (1982) argued that grammatical competence cannot be taught. His position, known as non-interface hypothesis, is that learning is different from acquisition, and each cannot be converted into the other. Therefore, formal instruction is rejected because it does not contribute to the development of implicit knowledge which is needed for normal communication. The learner's explicit knowledge, no matter how much he practices, cannot be converted into implicit knowledge. Krashen did not deny the fact that formal instruction can contribute to the learning of explicit knowledge, but he regarded this as of limited use because only rules that are formally simple and deal with meanings that are easy to explain can be "learnt"; most rules have to be "acquired". Krashen also claimed that explicit knowledge is of limited value because it can only be used to monitor production from the acquired system.

The zero position, as illustrated above, rejects not only planned instructional intervention by means of presenting and practicing language items and rules, but also unplanned intervention in the form of error correction. According to Krashen, error correction is regarded as a serious mistake, and should only be limited to rules that can be learnt. He claimed that it puts students on the defensive and encourages them to avoid using difficult constructions. Also, it is likely to disrupt the all-important focus on communication. However, negative feedback in the form of communicative response to learners' efforts to convey message is permitted. In other words, systematic correction is prohibited, but incidental feedback is allowed.

6.2.2　The facilitative position

Another theoretical position about the role of instruction in L2 acquisition is that although formal instruction is not necessary to acquire an L2, it helps learning, in particular by speeding up the process of "natural" acquisition. The facilitative position has several different versions. One is the interface hypothesis, claiming that by practicing specific structures learners can "control" them; the explicit knowledge gradually becomes implicit. According to the interface hypothesis, instruction facilitates acquisition by ①supplying learners with conscious rules, and ②providing practice to enable them to convert the conscious, "controlled" knowledge into "automatic" knowledge. The most spontaneous performance is attained by dint of practice. Declarative knowledge is converted into procedural knowledge by means of practice that involves the learner in communicative behavior (DeKeyser, 1998).

The second version of the facilitative position is the variability hypothesis, according to which instruction can directly affect the learners' ability to perform structures in some kinds of use but not in others. It is claimed that teaching learners new structures will affect their careful style but not their vernacular style. Therefore, its effects will be evident when learners are performing in planned language use but not in unplanned language use.

The third version is the teachability hypothesis, according to which instruction can only promote language acquisition if the interlanguage is close to the point when the structure to be taught is acquired in the natural setting (Pienemann, 1985). The hypothesis has a few corollaries: ①do not demand a learning process which is impossible at a given stage. That is, the order of teaching objectives should be in line with stages of acquisition. ②Do not introduce deviant (interlanguage) forms. ③The general input may contain structures which were not introduced for production. It must be noted that Pienemann's "teachability" only applied to developmental features, not to variational features (the features that could be acquired at any stage).

The fourth version is the weak interface hypothesis, according to which formal instruction acts as an aid to acquisition. In other words, instruction does not enable learners to fully acquire what is taught, but prepares the way for its subsequent acquisition. Instruction works by helping learners to pay selective attention to form and form-meaning connections in the input. It provides learners with tools that help them to recognize those features in their interlanguage which are in need of modification. Instruction directed at explicit knowledge can indirectly facilitate the acquisition of implicit knowledge by priming the processes involved in its development.

6.2.3 The necessity of FFI

While it is true that much of the L2 can be acquired naturally without any instruction, it is also true that most L2 learners, especially adults, do not achieve full target-language competence as a result of exposure and thus need assistance. That is, there may be certain linguistic properties that cannot be acquired by L2 learners unless they receive instruction in them. This indicates the necessity of form-focused instruction (FFI). There are occasions on which instruction may be necessary in L2 development. One occasion is when the learner is in danger of constructing an over-inclusive grammar. For example, certain types of "problematic overgeneralization" occur as when francophone learners of L2 English attempt to insert an adverb between the verb and the direct object, thus producing erroneous sentences like *John drank yesterday some coffee*. As argued by White (1989), this type of error cannot be eliminated purely on the basis of the positive evidence supplied by communicative input, because the learner could never be sure that such sentences were not possible. In such cases, negative evidence in the form of a grammar lesson or corrective feedback is necessary.

It has also been suggested that even for those errors that can be eliminated on the basis of positive evidence, instruction is still necessary. Learners may fail to expunge such errors on the basis of positive evidence because they have come to understand that language tolerates synonym. Therefore, noticing "went" in the input may not be sufficient to eliminate "goed", if the learner operates with the hypothesis that both forms are possible. This might explain why some learners fail to learn many of the morphological properties of a language even after years of intensive exposure. Such learners may need to have the fact that "goed" and "went" are not acceptable synonyms brought to their conscious attention.

Research indicates that even under favorable conditions, classroom learners fail to develop full L2 linguistic competence simply by communicating. It should be noted, however, that it does not follow that formal instruction is the answer. It is possible that many adult learners will fail to develop high levels of grammatical competence no matter what the instructional conditions. There may be limits to what is achievable through classroom learning for the simple reason that there are limits regarding what many learners are capable of achieving under any conditions, although there will always be exceptional learners for whom instruction may provide the assistance they need to achieve an advanced level of competence (Ellis, 2013: 847 – 848).

6.3　Effects and Durability of FFI on SLA

6.3.1　Effects of FFI

SLA research investigating how learners acquired an L2 in naturalistic settings indicated that learners tended to follow a natural order of acquisition and also manifested fairly well-defined sequences in the acquisition of specific target structures. Such findings led to a questioning of whether FFI was necessary for acquisition. Then followed research which compared the ultimate level of achievement and rate of learning of groups of learners who had received instruction with groups who had not. Long (1983) reviewed the literature on FFI and considered eleven studies, and concluded that most of the studies lent support to formal instruction. Three studies indicated that instruction did not help, while one study shows that exposure without formal instruction was beneficial. Long's general conclusion was that there is considerable evidence to indicate that L2 instruction does make a difference. Instruction was claimed to be advantageous ① for children as well as adults; ② for both intermediate and advanced learners; ③ irrespective of whether acquisition was measured by means of integrative or discrete-point tests, and ④ in acquisition-rich as well as acquisition-poor environments.

Long's conclusion was damaging to Krashen's zero position on FFI. Krashen (1985: 28 – 31) argued that the studies did not show an advantage for formal instruction, but only that learning in a classroom was helpful for beginners, who found it difficult to obtain the comprehensible input they needed in normal communication outside the classroom. The Long-Krashen debate continued and more studies were conducted to compare the relative effects of formal instruction and exposure. However, many L2 learners experienced both together. It is possible, therefore, that what works best is some form of combination of the two. In other words, those learners who had access both to formal instruction and to exposure showed the greatest gains in proficiency. That is, a combination of form-oriented and meaning-oriented language teaching was more beneficial than form-oriented teaching alone. FFI helps language learners, both foreign and second, to develop greater L2 proficiency, particularly if it is linked with opportunities for natural exposure. Foreign language learners appear to benefit by developing greater communicative skills, while second language learners benefit by developing greater linguistic accuracy.

6. 3. 2　Effects of FFI on production accuracy

The significance of research on the effects on production accuracy could be felt in both theoretical and pedagogic aspects. On a theoretical level, the studies sought to test the zero position that teaching grammar or correcting learner errors has no effect on the learner's "acquired" system. On the pedagogical level, the studies explored whether FFI could help learners to acquire those grammatical structures they had failed to acquire even after years of exposure to comprehensible input or those structures that were known to be difficult to acquire from studies of naturalistic learners.

Literature in research on the effects of FFI on production accuracy suggests mixed results. Some research results indicated that learner participation in classroom FFI activities is not related to gains in accuracy (Ellis, 1992). Why is it so? An explanation might be that the instruction was directed at a structure too far in advance of the learners' stage of development. Other studies, however, have produced results that are more supportive of FFI. For example, Lightbown, Spada, and Wallace (1980) reported that 175 French-speaking school learners of English improved by 11% on a grammaticality judgement test when instructed on a range of grammatical features whereas a control group improved by only 3%. Another study by Pica (1985) also provided evidence to suggest that some grammatical features are performed more accurately if learners have access to formal instruction.

In Pica's study, the subjects were divided into three groups: an natural group, an

instructed group, and a mixed group. She compared the accuracy with which the three groups performed a number of grammatical morphemes in unplanned speech. It was found that the instructed learners performed plural -s more accurately than the naturalistic learners. However, they performed the progressive -ing less accurately, while no difference between the groups was found for the use of articles. The results suggest that the grammatical structure that is taught may influence the effect of instruction: ① if the structure is formally simple, and displays a simple form-function relationship (such as plural -s), instruction may improve accuracy; ② if the structure is formally simple and salient but is functionally complex (such as -ing), instruction may help learners to learn the form but not its use. Therefore, learners make a lot of errors; ③ if a structure is not fairly salient, and functionally complex (such as articles), instruction has no effect.

Whereas the general picture emerging from the studies so far indicates that FFI often does not work, particularly when acquisition is measured in relation to spontaneous speech, a number of other studies suggest that grammar teaching can have positive effects on learning. These studies examined the role of FFI in the context of communicative language teaching. That is, the opportunities for communicating in the L2 are supplemented with grammar lessons. Harley (1989) devised a set of functional-grammar materials to teach French immersion students the distinction between *passé composé* and *imparfait* which is one of the features that is typically not acquired by immersion learners. She found that 8 weeks of instruction resulted in significant improvement in the accuracy with which the two verb tenses were used in a written composition and in an oral interview. The instructional effects were therefore evident in both planned and unplanned language use.

More studies supported the effect of FFI. White (1991) investigated the effects of instruction on adverb placement, examining whether it was successful in eliminating the error made by French learners of L2 English: *John kissed often Mary*. The learners were children in Grade 5 and 6 in an intensive ESL program. Two weeks of instruction in the use of frequency and manner adverbs was provided. The instructed learners showed significantly greater gains in accuracy in a number of tasks in comparison to control groups. Another study (White et al., 1991) investigated the effects of instruction on question formation on the same groups of learners as those used in the adverb study. Five hours of instruction over a two-week period were provided. Acquisition was measured by means of a cartoon task, a preference grammaticality judgement task, and an oral communication task. In comparison to a control group, the experimental group showed substantial gains in accuracy in all three tasks. The instructed learners in this case showed that they had learnt how to use inversion in questions.

The most powerful evidence for the positive effect of FFI on learners' accuracy of production comes from Norris and Ortega's (2000) meta-analysis of 49 studies. FFI was found to be more effective if learning outcomes were measured in ways that tapped into learners' explicit knowledge. The effect on implicit knowledge was still substantial. Another factor that was found to influence the overall effectiveness of FFI was the length of the duration of the treatment. Surprisingly, "brief treatment" (less than one hour) and "short treatment" (between 1 and 2 hours) resulted in larger mean effect sizes than medium treatments (between 3 and 6 hours) or "long treatments" (more than 7 hours). It was argued by Norris and Ortega that this difference probably reflected a number of moderator variables such as the intensity and type of instruction, which they were unable to investigate. The general conclusion that can be arrived on the basis of the studies investigating the effects of FFI on accuracy is that there is clear evidence to show that FFI can result in definite gains in production accuracy.

6. 3. 3 Durability of FFI effects

Even in cases, as is discussed above, where FFI appears to have worked, the beneficial effects may be only temporary. The improved levels of accuracy resulting from instruction may prove to be impermanent; the acquisition of a new grammatical feature may prove to be deceptive. As times passes, the effects of instruction may gradually wither away. Learners may return to similar levels of performance to those observed before instruction. Research indicates that the effects of grammar instruction may be limited. For example, it was found that the overall scores of the learners dropped to a level approximately halfway between that of the pre-test and the immediate post test in a follow-up test given 6 months after the instruction (Lightbown et al., 1980). The gains which one learner made in the accurate use of the copula as a result of instruction began to disappear after only one week (Pienemann, 1984). Also, it was found by White (1991) that gains in the correct positioning of adverbs were largely lost 5 months after the instruction. However, there were studies that found the effects of instruction were durable. For example, Harley (1989) retested her subjects 3 months after the instruction and found that the learners' improved ability to use French *imparfait* and *passé composé* had not only been maintained but extended even further. White et al. (1991) found that increased accuracy in the formation of questions did not slip back to pre-instruction levels. Norris and Ortega's (2000) meta-analysis of 12 FFI studies reported that the effects of instruction are durable.

The truth, however, is that sufficient evidence suggests that instruction does not always have a long-term effect. Why is it so? Lightbown (1992) shared her explanation: when FFI is introduced in a way which is divorced from the communicative needs and activities of the students, only short-term effects are obtained. In other words, learners benefit most from instruction that is embedded in communicative activities. This explanation sounds attractive, but it does not seem to account fully for the results of many studies. For example, it is reasonable to assume that the structures like various -s morphemes, copula "be", locative prepositions are frequent in classroom input and that opportunities for using them were available to the learners. However, the effects of instruction directed at these features tended to disappear. Therefore, it would seem that other factors are involved in accounting for FFI's lack of long-term effect. One possibility is the saliency of the target structure. Features such as copula "be" and -s morphemes are not very salient. Even if they occur frequently, they may not easily be perceived in communicative speech. What's more, these features may also not be seen as very important for message conveyance. So they are often neglected. If learners are motivated mainly by communicative need, then they will probably remember only those features or structures that they think are important for communication.

Another possible account for the absence of durable effects is related to the nature of instruction. The effects of FFI might be lost if learners receive instruction in a related structure and are unable to sort out the two structures in their interlanguage systems. For example, it was found that explicit instruction had a positive effect on Japanese high-school students' acquisition of copula "be". Such an effect declined somewhat but was still evident in a delayed post-test. But the effect subsequently disappeared after the same learners had been provided with instruction in progressive "be" (Tode, 2007). It is clear that the instruction in progressive "be" interferes with effect of instruction in copula "be".

As for the phenomenon that statistically significant effects for instruction were not immediately evident but only emerged in the delayed post-tests, the likely explanation lies in the nature of the target structure. For example, explicit corrective feedback had an immediate effect on the acquisition of comparative adjectives; it only had a delayed effect on the acquisition of past tense -ed. This might be because the learners possessed solid explicit knowledge of past tense -ed but not of comparative -er before instruction. The instruction served to develop the learners' explicit knowledge of comparative -er, resulting in an immediate effect. As for the past tense -ed, however, the instruction activated learners' existing explicit knowledge, which primed them to attend to this feature in subsequent input with the result that gains became apparent in the delayed test (Ellis, 2007).

6. 4   Different Types of Formal Instruction

So far we have attempted to answer the question as to whether formal instruction results in the acquisition of the features that have been taught. The research cited above has viewed formal instruction generally as involving attention to form and the provision of corrective feedback. Researchers have gained insight into the nature of the complex relationship between instruction and L2 learning. In this section, we will discuss, from the teacher's perspective, different types of instruction and deal with another question of equal importance: what kind of instruction works best in the classroom.

6. 4. 1   Focus on form and focus on forms

One approach to L2 instruction that has been proposed to develop learners who can communicate fluently but also accurately is focus on form (Long, 1996). Focus on form occurs when learners briefly pay attention to linguistic forms within a larger meaning-focused context. In this way, learners are still engaged in interaction, which is beneficial for communicative fluency, but they are also developing their linguistic competence by attending to the accurate use of language during communication (Loewen, 2015). In order to illustrate the unique aspects of focus on form, Long (1996) contrasted it with focus on meaning and focus on forms. Focus on meaning consists of those activities in the classroom that are entirely communicative with no attention to specific language items unless there is a breakdown in communication. Focus on forms, on the other hand, encompasses explicit types of L2 instruction in which language and language rules are the overt objects of instruction.

It is necessary to make a distinction between focus on form and focus on forms. Focus on

form requires a need for meaning-focused activities, and an attention to form is embedded into these activities. As Long put it, focus on form "overtly draws students' attention to linguistic elements as they arise incidentally in lessons whose overriding focus is on meaning or communication" (Long, 1991: 45 – 46). Focus on form occurs when teachers follow a task-based syllabus, focusing the learner's attention on specific linguistic properties in the course of performing communicative activities. Focus on forms, however, refers to the earlier teaching methodologies in which the main organizing principle for language classrooms was the accumulation of individual language items. Focus on forms occurs when language teaching is based on a structural syllabus. Loewen (2011) divides L2 instruction into two main categories: meaning-focused instruction and form-focused instruction, as is shown below:

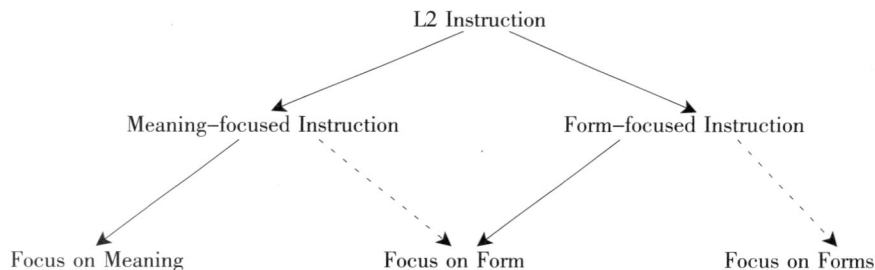

Figure 6.1　Types of L2 Instruction

Much research has been done in this field of study. For example, Williams (1999) studied eight classroom learners at different levels of proficiency. The results show numerous examples of learner-generated attention to form and great variation. It is suggested that learners at low levels of proficiency do not often spontaneously attend to language form. This is because there is a demand to maintain communication in L2, especially when L2 knowledge is scant. It is also found that when there is learner-generated attention to form, it is often given to words rather than to other linguistic features.

Another study by Gass et al. (1999) supports the concept that freeing up the cognitive burden of focusing on both form and meaning allows greater opportunity to focus on form. In the study, subjects perform an online telling of a short video clip. After seeing the same video multiple times (they did not have to focus on meaning during the latter viewings), participants showed improvement on overall measures of proficiency, morphosyntax, and lexical sophistication (Gass and Selinker, 2008: 381).

Still another study investigated learners' noticing of corrective feedback in a classroom context (for example by Mackey, 2006), with the linguistic focus on question formation and two morphological forms: English plurals and past tense. It was found that there exists a relationship between noticing and learning for question formation, but not for the two morphological forms. This can be explained by salience. Obviously, question formation, with syntactic movement and the addition of an auxiliary, is more salient than the addition of a plural or past tense marker. Another issue is the type of feedback offered. As is reported by Mackey, there were more instances of negotiation for questions than for the morphological forms. The latter were more often recast rather than negotiated.

It should be pointed out that one cannot use focus on form instruction with all grammatical constructions. Some structures are complex, and involves movement. Thus it is not clear about what could be focused on. For example, Williams and Evans (1998) examined the effect of focus on form on two structures: ①participial adjectives of emotive verbs (*I am boring* vs. *I am bored*) and ②passives (*The dog was chased by the cat*). It was found that participial adjectives were used by the learners incorrectly and passives were used rarely. Among the three groups, the group that had explicit instruction and feedback outperformed the other two groups in learning participial adjectives. The other two groups are the group which receive input only and the control group. The results of the study suggest that learners' "readiness" contributes to their ability to focus on and take in new information. Another finding is that not all structures are created equal with regard to input type. Here explicit instruction was more effective than offering input only. In general, however, we have to carefully consider what is being targeted to focus on and how best to relate that information to a learner's individual knowledge state and to the means by which a form is focused on.

6.4.2 Input-based instruction and output-based instruction

Input-based instruction is directed at enabling learners to ①notice the presence of a specific feature in the input, ②comprehend the meaning of the feature, and ③rehearse the feature in short-term memory. Input-based instruction is also known as comprehension-based instruction. In input-based instruction, learners are provided with verbal or written input, which is manipulated in order for learners to create form-meaning mappings (Shintani, Li

and Ellis，2013）. Input-based instruction does not necessarily involve learners in producing language；instead，this type of instruction focuses on comprehension of specific structures，with learners indicating their comprehension through tasks such as choosing from a set of pictures the one that matches the input. However，output is not prohibited，and learners may produce language if they want. It is suggested that input-based instruction can be good for lower level learners because it can provide exposure to new structures in the input，and it can help reduce learner anxiety. It is assumed that input-based instruction is psycho-linguistically easier to manipulate the processes involved in intake than it is to induce learners to restructure their interlanguage systems.

Learners' L2 production，according to Swain's（1995）Comprehensible Output Hypothesis，can actually play a facilitative role in the L2 development process. Output-based instruction draws upon this perspective to involve learners in classroom activities in which they produce language. One such activity is a dictogloss task，which involves learners in text reconstruction task. Learners are given a text，usually orally，but it is also possible for the text to be provided in writing. After hearing or reading the text once or twice，learners are asked to reconstruct the passage either on their own or in pairs or groups. During the reconstruction process，they should pay attention to forms that were used in the original text，and they may need to discuss and negotiate the correct linguistic forms in order to achieve an accurate reproduction of the text.

The input-based instruction emphasizes input processing while the output-based instruction is the traditional grammar teaching which emphasizes output production. Here，our concern is which is better for L2 learning. A related experiment conducted by Bill VanPatten and Teresa Cadierno（1993）may give us the answer. In that experiment，one group of learners was exposed to the traditional production-based instruction. Another group of learners was exposed to input-based instruction，in which they had to listen to and respond to sentences containing the target structure. When the experiment was over，both groups completed two tests：a production test and a comprehension test. The results show that the group receiving input-based instruction did far better on the comprehension test and just as well on the production test. This study has the implication that form-focused instruction emphasizing input processing may be very effective. It also lends support to the theories of L2 acquisition which emphasizes the role of conscious noticing in input. That is，input-based instruction may work because it generates noticing in learners.

6. 4. 3　Enriched input and structured input

Enriched input can take the form of oral or written texts learners simply listen to or read
(i. e. input-flooding) or texts where the target structure has been highlighted in some way
(for example, through the use of underlining or bold print) . Ellis (2013) identified
several groups of enriched input studies. The first groups are those studies designed to
investigate whether the forms targeted in the enriched input are noticed by
learners. According to the Noticing Hypothesis, enriched input can only work for acquisition
if learners actually pay attention to the target structure. So it is important to demonstrate that
noticing does take place. It was found in a study (Jourdenais, et al, 1995) that English
speaking learners of L2 Spanish were more likely to make explicit reference to preterite and
imperfect verb forms when thinking aloud during a narrative writing task if they had
previously read texts where the forms were typologically highlighted. It was also found that the
learners exposed to the enhanced text were more likely to use past tense forms than the
learners who read the non-enhanced text even if both texts had been enriched. In another
study (Yoshimura, 2006), groups of Japanese L2 English learners were asked to read a
text under three conditions: to memorize it, to retell it, and to draw a picture based on
it. The result led the researcher to hypothesize that more noticing would occur in the first two
conditions than the third. This was supported in a fill-in-the-blanks production post-test of
verbs in the text.

The second groups of studies were designed to investigate whether enriched input
promotes acquisition, and produced mixed results. For example, Trahey and White (1993)
examined whether enriched input was sufficient to enable francophone learners of L2 English
to learn that English permits adverb placement between the subject and the verb but does not
permit placement between the verb and the object. Exposure occurred one hour a day for ten
days. The learners succeeded in learning the SAV position but failed to "unlearn" the
ungrammatical SVAO position. J. White (1998) compared the effects of three types of
enriched input: ①typographically enhanced input flood plus extensive listening and reading,
②typographically enhanced input by itself, and③typically unenhanced input flood. It was
found that all the three types of enriched input worked equally effectively in assisting
francophone learners to acquire the possessive pronouns "his" and "her" . This led White to
conclude that the target structure was equally salient in all three types of enriched input.

The third groups of studies compared the effects of enriched input with some other instructional option. There is some evidence that enriched input involving either highlighting or orienting learners to attend to form induces noticing of target features. But little is known about which approach to enrichment works best. Fairly convincing evidence indicates that enriched input can help L2 learners acquire some new grammatical features and use partially learnt features more consistently, although it may not enable learners to eradicate erroneous rules from their interlanguage.

Structured input differs from enriched input in that it presents learners with input in a context that requires them to demonstrate that they have correctly processed the target structure for meaning. The demonstration takes the form of a learner response to an input stimulus. The response is either non-verbal or minimally verbal. The non-verbal response takes different forms, such as choosing the picture that matches the stimulus, while the minimally verbal response indicates whether learners agree or disagree with some statement. This is achieved by means of interpretation tasks. Ellis (1995) provided a set of guidelines for designing interpretation tasks: ①An interpretation task consists of a stimulus to which learners must make some kind of response. ②The stimulus can take the form of spoken or written input. ③The response can take various forms (for example, indicate true/false, check a box, select the correct picture, draw a diagram, perform an action) but in each case the response will be completely nonverbal or minimally verbal. ④ The activities in the task can be sequenced to require first attention to meaning, then noticing the form and function of the grammatical structure, and finally error identification. ⑤Learners should have the opportunity to make some kind of personal response (that is, relate the input to their own lives).

6.4.4　Processing instruction (PI)

Processing instruction is a model of instruction put forward by VanPatten. It refers to a type of instruction that takes as its basis how learners process input. In particular, it deals with the conversion of input to intake and specifically focuses on form-meaning relationships (VanPatten, 1995). According to VanPatten, PI is a type of grammar instruction whose purpose is to affect the ways in which learners attend to input data. It is input-based rather than output-based. In a series of experiments, VanPatten and his colleagues presented a model for instructional intervention that relied heavily on the notion of attention to form and its crucial role in a learner's movement from input to intake and finally to output. They compared two instructional models. In one model, input is practiced as a form of output manipulation, a model of traditional grammar instruction in which information is presented to learners for practice. The other is one in which an attempt is made to change the way input is perceived and processed, hence the name processing instruction. What is new here is that rather than passively allowing an internalized system to develop, the attempt of PI is to actively influence the way that input is processed and hence the way the system develops. The difference between the above mentioned two models is presented in the following two figures:

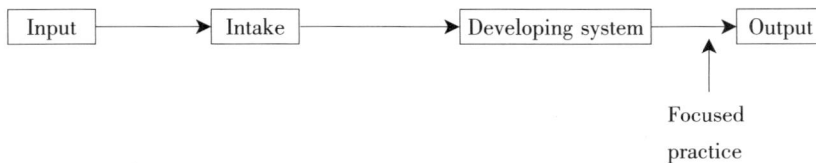

Figure 6. 2 Traditional Instruction in Foreign Language Learning (**Gass and Selinker**, **2008**: **373**)

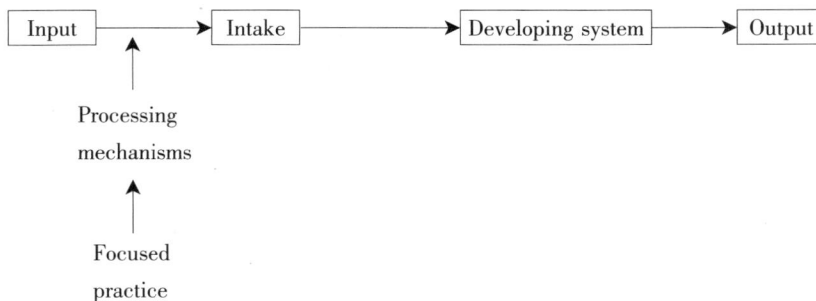

Figure 6. 3 Processing Instruction in Foreign Language Teaching (**Gass and Selinker**, **2008**: **373**)

According to VanPatten (2008), there are three premises that constitute the basis of processing instruction.

(1) Learners need input for acquisition;
(2) A major problem in acquisition might be the way in which learners process input;

（3）If we can understand how learners process input, then we might be able to devise effective input enhancement or focus on form to aid acquisition of formal features of language.

VanPatten （2007b） also outlines three fundamental characteristics of processing instruction.

（1）Giving learners information about a structure or form.

（2）Informing learners about a particular processing strategy that may get in the way of selecting the form/structure during comprehension.

（3）Structuring input so that learners must rely on form/structure to get meaning and not rely on natural processing tendencies.

Here let us look at an example given by VanPatten to illustrate the process of processing instruction of the French causative:

Jean fait promener le chien à Marie. （French）
John makes to walk the dog to Mary.
"John makes Mary walk the dog."

First, ask learners the question *Who walks the dog?* The majority of the English learners say that John does because John is the first noun. This is part of the first stage in which information is provided to learners about the causative construction in French. The next stage is structured input activities, in which other causative constructions are read aloud, and learners have to respond by saying who is doing the action. These are called by VanPatten referential activities, because the answer might be right or wrong. In the final stage, affective structured activities, which are more open-ended, learners are requested to use information from the real world.

The results of relevant studies （both sentence-level and discourse-related） suggest a positive effect for processing instruction. Learners in the processing instruction group were better able to understand and produce the target structure （direct object pronouns in Spanish） than learners in the traditional instruction group （VanPatten and Cadierno, 1993）. Other studies have been conducted with languages other than Spanish, for example,

VanPatten and Wong (2004) in French, Benati (2004) in Italian, all showing support for the effect of processing instruction.

Here we think it necessary to give a mention of the relationship between comprehension and acquisition. Comprehension is based on meaning, while acquisition is based on the understanding of the syntax of a language. The former is not synonymous with the latter. Some input will be used for meaning, while other input is used for grammar development. It is argued that semantic comprehension is a necessary condition for syntactic comprehension and syntactic comprehension is a necessary condition for acquisition. But neither assures the next step to take place. That is, semantic comprehension is prerequisite to syntactic comprehension but does not guarantee it. If we assume that the notion is valid, then it might follow that comprehension does not serve much in helping a learner understand the syntax of the language, which is an ultimate aim of language learning. To put it in Cook's words (Cook, 1996: 76), the ability to decode language for meaning— "processing language to get the 'message'" is not the same as code breaking—the determination of the nature of the linguistic systems used for conveying meaning or the "processing of language to get the 'rules'".

6.4.5 Explicit and implicit instruction

Form-focused instruction may take different forms, two of them being explicit FFI and implicit FFI. In an explicit instruction class, learners are given a rule, and then they practice using it, and the knowledge gained is called explicit knowledge. In an implicit instruction class, learners are required to induce rules from examples given to them, and gain implicit knowledge. It is generally accepted that explicit knowledge is acquired through controlled processes in declarative memory, while implicit knowledge is acquired through much less conscious or even subconscious processes (Macaro and Masterman, 2006). Housen and Pierrard (2006) differentiated explicit FFI and implicit FFI in terms of a number of characteristics, as shown in Table 6.2.

Table 6. 2 Explicit FFI and Implicit FFI

Explicit FFI	Implicit FFI
—directs attention to target form —is predetermined and planned (e. g., as the main focus and goal of a teaching activity) —is obtrusive (interruption of communicative meaning) —presents target forms in isolation —uses metalinguistic terminology (e. g., rule explanation) —involves controlled practice of target form	—attracts attention to target form —is delivered spontaneously (e. g., in an otherwise communication-oriented activity) —is unobtrusive (minimal interruption of communication of meaning) —presents target form in context —makes no use of metalanguage —encourages free use of the target form

It must be pointed out that the terms explicit FFI and implicit FFI can only be defined from a perspective external to the learner—the teacher's, material writer's, or course designer's perspective. In contrast, the terms explicit/implicit learning and intentional/incidental L2 learning refer to the learner's perspective. These distinctions should not be treated equal. That is, it does not follow that implicit instruction results in implicit or incidental learning nor that explicit instruction necessarily leads to explicit/intentional learning.

Quite a number of studies have been conducted to establish which type of instruction was most effective. The results were uncertain, although some research showed the advantages of explicit instruction. For example, the explicit method of teaching seemed to be more beneficial for adult and female adolescent learners of above average intelligence (Ellis, 1994: 642).

Whether or not explicit instruction works better partially depends on the features of the grammatical structures. It is found that some grammatical structures are more susceptible to a deductive method of teaching while others are more suited to an inductive method. This is supported by psychological research on explicit learning and implicit learning. For example, a series of studies performed by Reber et al. (1980) showed that explicit instruction works better if the material to be learnt is relatively simple, but not when the material is complex. There are some important factors which affect the ease of learning, with the first being the number of variables to be learned, and the second being the saliency of the features in the input.

Another factor is whether the rule is presented separately or with examples. For example, N. Ellis (1991) compared the effects of three kinds of instruction on adult learners' ability to acquire the rules of soft mutation in Welsh. These rules require that initial consonants in Welsh nouns mutate (for example, /t/→/d/) in accordance with a complex set of contextual factors. One group of learners were taught implicitly. That is, they were given randomly ordered examples of mutating and non-mutating nouns in different contexts. The result showed that the knowledge of the rules of soft mutation is very uncertain. A second group received explicit instruction; they were given an explanation of the rule for soft mutation. Results showed that they developed a solid knowledge of the rules, but could not always make correct use of them when they were asked to judge correct and incorrect noun forms. A third group of learners were given a "structured" treatment. That is, they were taught the rules and given examples of how to apply them. Compared with other two groups, this group did the best in that they learnt the rules and were successful in using them judging the grammaticality of sentences. As can be seen, the final results showed that explicit instruction in conjunction with examples works best. The result was supported by studies carried out by Michas and Berry (1994) on the native English speakers' acquisition of Greek words' pronunciation, by the research of Rosa and O'Neill (1999) who studied native English learners of Spanish subjunctive mood clauses and by that of Norris and Ortega's (2000) meta-analysis of 69 experiments on explicit learning.

Further research shows that the degree of difficulty of grammatical rules determines whether explicit instruction works. The difficulty can be divided into five degrees: very easy, easy, moderately difficult, difficult and very difficult. It is supposed (DeKeyser, 2003) that when the grammatical rule is moderately difficult, explicit instruction yields the best results; when the rule is very easy or very difficult, explicit instruction does not work. Therefore, the relationship between rule difficulty and explicit instruction can be described in a quadratical curve, as shown in Figure 6.4.

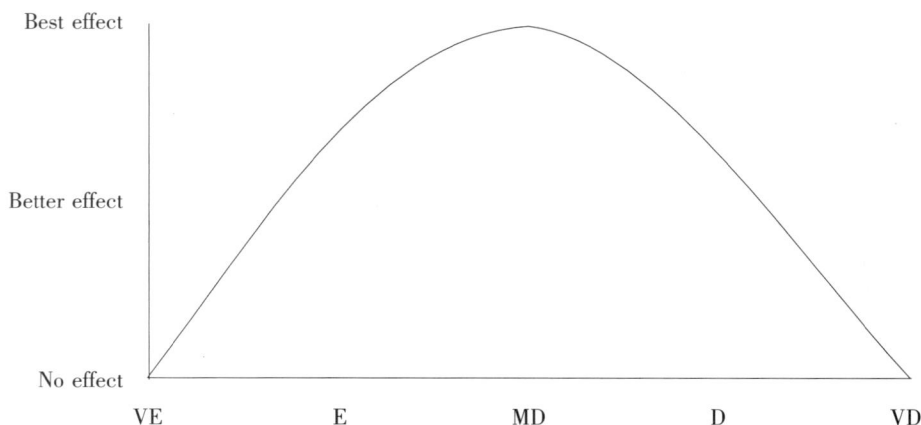

Figure 6. 4   Relationship Between Degree of Difficulty and Effect of Explicit Instruction
(VE = very easy; E = easy; MD = moderately difficult; D = difficult; VD = very difficult)

In recent years, research has been concerned with the effect of explicit grammar instruction on grammatical knowledge and production tasks. Results show that explicit grammar instruction results in gains in explicit knowledge, and its application in specific grammar related tasks, but there is less evidence that it leads to gains in production tasks, such as translation and free writing (Macaro and Materman, 2006).

An implicit way of instruction is to provide learners with more natural input through communicative and content-based language teaching, in which the emphasis is on meaning instead of linguistic forms. What language learners are exposed to is not presented according to a sequence of grammatical forms, but to a theme or a school subject such as science and history. In such classes, learners develop more comprehension and communication skills than they do in traditional language teaching approaches. However, even in such a rich communicative environment, there exist limitations on the input which is available for acquisition. This is because of the fact that some language features do not appear frequently in the "natural language" and from the absence of certain kinds of situational context in the classroom. For example, in history lessons in French immersion classes, learners may not hear regularly-used past tense (Swain, 1988). In a history class, the teacher often uses the historical present tense, intending to make the narrative events interesting to the students. Besides, classroom language is likely to have a limited range of sociolinguistic and discoursal features. Another finding is that students having had several years of French immersion were still uncertain about the use of formal and informal address forms *vous* and *tu* (Lyster, 1994) . It seems that in an immersion class the only proficient speaker is the teacher, and the speech and discourse characteristics which are typical of adolescent interaction are rare or absent (Tarone and Swain, 1995) . Therefore, such learners who can only get access to L2 exposure in the classroom will inevitably suffer from the gaps in their knowledge of the language and the way it is used outside the classroom.

Another limitation in such a meaning-oriented and content-based setting, without any form-focused instruction, is that learners may not develop high levels of accuracy. It is true that these L2 learners develop comprehension and fluency abilities; it is also true that they continue to experience problems with grammatical accuracy and lexical precision (Lightbown and Spada, 1990) . Why? While learners understand the meaning, they may neglect the forms that are required to express these meanings. When they can successfully communicate with inaccurate language, and when there is no corrective feedback, it is very likely that they are not motivated to move beyond their current level of language use.

Much more studies supported Norris and Ortega's (2000) finding that explicit instruction is more effective than implicit instruction. It was found that learners receiving explicit instruction outperformed learners receiving implicit instruction. This general conclusion applies irrespective of how the implicit instruction was operationalized, whether in terms of enriched input or through an instruction to memorize a set of sentences. Despite such success in explicit FFI, a number of caveats should be taken into consideration. First, the studies suggest that explicit instruction is more effective when it is directed at easy rather than difficult structures. Research indicates that there is no statistically significant differences between implicit and explicit learners for the complex structures. Another caveat concerns how acquisition was measured. For example, the beneficial effects of explicit instruction, in a study, were evident in the sentence-completion test but not in the narrative test. The key question here is whether explicit instruction is effective when learning is measured in terms of free constructed responses. Ellis (2008) reviewed a number of studies that suggest it is effective and found that in all those studies explicit instruction was combined with some other instructional option such as production practice. Evidence showing that explicit instruction by itself results in improved accuracy in free production is still lacking.

6. 4. 6　Consciousness-raising

The term consciousness-raising (CR) has been widely used in SLA research by researchers who are interested in the role of formal instruction. It is frequently used to refer to any attempt to focus the learner's attention on a specific target structure, as a synonym for form-focused instruction. In contrast, the traditional focus-on-forms approach has emphasized the value of practice. Learners are required to produce sentences containing the target language structures; they must do this repetitively; and they are expected to do it correctly. During the whole process learners receive corrective feedback. Then, an alternative type of formal instruction is the one in which learners are not expected to produce the target structure. Instead, they are only supposed to understand it by formulating some kind of cognitive representation of how it works. This kind of formal instruction is called consciousness-raising. In contrast to practice, which aims at developing implicit knowledge of the rule, CR is directed only at explicit knowledge. That is, there is no expectancy that learners will be able to use the rule in communicative output.

Many scholars advocate the role of practice in classroom teaching and hold the view that participation in classroom practice can result in learning. But the overall results of related studies show that there is no evidence to support this claim. What's more, there are studies suggesting that the extent to which individual learners practice specific grammatical features is not related to the accuracy with which they subsequently perform them in communication (Ellis, 1999: 643). Why does practice fail to result in learning? One possible reason is that learners are not ready to learn the grammatical features being taught in class.

Then consciousness-raising comes as an alternative. One reason for its existence is that CR need not involve production by the learner, as practice does. What's more, CR is directed at explicit rather than implicit knowledge; it does not go against teachability hypothesis. What consciousness-raising can help learning is that it results in noticing the structures in input and that this noticing may help retention of the structures.

Research (for example, Fotos and Ellis, 1991) indicates that both teacher-provided metalinguistic explanation and a CR task resulted in significant gains in understanding of the target structure, although the former seemed to produce the more durable gains. CR tasks are those tasks in which learners discover rules for themselves. It can be equated with a type of inductive FFI. Mohamed (2001) found that a CR task was more effective than metalinguistic explanation with groups of high-intermediate ESL learners from missed L1 backgrounds but not with a group of low-intermediate learners. This study suggests that the effectiveness of CR tasks may depend on the proficiency of learners. Although no convincing evidence indicates that deductive explicit FFI results in L2 implicit knowledge, Fotos (1993) was able to show that the explicit knowledge the learners gained from her CR tasks may have aided the processes believed to be involved in the acquisition of implicit knowledge. Fotos showed that completing the CR tasks aided subsequent noticing of the targeted features. Several weeks after the completion of the CR tasks, the learners in her study completed a number of dictations that included exemplars of the targeted structures. They were then asked to underline any particular bit of language they had paid special attention to as they did the dictation. Fotos found that they frequently underlined the structures that had been targeted in the CR tasks.

6. 5   The Teaching of Pragmatics

6. 5. 1   Expanded definitions of pragmatic competence

The concept of pragmatic competence originated in Hymes's (1972) framework of communicative competence. Language knowledge, as was proposed by Hymes, entails grammatical and sociocultural knowledge. These two types of knowledge help us understand how to speak appropriately in a social context. Since then, the definition of pragmatic competence has evolved into multiple directions. Currently, pragmatic competence is viewed as a multi-dimensional construct involving different knowledge and skill areas, as summarized below by Taguchi (2023).

The first component of pragmatic competence is the knowledge of form-function-context mappings. Pragmatic knowledge involves understanding what forms to use to achieve a communicative goal in context. It entails a repertoire of linguistic forms and sociocultural knowledge of how those forms work in context. The concept of form-function-context mappings was introduced by Thomas (1983), who claimed that pragmatic knowledge involves two distinct yet complementary dimensions—pragmalinguistics and sociopragmatics. The former refers to the knowledge of linguistic forms for performing a communicative function, while the latter involves the knowledge of social conventions and norms of behavior in the society. These dimensions largely parallel to functional and sociolinguistic knowledge in the modes of communicative competence. Functional knowledge involves the knowledge of form-function mappings, while sociolinguistic knowledge extends the form-function mappings to contexts of use.

The second aspect of pragmatic knowledge is the interactional ability. The knowledge of form-function-context-mappings has long been considered as the core of pragmatic competence. However, with the advent of discourse pragmatic and interactional competence, pragmatic competence is no longer viewed simply as fixed knowledge of form, function, and context of use. Rather, it is understood to involve interactional abilities to use this knowledge in a flexible manner, adapting to the changing course of interaction. It is crucial to understand that the context is never stable. It changes moment-by-moment depending on how a conversation unfolds. Therefore, an essential aspect of pragmatic competence is interactional ability, the skill to navigate the dynamic course of interaction by adapting our interactional resources to changing realities.

The third part of pragmatic competence is learner agency. While the knowledge of form-function-context mappings and interactional ability enable us to communicate appropriately in a variety of social settings, our manner of speaking is also shaped by agency. Agency is a self-reliant capacity that works with volition to bring about an effect on one's behavior. Our linguistic choice is influenced by our own beliefs and values—how we want to be perceived by others and what social positions we want to create for ourselves. When applied to L2 learning, we need to understand that learners are active agents who make their own linguistic choices.

In a word, pragmatic competence is a multi-dimensional construct involving the above three multiple knowledge and skill areas. L2 learners need to be equipped with the knowledge of form-function-context mappings and be able to adapt their knowledge to interaction-in-progress. At the same time, they must have the agentic capacity to decide whether or not to actually use the knowledge in a situation. The teaching of pragmatics should, ideally, address each of these three areas.

6.5.2　Teaching methodologies

There are quite a few methods of teaching pragmatical knowledge. Explicit and implicit teaching methods have been widely adopted to teach pragmatics. The explicit method typically involves a direct metapragmatic explanation (e. g. , information about which forms to use when greeting a boss vs. a family member). The implicit method holds back metapragmatic explanation, but tries to develop learners' understanding of pragmatic features indirectly through input exposure, consciousness-raising tasks, and implicit feedback. Explicit and implicit methods are motivated by Schmidt's (1993) noticing hypothesis that capitalizes on the role of consciousness and attention in learning. According to Schmidt, learning occurs when learners attend to linguistic forms, their functions, and relevant contextual factors. When the focal form-function-context mapping is noticed and processed, it is internalized and stored in long-term memory.

A second method is based on skill acquisition theory which focuses on the transition from the initial stage of conscious rule learning (declarative knowledge) to the end stage where learners can use rules unconsciously and fluently (procedural knowledge). The declarative knowledge refers to the knowledge of "what" (for example, knowing which greeting expressions to use in what contexts), while procedural knowledge is concerned with "how", or automatic and fluent use of the rules (for example, performing greetings in a variety of settings without thinking). The transition from declarative to procedural knowledge occurs through intensive practice. Skill acquisition theories provide implications for the design of instruction, especially how to sequence instruction so learners can transition from declarative to procedural knowledge stage. First, teachers can develop learners' declarative knowledge by providing explicit information about the target form-function-context mapping. Then, they can provide systematic, repeated practice so learners can use the declarative knowledge in a series of communicative tasks. Focused, systematic feedback can be incorporated into the practice to ensure the correct use of declarative knowledge.

Other methods involve how role play, simulations, and computer-mediated communication (CMC) can be used to develop L2 learners' pragmatic competence in interaction. In a typical role play, learners read a situational scenario and act out the scenario with an assigned interlocutor, usually a peer student. The scenarios are written in a way that they elicit the targeted pragmatic language use (such as speech acts) while interacting with another person. There are two types of role play: closed and open. In closed role plays, learners act out a situation to achieve pre-defined outcomes. Open role plays, however, do not specify any outcomes of interaction in a scenario. They are more reflective of learners' interaction abilities because learners have to navigate through unpredictable sequences of interaction and negotiate interactional outcomes with their interlocutors.

Recently, virtual reality (VR) technology has significantly advanced the role play format in terms of contextualization of L2 use. VR games for pragmatics teaching have been developed, such as *Croquelandia*, a 3-dimensional interactive game where L2 Spanish learners interacted with built-in characters and performed speech acts of request and apology (Sykes, 2013) and *Questauant*, a scenario-based digital game where learners took the role of a robot who works in a restaurant in China and runs quests by interacting with built-in characters using formulaic expressions (Tang and Taguchi, 2021). Given the nature of pragmatics that capitalizes on language use in a social context, VR serves as a useful platform for pragmatic teaching. Despite the fact that VR-based role play and simulations are never "real", the sensory-rich VR environment can offer an immense space where learners can interact in diverse roles and social settings.

Compared with VR, which provides typically a short exchange involving one or two turns rather than an extended conversation, CMC can offer opportunities to perform a variety of pragmatic functions while directly interacting with members of the target culture. Two types of CMC have been applied to pragmatics teaching. One is asynchronous, such as e-mail, blogs, and discussion forms. The other is synchronous, such as text and voice-based chats and teleconferencing. Synchronous CMC is a promising venue for developing learners' interactional abilities in pragmatics.

It is true that pragmatics-learning opportunities can emerge naturally in interaction without instruction. It is also true that explicit focus on form-function-context mappings mentioned above can make interaction more pedagogical. When interactional tasks are designed to promote the use of specific pragmatic features, the tasks can help orient learners to their learning goals, contributing to their maximum use of interactional opportunities.

6.5.3   Effects of instruction on L2 pragmatic development

Even though most FFI studies have addressed second language grammatical development, there is a growing interest in the effects of FFI on L2 pragmatic development. Such studies have focused on speech acts such as requests or compliments, and other areas of pragmatics such as socio-pragmatic aspects of politeness and implicature. A number of issues that have been addressed in relevant studies are: ①whether the teaching of L2 pragmatics is necessary, ②the differential effectiveness of different instructional options,

③whether the method of measurement of learning affects the results obtained, and ④the effect of different lengths of instruction on learning (Jeon and Kaya, 2006).

Some studies investigated the effects of FFI on pragmalinguistic features, including both formulaic devices associated with early L2 development and more complex devices likely to be found in more advanced learners. The studies were conducted mainly in foreign language classroom contexts, possibly because instruction is seen as less important when learners have exposure to communicative language use outside the classroom. Now we will briefly review the effects of FFI on L2 pragmatic development in terms of the four issues mentioned above.

First, as for whether L2 pragmatic instruction is necessary, studies showed mixed results. For example, research indicated that instruction had no overall effect on the acquisition of the pragmalinguistic devices for performing compliments (Rose and Kwai-fun, 2001). However, Lyster (1994) reported clear gains in both an oral and written production test and in awareness of the appropriate use of "tu" and "vous". It was also found in another study that instruction resulted in a more native-like performance of a specific communicative task. It can be seen that FFI directed at pragmatic features is effective at least some of the time. Jeon and Kaya's meta-analysis of 13 FFI studies reported a considerable range of effect sizes. These effect sizes showed that L2 pragmatic features are teachable. As for to what extent the choice of target features affects the success of instruction, it is possible that instruction is successful when it is directed at relatively simple features (for example, formulaic expressions) but is less successful when it is directed at syntactically complex realization devices (for example, bi-clausal requests).

Second, as for the relative effectiveness of different instructional options, studies have focused mainly on the implicit versus explicit instruction. Some studies found no difference between explicit and implicit instruction, while other studies reported a clear overall effect for instruction. Existing studies have shown that explicit instruction leads to great gains in pragmatic knowledge than implicit instruction. Plonsky and Zhuang's (2019) meta-analysis of 50 studies found that studies using the explicit method had a larger effect size than those using the implicit method. Taguchi's (2015) narrative review, however, showed that the implicit method can be as effective as the explicit method if instructors can strategically guide learners to notice focal pragmatic features and process them at a deeper level.

Third, the method of measuring learning outcomes is important for evaluating FFI effect. It is of particular importance whether the instruction can be shown to have an effect on both natural language data and elicited data. Some research results showed that the instruction led to improvements in oral language use suggesting that FFI can result in implicit knowledge of pragmatic features. Jeon and Kaya (2006) compared studies that collected just elicited language data with those that collected both elicited and natural language data. They reported that there was a large difference in the mean effect sizes in favor of the elicited plus natural data, although they acknowledged that this finding was not reliable, given the low number of observations they were able to include in their analysis. Also, their analysis showed that FFI has a stronger effect on the pragmatic ability when multiple as opposed to single measures of learning are obtained; that is, it did not address the crucial question of the effects of FFI on implicit and explicit pragmatic knowledge.

Fourth, as for the differential effect of length of instruction, it is believed that extended instruction is more beneficial. This is supported by Jeon and Kaya who compared studies that provided less than 5 hours of instruction with those that provided more than 5 hours. The results indicated that the mean effect sizes for the latter were notably larger than those for the former. However, they cautioned about reaching a firm conclusion, pointing out that their finding contradicted Norris and Ortega's (2000).

It should be noted that the research investigating the effects of FFI on second language pragmatics has a few shortcomings, as summarized by Ellis (2013: 894 – 895) below. First, there are still relatively few studies. Second, the research suffers from a failure to operationalize FFI in precise and systematic ways, reflecting perhaps the pedagogical as opposed to theoretical orientation of many of the studies. Third, there are a number of other design problems—for example, insufficient attention to ensuring the reliability and validity of measurements of learning outcomes and a general failure to include delayed post-tests. There is no denying, however, that FFI can lead to improvements in pragmatic ability at least in the short term. It is not yet possible to conclude with confidence which type of instruction is more effective or whether FFI results in gains in implicit or explicit knowledge or both.

6. 6   Teachability/Learnability and Uniqueness of Classroom Instruction

6. 6. 1   Teachability/learnability

We have discussed in the previous sections the effect of instructional intervention in L2 acquisition. Although FFI plays an important role in facilitating L2 learning in certain contexts, there are theoretical grounds for believing that instruction does not have a long-term effect on learners' construction of interlanguage systems. It is often said that L2 learners may be endowed with an "internal syllabus" (or "built-in syllabus") for learning the language. The internal syllabus will determine, to a large extent, the learning path that they will follow. That is, it will control how and when learners acquire particular grammatical structures. This special "syllabus" is not susceptible to the outside modification. The classroom learner is also provided with an external syllabus, in which items have been placed into a teaching sequence. This may conflict with the learner's internal syllabus, but will not necessarily override it. That is, the learner may still be employing his natural strategies in order to process the data and internalize it. In other words, the learning sequence may not be the same as the teaching sequence. Teaching cannot keep pace with learning in rate and path in some aspects.

The morpheme order studies showed that acquisition takes place in some sort of natural order. Krashen also claimed in his Natural Order Hypothesis that elements of language are acquired in a predictable order. The order is the same regardless of whether or not instruction is involved. The "natural order" is the result of the acquired system without interference from the learned system. The implication of acquisition order is that pedagogical intervention cannot, or can alter in only a trivial manner, the natural acquisition orders (Lightbown, 1983).

Findings based on the natural progression within a classroom context are supported by a number of studies. For example, Pienemann (1984) argued that the stages in this developmental sequence cannot be skipped even as a result of instruction. He investigated German word-order development among 10 Italian children ranging from 7 to 9 years old. These subjects all had two weeks of instruction on a particular stage. Some were at the immediately preceding stage, and others at a much earlier stage. Results showed that only the former group learned the instructional target. This indicates that the other children could not learn because they were not developmentally ready. Such a study led Pienemann (1985) to propose the teachability hypothesis: Instruction can only promote acquisition if the interlanguage is close to the point when the structure to be taught is learnable without instruction in natural settings.

Mackey's (1995) study set up to determine the extent to which conversational interaction could alter the developmental progression of the acquisition of questions. A positive relationship was found between interaction and development. Learners who were involved in structure-focused interaction moved along a developmental path more rapidly than learners who were not. As she noted, interaction was able to "set up the pace" of development, but was not able to push learners beyond a developmental stage. In other words, developmental stages could not be skipped. There are constraints on learning such that even pedagogical intervention is likely to be unsuccessful in altering the order.

According to this hypothesis, instruction does not change the natural sequence of acquisition but rather speed up the learner's passage through it. However, the problem is that teachers are not always clear about which learners in their class are ready to be taught a particular structure; it is not easy to find out. As noted by Lightbown (1985b), our knowledge of natural acquisition sequences is too limited to make specific recommendations about how they should be related to teaching sequences. Pienemann and his fellow researchers subsequently attempted to overcome this problem by developing a broad theoretical framework with predictive power for when specific structures will be acquired.

Here it is necessary to have a brief review of Pienemann's processability theory, as it seeks to explain what is known about acquisitional sequences in terms of a set of processing procedures. As he put it: once we can spell out the sequence in which language processing routines develop we can delineate those grammars that are processable at different points of development (Pienemann, 2005a: 2). He proposed that language production could only be explained with reference to a set of basic premises: ① speakers posses relatively specialized processing components that operate automatically and in parallel, ②processing is incremental, ③in order to cope with non-linearity, speakers need to store grammatical information in memory, and thus it follows that ④grammatical processing must have access to a grammatical memory store, which is procedural rather than declarative. It is proposed that the processing procedures are hierarchical and are mastered one at a time. Thus, the failure to master a low-level procedure blocks access to high-level procedures and makes it impossible for the learner to acquire those grammatical features that depend on them.

According to Pienemann (2005a), L2 learners follow the following language generation processes: ①word/lemma; ②category procedure (lexical category); ③phrasal procedure (head); ④S-procedure and word order rule; ⑤matrix/subordinate clause. In the beginning, learners can access L2 words but these are invariant in form and are used in single constituent utterances. At the lexical category stage, lexical entries are now annotated with a number of diacritic features such as "possessive" and "number". These lexical items can be accessed but only within a single constituent and are matched directly with the underlying conceptual content of a message, so still no exchange of grammatical information is required. At this stage, the learner is still not able to handle structures where diacritic features need to be matched across elements within a constituent or between constituents. Such ability begins at the third stage—the level of phrasal procedure. Now it is possible for learners to handle such structures as articles, plural agreement, and do-fronting. Exchange of information in the phrasal procedure is required to check the value of a diacritic feature of one lexical entry (for example, "child") with that of another (for example, the indefinite article "a") to ascertain that they match and thus enable the production of a structural phrase (for example, "a child"). Similarly, exchange of information between structural phrases at this stage is still not possible. This ability is activated at the next stage—the S-procedure. How does it happen? This involves exchange of information between heads of different phrases, as in subject-verb agreement. The features of one constituent (the subject noun phrase) are deposited in the S-procedure and subsequently placed in another constituent (the verb phrase). When this becomes possible learners are able to mark the third person of the present simple tense with the -s morpheme. The final procedure to be acquired enables learners to process the word order of subordinate structures such as that found in embedded questions (for example, "He asked where I lived").

6.6.2 Uniqueness of classroom instruction

Although FFI does not always produce desirable effects and classroom instruction does not always keep pace with natural acquisition order, the uniqueness of classroom instruction, compared with an informal environment, can never be neglected. That is, whether instruction is given or nor may produce quite different results. Here in this part, we will review some unique repercussions that instruction has for second language learning.

First, formal classroom instruction may provide richness that an informal environment may not have. A relevant study (Pavesi, 1986) was done between two different groups of Italian ESL learners in how they acquire relative clauses. In one group were naturalistic learners, while in the other were instructed learners. The instructed learners were high school students aged 14 ~ 18 who had studied English for 4 years on average. They had had no informal exposure to English. Their instruction had been grammar-based, and had had much written input. The other group of learners was made up of Italian workers, ranging in age from 19 to 50, and had lived in the United Kingdom for an average of 6 years. Their exposure to English was almost entirely informal. The results showed that learning proceeds from the unmarked to the marked structure, which is commonly accepted order of acquisition. Such an order is not affected by the context of learning. However, a noticeable difference was found in the number of marked relative clauses used by learners: the instructed group used more. Another interesting finding was that the informal group learners used more noun copies (for example, *Number Five is the boy who the dog is biting the boy*) than the formal group while the instructed learners used more pronoun copies (for example, *Number Five is the boy who the dog is biting him*).

Second, instruction may speed up the rate of acquisition. Grammar development in both L1 and L2 occurs in stages that are similar for most learners. According to teachability hypothesis, if learners are developmentally ready to acquire certain grammatical structures, instruction will result in acquisition. The ideas proposed by Processability Theory have implications for what teachers and learners should expect as a result of classroom instruction. Although a grammatical structure taught in the classroom does not mean that it can be used productively by learners unless they are developmentally ready, instruction may help learners progress through the stages more rapidly.

Third, instruction may help prevent fossilization and allow learners to achieve higher levels of accuracy than they might have otherwise (Nassaji and Fotos, 2011). In contrast to naturalistic learning environment, classroom instruction provides opportunities for teachers to point out learners' errors and correct them through explicit feedback. It is more likely that learners in the classroom will notice the difference between their poorly organized utterances and target norms with the help of the teacher and other more competent learners.

Fourth, instruction facilitates the acquisition of pragmatic and lexical knowledge. Kasper and Rose (2002) claimed that L2 pragmatics can be taught and that instructional intervention is better than no instruction. Specifically, they made a claim that explicit instruction coupled with practice provide the best chance for success. Pragmatic studies conducted in a study-abroad context show that appropriate pragmatic behavior is not always acquired just by living abroad. Instruction coupled with a study-abroad experience offers the optimal condition for pragmatic learning. As was commented by Kasper and Rose (2002: 230), "For developing pragmatic ability, spending time in the target community is no panacea, length of residence is not a reliable predictor, and L2 classroom can be a productive social context."

Focus-on-form instruction is essential to vocabulary learning. It is proposed that instruction does not need to be conducted within the context of a communicative task. The language-focused learning includes various ways of giving attention to vocabulary. Some of the ways involve classroom teaching and others involve the learners taking responsibility for their own learning. A course in English as a foreign language which includes deliberate attention to vocabulary will have advantages over incidental or naturalistic learning that does not have a focus on vocabulary (Nation, 2023).

Multiple studies showed the effects of explicit instruction on L2 vocabulary acquisition. For example, Laufer and Girsai (2008) investigated the effects of explicit contrastive analysis and translation activities on the incidental acquisition of single words and collocations. High school learners of English were provided with either: (a) meaning-focused instruction in which there was no focus on target words; (b) form-focused instruction, with contextualized focus on the target words; or (c) contrastive analysis and translation, in which learners translated sentences from L2 into L1, and vice versa. Learners who were given both active and passive recall tests, and the contrastive analysis and translation group significantly outperformed the other two groups. Methods that have been used to make vocabulary instruction more explicit, such as rote copying, single coding (verbal only), dual coding (verbal plus imagery), as well as contrastive analysis and translation, are all effective in facilitating vocabulary development.

6. 7   Teaching of Grammar

6. 7. 1   Concepts of grammar

Grammar can be conceptualized in several different ways, so it is necessary to determine what is meant by grammar. Grammar is the internal cognitive system of rules about the morphology and syntax of a language. Knowledge of this system is what allows speakers to produce accurate and grammatical language that conforms to the target language norms. Native speakers' use of language is usually considered to be grammatical in the common sense of the term; however, there is sometimes a difference between prescriptive grammar, which is how so-called experts think people should speak, and descriptive grammar, which is how people really speak in everyday life.

Prescriptive grammar refers to some *Dos and Don'ts* such as "Don't split infinitives", "Don't end a sentence with a preposition", and "Use *who* as a subject pronoun and *whom* as an object pronoun". In spite of this, these supposed grammar rules are often violated by many native speakers of English. For example, many English L1 speakers find the prescriptively correct phrase *For whom are you calling*? to be stilted and old-fashioned. Instead many people might say *Who are you calling for*? Many instructed second language acquisition researchers are not concerned with prescriptive grammar; rather, they are concerned with descriptive grammar, that is how L1 speakers actually use the language in everyday life. Descriptive grammatical rules can also be referred to as pedagogical grammar, which consists of explicit descriptions of the surface structure of grammatical rules in order to help with learning the language.

Another characteristic of grammar is that while much of it is considered to be rule-based, there are also some components that are item-based. For much of grammar, there are rules that can be used to produce target-like language, but sometimes there are no rules and these items must be memorized. For instance, English regular past tense is rule-based. There is a rule that can be applied to all regular verbs. However, English irregular past tense is memorized and recalled as individual items. Much SLA research is concerned with rule-based learning, or how learners develop rule-based, implicit grammatical knowledge.

It is quite natural for L2 learners' production to be different from the grammatical norms of native speakers. However, L2 learners' production is also systematic and rule-governed, even if those rules are not the same as those of L1 speakers. The term "interlanguage" has been used to acknowledge the fact that learners do not immediately gain native-like knowledge of L2 grammar. The truth is that many learners never achieve native-like mastery of the L2. Instead, learners have an interlanguage system that is rule-governed and dynamic, allowing them to produce grammatical forms at their current level of development. Interlanguage theory takes into consideration the developmental nature of learners' grammatical system. It also proposes that learners' L2 knowledge will not be the same as native speakers' knowledge of that language.

6.7.2　The scope of grammar teaching

Grammar teaching does not only deal with the major word classes, but also it can cover the full range of concerns that linguists call grammar. Indeed, it can be taken even more broadly to include all aspects of language structure. In this very broad sense, therefore, grammar teaching could include all the following topics (Hudson, 2010): ①word classes, feeding all the other kinds of analysis; ②syntax, including sentence and clause analysis; ③ morphology, which is particularly important for English spelling; ④ phonology, graphology, and spelling; ⑤ punctuation; ⑥ lexical relations, including semantic and morphological relations; ⑦semantics (lexical and syntactic); ⑧pragmatic and discourse structure; ⑨ sociolinguistics, style, and dialectology; ⑩ language change. However, syntax has always had a central place in language teaching, especially in the debate about whether grammar teaching improves writing.

Another variable in grammar teaching concerns the language to which it is applied: the children's L1 or a second language or foreign language. Cross-language teaching can work well or badly, according to how sophisticated the teacher's and pupils' grasp of grammar is. The recent history of the English-speaking world has seen much the same rejection of grammar teaching in L2 teaching as in L1 teaching, but the pendulum has now swung back in its favor as a result of a large body of supportive research (Norris and Ortega, 2000). Grammar teaching could, in principle, be embedded in a much broader framework of work on language, including psycholinguistic questions about child language, speech processing, animal communication and sociological questions about how language perpetuates prejudices, power structures, and so on. This broad program would be a course in general linguistics in

all but name, and it is being actively pursued under the name of language awareness (Hawkins, 1994).

6.7.3　The aims of grammar teaching

Since its origins in classical Greece, the main aim of grammar teaching has been to support the learning of literacy skills. However, it is important to remember that the grammar of any language itself is a complex system rather than a disconnected list of categories or facts, so even if the ultimate aim is to improve writing, the immediate aim has to be an understanding of the system of grammar itself. Merely teaching the names and definitions of the word classes by rote is unlikely to have any benefit for writing. Hudson (2011) mentioned two versions of grammar teaching. At its weakest, grammar teaching targets a prescriptive list of errors to improve writing. Healthy grammar teaching, however, encourages growth, even though this typically leads to temporary errors at growth points. According to Hudson, grammar teaching helps young writers to develop richer grammatical repertoires: ①by providing a meta language for discussion of new constructions and weaknesses in the children's writing. ②by providing a deeper understanding of how language works, including a more or less conscious awareness of the resources available for particular functions. ③by directing learners' attention to the form of what they read, in the hope that they will notice new patterns and remember them.

An essential question to consider here is whether grammar can in fact produce these benefits. The improvement of writing (and reading) is only one of the possible aims of grammar teaching. There are more others: First, provide a metalanguage for L2 learning, and perhaps even for explicit comparisons between L1 and L2 structures. Second, teach children, as part of a liberal education, about an important part of themselves. In this approach, grammar is taught, alongside other areas of language, on much the same basis as, say, history—something every citizen ought to know something about. Third, use grammar as a vehicle for teaching scientific method. A number of small-scale experiments have shown that children can learn to formulate and test hypothesis about grammar, and that even small amounts (for example, two weeks) of this activity can produce measurable improvements in general scientific reasoning.

6. 7. 4　Methods of grammar teaching

As for how to teach grammar, a wide range of methods have been used, ranging from didactic teaching by rote, with a question-and-answer dialogue that included "parsing", to discovery-based learning in which children induce grammatical generalizations from their own data. The methods used obviously depend on the aims of teaching. Even when the aim is to improve writing, there is a major choice about the timing of the grammar teaching in relation to writing activity. Below are the three options:

First, separating teaching teaches grammar separately from writing so that topics in grammar are not related to topics in writing.

Second, reactive teaching teaches grammar as and when needed. This is an approach strongly favored under the title "grammar in context". When taken literally this approach generally means in fact that grammar is never taught because of the time needed to teach most grammatical concepts.

Third, proactive teaching anticipates the needs of a class and teaches a particular point of grammar with immediate links to those needs. This has probably been the basis for all successful grammar teaching. The advantage of this approach is to allow grammar teaching to have its own systematic structure (for example, teaching about verbs before teaching about tenses) while still being closely integrated with writing.

The above choices lead to further choices about methods, for example, the choice of whether or not to teach and use sentence diagramming, and if so, what kind of diagrams to use. These questions lead in one direction into pedagogy and in another direction into linguistic theory.

Does grammar teaching work? Does it improve writing and reading skills? The answer is uncertain. On the one hand, research showed it did not. Elley (1994) gave a typical summary: "Formal grammar instruction appears to contribute nothing to the development of writing and reading skills." It is not difficult to find examples of grammar teaching that were unsuccessful (by any criteria), but this merely shows that grammar can be taught unsuccessfully. On the other hand, there is also a great deal of solid research evidence that grammar teaching does in fact work if teachers are sufficiently well-informed about grammar and if the teaching is provocative, that is, closely integrated with activity to which grammatical instruction is relevant. Hudson (2010) listed some representative examples:

Example 1：

The exercise known as "sentence combining" has been shown to improve writing. In this method, students combine a list of simple sentences into a single sentence, with or without explicit comment on the structures concerned. This activity combines focus on a specific aspect of grammatical form with an immediate writing activity. Its effectiveness is an important demonstration that grammar teaching does not have to be "in context", in the sense of reacting to children's own writing.

Example 2：

Instruction about specific aspects of spelling such as the possessive apostrophe and irregular past tense forms produced immediate improvements in these areas, as measured by tests before and after the instruction.

Example 3：

Teaching about complex noun phrases helped 18-year-olds to understand such phrases in reading. Research was designed to separate the effects of grammatical knowledge from those of working memory differences, and showed that explicit instruction in grammar improved comprehension. In fact, it brought a "low-academic-ability" group up to the same level of comprehension as a high-ability group who received no instruction.

Grammar is playing, and will continue to play, a central role in second language teaching. Current textbook materials and SLA theories have evidence that zero grammar approach (that is, there should be no necessity to teach grammar) never really took hold. Ample evidence shows that grammar teaching works. However, it has to be admitted that the research basis for such work is still thin, and it is not clear exactly what distinguishes successful and unsuccessful grammar teaching.

Assignment

1. Questions for self-study.

(1) What is the difference between focus on form and focus on forms?

(2) Why do some structures seem to be permanently affected by instruction and others not?

(3) What is the difference between explicit instruction and implicit instruction?

(4) What are the limitations in the meaning-oriented implicit teaching?

(5) What caveats should we take into account when considering the success in explicit FFI?

(6) What is consciousness raising (CR)? What are the advantages of CR over the deductive explicit FFI?

(7) How do you define pragmatic competence? What kinds of knowledge and skill areas are included in pragmatic competence?

(8) What is learner agency?

(9) What implications does the skill acquisition theory produce for instruction design?

2. Match the following items in column I to their corresponding main concern in column Ⅱ.

I	Ⅱ
(1) linguistic concern about SLA	a. why some are more successful than others
(2) psychological concern about SLA	b. what to learn
(3) social concern about SLA	c. how to learn

3. Fill in the blanks in the following passage.

The traditional focus-on-forms approach has emphasized the value of _____ . Learners are required to produce sentences containing the target language _____ ; they must do this repetitively; and they are expected to do it correctly. So during the whole process learners receive corrective _____ . Then, an alternative type of formal instruction is the one in which learners are not expected to produce the target structure. Instead, they are only supposed to understand it by formulating some kind of cognitive _____ of how it works. This kind of formal instruction is called consciousness-raising. In contrast to practice, which aims at developing implicit knowledge of the rule, consciousness-raising is directed only at _____ knowledge. That is, there is no expectation that learners will be able to use the _____ in communicative output.

4. Open discussion for pair or group work.

(1) A native Chinese English teacher has drilled his students in class on indirect questions like:

Do you know where my watch is?
Do you know what time it is?
Did he tell you what time it is?

As a direct result, all students in the class were able to produce the indirect questions correctly in class. After class, one student came up to the teacher and asked, "Do you know where is our Physics teacher?" The truth is that only a few minutes after the class, in a spontaneous talk, the student used the indirect question incorrectly, though she practiced correctly in class perfectly. What do you think is the reason for her failure in using the right form? Was the lesson a waste of time? How might you go about finding answers to these questions?

(2) What do you think of the relationship between second language acquisition and second language pedagogy? How are they different from each other? How might they affect each other and how might the study of one influence the study or practices of the other? Try to relate your answers to a specific learning situation. When you are thinking about the relationship, also think about whether or not all aspects of SLA relate to classroom practice.

(3) In Chapter 3, we discussed Krashen's view on the function of the Monitor and how it can "get in your way" with its focus on form. Does this mean in a language class there should never be a focus on form and that teachers should only provide well-organized input? When might grammar instruction, that is, form-focused instruction be appropriate or necessary?

(4) In your experience of L2 learning, what are some examples of your being conscious of your language output? How would you attend to that output? Did your teacher favor implicit or explicit treatment, and which one was more effective?

Chapter Seven   Second Language Acquisition Research: Data Collection and Analysis

In the previous chapters, we have reviewed numerous questions and findings in second language acquisition. You may wonder how these findings come into existence. To put it simply, they are the results of SLA research. Researchers ask questions and find answers to these questions through studying the data collected from L2 learners. In this final chapter, we will present a means for data analysis and review the methods for data elicitation and data analysis.

7. 1   Data Collection

In the field of second language acquisition, recent years have seen the publication of numerous books on specific data collection methods, such as questionnaires, case studies, stimulated recall, and conversation analysis. This indicates an increasing interest in, and attention to, data collection and data analysis. Findings in second language research are often influenced by the way data are collected. As could be seen in the previous chapters, there are different ways of approaching the study of second language acquisition, and each approach has its unique way of gathering data. For example, when investigating learners' interlanguage development, we may consider the data needed to examine learners' errors. To investigate pragmatic features of learner language, we may consider the merits of discourse completion questionnaire. To understand learners' implicit knowledge, we may use data from grammaticality tests. Also, think-aloud method may be used if we want to know what strategies learners employ in L2 learning.

While there exist typical data collection approaches, there is also overlap in data elicitation methods. The choice of one method over another is highly dependent on the research question being asked（Gass and Mackey, 2007: 4）. Many L2 research methods are derived from those of other disciplines, especially linguistics, child language acquisition, sociology, and psychology. In this section, we will introduce three main types of data and their corresponding elicitation techniques.

7. 1. 1　Three types of data

The data chosen should serve the purpose of research. Research itself determines the type of data. There are different ways to categorize data, and different researchers have their principles. Ellis and Barkhuizen（2005）identified three broad types of data: ① non-production performance data, ②samples of learner production, and ③reports from learners about their own learning. Non-production performance data consist of measurements of learners' non-verbal responses to linguistic stimuli. They include measures of learners' reaction times to linguistic stimuli as in sentence matching tests, non-verbal measures of learners' comprehension of linguistic input as in picture-matching tests, and measures of learners' intuitions about the grammaticality or acceptability of utterances. Learner production data, however, consist of oral or written samples of naturally occurring language use or elicited data. Elicited data can be further categorized into clinical elicitation and experimental elicitation. Verbal-report data can be divided into self-report, self-observation, self-revelation, and self-assessment.

It must be pointed out that different kinds of SLA research tend to favor different data types. Early descriptive work about the order or sequence of acquisition showed a preference for language-use data in the early case studies, and clinical and experimental elicitation in the cross-sectional studies. However, the study of interlanguage pragmatics relied largely on experimentally elicited data, using discourse completion questionnaires. In contrast, research of UG and the competition model relied heavily on non-linguistic performance data. Studies on individual learner differences seldom employ language-use data, but turned to various kinds of verbal reports. In a word, what type of data to be used depends on what the research goal is. We will discuss some of the main types below.

7. 1. 1. 1　Non-production performance data

By measuring learners' non-production data, researchers can make inferences about learners' linguistic knowledge based on their ability to process language receptively. The following are some methods of measuring non-production data.

(1) Method of measuring learners' reaction time. An example of using this measure can be found in sentence-matching. Learners are presented with two sentences, which are either both grammatical or both ungrammatical, and then are asked to decide whether the two sentences are identical or not. The time it takes learners to make an online judgment is measured. The procedure is like this: the researchers presents one sentence (grammatical or ungrammatical) to the subjects and, after a short delay, a second sentence. Subjects are asked to decide as quickly as possible if the two sentences match or do not match. The time from the appearance of the second sentence to the subject's response is recorded and forms the data base for analysis. What's the use of this reaction time? It is used to determine the status of learners' L2 knowledge. That is, by examining the reaction times, it is possible to determine to what extent specific structures are deemed to be grammatical or ungrammatical by a particular learner.

(2) Method of measuring learners' comprehension. This measure has been used to establish whether learners are able to process specific linguistic features in the input. In a picture-matching test, for example, subjects are presented with a sentence and then asked to select which picture (from two or three) the sentence matches. For example, they might be shown the sentence *The dog was bitten by Thomas* and then asked to match the sentence with the correct picture from a pair of pictures with one showing a dog biting a man and the other a man biting a dog. Obviously, comprehension test such as picture matching only work with grammatical structures that have clear, identifiable functions such as the passive voice in English. They cannot be used for structures that are semantically redundant such as third person -s in English or noun-adjectival agreement in French.

(3) Grammaticality judgements tests. Two factors are to be considered in grammaticality judgment test (GJT): the design of the GJT and the procedures for implementing the test. As for the design, variables relate to the way in which learners are asked to make their judgments and in whether they are asked to perform some additional operation. In the standard GJT, learners are simply asked to judge whether the sentences are grammatical or ungrammatical (sometimes with the additional option of choosing a "not sure" option). They can also be offered a wider selection of choices in a multiple choice format or given a scale of grammaticality to respond to.

As for procedures, perhaps the most important variable is whether the test is authorized in a speeded or un-speeded format. The former is one in which learners are given a specified amount of time to judge each sentence. It is intended to elicit judgments based on implicit knowledge by preventing learners from consulting their metalinguistic knowledge. The latter is one in which learners have as much time as they want to judge each sentence. In an un-speeded test, learners are more able to utilize their explicit knowledge.

Researchers can gain three kinds of data from GJTs. First, they get information about learners' intuitions as to what is grammatical and what is ungrammatical. Second, if the time it takes learners to judge each sentence is recorded, GJTs provide information about reaction times which can be used to evaluate what kind of knowledge, explicit or implicit, the learners used to make judgments. Third, if learners are asked to correct ungrammatical sentences, the GJT can serve as a device for eliciting samples of learner language. These different types of data are used to draw conclusions about the nature of learners' L2 grammatical representations.

7.1.1.2　Learner production data

As mentioned above, learner production data has three main types, which constitute a data continuum. At one end of the continuum are the naturally occurring samples, and at the other end the experimentally elicited samples. Staying between these two poles are the clinically elicited samples, where some control is exercised through the choice of task but learners are exposed to be primarily engaged in message communication for a pragmatic purpose. Here, we introduce the methods of collecting these three different types of data.

(1) Collecting naturally occurring samples. Oral samples of naturally occurring learner language can be collected by different means. The most preferred methods are audio recording and video recording. Audio recording is widely used in sampling naturally occurring language use. But the disadvantage of this method is that the presence of a recorder may induce learners to attend to their speech, thus making it less likely that samples will reflect their vernacular style. Clip-on radio microphones and mini-disc recorders can be used to minimize this problem. Video recording has the obvious advantage of providing detailed visual information relating to the context of an utterance, including important paralinguistic information such as gestion and facial expressions.

(2) Collecting clinically elicited samples. Clinically elicited samples, different from naturally occurring samples, are collected specifically for the purpose of research. There are

two broad types of clinically elicited data: general samples and focused samples. In the case of a general sample, the elicitation instrument is designed to provide a context for learners to speak and write in the L2 in a purposeful manner. In the case of a focused sample, the elicitation instrument is designed to induce learners to use some specific linguistic feature when speaking or writing. In the former case, there is no attempt to pre-determine what linguistic forms to be used by learners whereas in the latter case there is.

Tasks are important in the elicitation of general samples of learner language. A task can be authentic or pedagogic. By "authentic", it means the task corresponds to some real-world activity. By "pedagogic", it means the task is only fulfilled in an instructional setting. Tasks can be used to gain both oral and written samples. Some common types of tasks used in SLA research are: a) tasks that involve some kind of gap, b) open role-plays, c) text reconstruction, d) picture narratives, and e) oral interviews.

(3) Experimentally elicited samples. What we get from experimental elicitation is the constrained constructed responses; that is the production of short L2 segments within highly controlled linguistic contexts. As for many linguistic features, experimental elicitation may serve as the only way of obtaining sufficient data. However, experimental elicitation may only tell us what learners can produce under experimental conditions and may or may not reflect what they can do under more natural conditions of language use.

7. 1. 1. 3   Verbal reports

Verbal reports can serve the double purpose of providing samples of learner language and important information about "learners" subjective theories, which can assist in providing explanations of L2 acquisition. Verbal report methods include self-report, self-observation, self-revelation and self-assessment. It should be noted that there is some disagreement over the validity of verbal reports, with some researchers arguing that much of language learning is unconscious and thus not reportable by learners. Therefore, it is advisable to combine two or more self-report methods when collecting verbal report data.

7. 1. 2   The longitudinal data/study

A longitudinal study, which is often called a case study in the SLA field, involves observing the development of language performance. It usually refers to the spontaneous speech of a subject when the speech data are collected at periodic intervals over a span of

time, for example, weekly, biweekly, or monthly. A longitudinal study has the following characteristics:

First, the data in most longitudinal studies come from spontaneous speech. It is not that the researcher fails to set up a conversation to generate a specific type of data; it is that longitudinal studies do not fit into the experimental paradigm, which consists of a control group, an experimental group, a counter-balancing group, and so on. Relevant to the spontaneous speech data collection is an important methodological question: How can one generate a particular type of data through spontaneous speech? It is not always possible that certain designated interlanguage structures will appear. However, during the course of data collection, the researcher can ask certain kinds of questions that will likely lead to specific language forms. For instance, if one were interested in learners' development of the past tense, they could ask them to describe an event that took place on the previous day. In such a way, the needed data can be obtained.

Second, longitudinal data often involve detail provided on a learner's speech, on the setting in which the speech event took place, and on other relevant information relating to analysis of the data, such as who participated in the conversation and what their relationship was with the subject. In other words, while a researcher is doing a longitudinal study, he or she often gives a detailed account of the background information on the object of investigation.

Third, analyses of longitudinal data are often the descriptive qualitative comments or narrative expositions. Although the quantification of data may not be the goal of such studies, the research may report the frequency of occurrence in some form. Longitudinal data are highly useful in determining developmental trends as well as in interpreting a variety of social factors and input influences on the learner's speech.

Now let us look at Lardiere's (2007) study of Patty as an example to see how a longitudinal study was carried out. Patty was born in Indonesia in 1953 but was of Chinese origin. In 1969, Patty left Indonesia for the Chinese mainland and lived in China for two years. Then she moved to Chinese Hong Kong, where English was the primary language of instruction. When she finished high school she worked in an import-export company in Hong Kong, and rarely spoke English there. She arrived in the United States in 1976 at the age of 22. She lived with her Vietnamese fiancé's family and began college-level study and later took a waitressing job. In 1985 she separated from her husband and began to live by herself but married again in 1989 to a native English speaker.

Lardiere collected naturalistic production data from Patty on three occasions. The first recording was made in 1986 when Patty had been living in the U. S. for about ten years. The second and the third recordings were made two months apart in 1995. Lardiere also collected written samples from email messages. Lardiere examined a number of grammatical features in Patty's English speech and writing, including finiteness, the acquisition of past tense, clausal word order and movement, and nominal phrases. This constitutes perhaps the most exhaustive account of an L2 learner's acquisition of grammar currently available (Ellis, 2013: 15 – 16).

It was found that Patty had not achieved a native-like grammar by the end of the study. But there was a clear difference in her ability to use morphophonological aspects of English grammar and her ability to employ English syntactical constructions. The former continued to be problematic (for example, in the frequent omission or over use of inflectional markers on verbs and nouns) while the latter were surprisingly target-like (for example, perfect knowledge of pronominal case marking, near perfect use of possessive, and accurate placement of adverbs). A further finding was that Patty's written English was more accurate than her spoken English. The results suggest that three questions should be answered. ①Why did Patty fail to achieve accuracy in the use of morphological features despite the fact that she had been in the U. S. for 10 years and that she had experienced favorable acquisition circumstances? ② Why was there such a difference between the morphological and syntactical aspects? ③Why was her written English more accurate than her spoken English?

Lardiere gave a number of answers to the above questions. First, although Patty's L1 may have played a role in her acquisition of English grammar, it cannot fully account for the findings of the case study. Instead, Patty's continued variability in the use of morphological features (despite highly favorable conditions for learning) might be explained by the age factor. Thus Patty failed to achieve full accuracy in the use of features like plural -s because she did not begin to learn English until her adolescent years. To account for Patty's differential acquisition of morphophonology and syntax, Lardiere appeals to the notion of modularity in grammatical systems, suggesting that some domains are inherently more susceptible to failure than others, possibly because they are not governed by the "language faculty" that governs L2 acquisition as it does L1 acquisition. The difference in accuracy in

Patty's spoken and written English was not addressed. This is perhaps because Patty possesses metalinguistic knowledge of English grammar and was able to use it more easily when writing than when speaking.

The longitudinal data is useful in determining the learner's developmental trends and in interpreting different social constraints and input influences on the learner's speech. However, the longitudinal study also has weaknesses. First, a major disadvantage is the time involved. Conducting a case study requires much time in collecting data at regular intervals, and in transcribing the speech into the text. Besides, a speech event often takes place in particular social, personal, and physical settings, so much detailed work must be involved. Second, a longitudinal study is short of generalization. Because a longitudinal study is often limited in the number of subjects investigated, it is difficult to draw a general result. It is also difficult to know whether the results obtained can only be applied to the one or two subjects studied, or whether they are characteristic of a large number of subjects.

There exists another difficulty with the longitudinal data, which is often spontaneously collected, and which is perhaps the most serious one. That is, when learners produce a linguistic form, it is hard to probe their knowledge any further than what they have produced spontaneously. This is true if the researcher has not collected the data or if the researcher has not generated particular hypotheses and are not inclined to gather information about specific forms of speech. For example, if a learner, in a specific set of spontaneously elicited data, only produces the present tense of verbs, does it mean that this is all that the learner knows? Obviously, we cannot interpret the data only on the basis of what is present. This is because we can never be sure that absence of forms means lack of knowledge of the forms.

7. 1. 3　The cross-sectional data/study

In addition to the longitudinal type of data, there is a second type of data-elicitation method which involves cross-sectional studies. In a cross-sectional study, the linguistic performance of a large number of subjects is observed, and the performance data are usually collected at only one session. Besides, the data are usually elicited by asking subjects to perform some verbal tasks, such as having subjects describe a picture.

The cross-sectional studies are different from longitudinal studies in a number of ways. The first one lies in time. Cross-sectional data are often gathered from a large number of subjects at a single point in time, so that we are able to see a slice of development, which is used to piece together the actual development. Second, unlike case studies, which are based mainly on spontaneous speech, cross-sectional data are often based on controlled output. That is, the data collected by a researcher are based on a particular research hypothesis. The data come from the subjects' performance on some pre-designated tasks. The third point is the type of background information. In contrast to longitudinal studies, the participants in cross-sectional studies are not identified individually, nor is the detailed descriptive information supplied. The background information in a cross-sectional study is likely to be presented in tabular form, as is shown in Table 7.1. Fourth, the results in a cross-sectional research are more quantitative and less descriptive than in longitudinal studies, and the statistical analyses and their interpretation are the integral parts of the research report.

Table 7.1 An Example of Cross-sectional Data Presentation (Gass and Selinker, 2008: 56)

Language Background	No. of Participants	Gender	Age	Proficiency
Arabic	24	13F; 11M	23 ~ 26	8Beg/8Int/8Adv
Spanish	24	12F; 12M	23 ~ 28	12Beg/12Adv
Japanese	24	11F; 13M	21 ~ 23	20Beg/4Adv

An advantage of cross-sectional data is that the results are, in contrast with longitudinal data, more likely to be generalized to a wider group of subjects since there are a large number of subjects involved in such a study. The disadvantage is that there is often no detailed information about the subjects and the linguistic environment in which production was elicited.

7.1.4 Mixture of research paradigms

As discussed above, longitudinal studies often contain descriptive, or qualitative data; cross-sectional studies often involve quantitative, or statistical measures. However, it does not mean one type of research is only associated with one type of approach. Statistical analyses on longitudinal data can be easily conducted, and descriptive analyses of cross-sectional data can also be provided. It is wrong to assume that longitudinal data cannot be generalized. A researcher may be able to put together a profile of learners based on many

longitudinal studies.

So, why would a researcher choose one type of data-collection method over another? This is decided by the relationship between a research question and research methodology. There may not always be a one-to-one relationship; certain types of questions and certain types of external pressures would lead one into choosing one kind of methodology over another. For instance, if we want to collect information about how nonnative speakers learn to apologize in an L2, we could observe learners over a period of time and note those instances of apologizing. In comparison, we could use a cross-sectional approach by setting up a situation and asking a large number of L2 speakers what they would say. The difference is that the former waits until it happens while the latter forces production.

It would be inappropriate to think that there are rigid boundaries between these paradigms; it would also be improper to think of longitudinal studies in connection with naturalistic data collection. A longitudinal study can be conducted with a large number of subjects. Data can also be collected longitudinally using an experimental format. A mixture of the two approaches is possible. For example, Dato (Larsen-Freeman and Long, 2000: 13) designed a study of the acquisition of Spanish by English-speaking children using three groups of English speakers with varying levels of exposure to Spanish, as shown in Table 7. 2. At the beginning of the study, Group A were exposed to Spanish for one month, while Group C had three months of exposure. The data were being collected four times from each of the three different groups. The data collected at any one time constitute a cross-sectional study; all the data for a particular group provide a longitudinal view.

Table 7. 2　An Example of a Mixed Paradigm (Larsen-Freeman and Long, 2000: 13)

	Data collection times (months)				
	Group	Time 1	Time 2	Time 3	Time 4
English children's length of exposure to Spanish	A	1	2	3	4
	B	2	3	4	5
	C	3	4	5	6

Another example is a study on relative clause studies (Gass, 1979a, 1979b). Gass gathered data from seventeen subjects at six points in time, at monthly intervals. Thus, the study can be regarded as longitudinal. On the other hand, given the experimental nature of the study, which involved forced production of relative clauses, it is more likely to be a cross-sectional study. In a word, the categories we have discussed are only suggestive. There are no rigid boundaries between them. Therefore, in categorizing research, it cam be flexible.

7.1.5 Linguistic production data elicitation

In second language acquisition research today, there are a number of data elicitation procedures which are employed in collecting L2 data. Larsen-Freeman and Long (2000: 27 – 30) have briefly summarized those data collection methods. Although some of the data elicitation methods have been mentioned in the previous section, we still think it necessary to present them, here and now, in a rough order from those that have more control over the subjects' performance to those that have less control.

7.1.5.1 Reading aloud

This method of data elicitation has been used in studies of pronunciation in an L2, in which the subjects are asked to read aloud word lists, sentences or passages which contain a great number of particular sounds in a representative environment. The reading is often recorded for future analysis.

7.1.5.2 Structured exercises

Researchers ask L2 learners to perform some grammatical manipulation in order to study the subjects' performance with regard to particular morphemes or syntactic patterns. The exercise types can be in various forms, such as transformation exercises, blank-filling with the correct form, sentence-rewriting, sentence-combining, and multiple choice.

7.1.5.3 Completion task

This task may take different forms. One form is that subjects listen to or read the beginning of a sentence and are asked to complete it using their own words. For example, this method can be used to investigate learners' mastery of infinitive and gerund complements. The researcher may give the learner the beginning of a sentence including a verb which could take either of the two complements. The learners are asked to complete the sentence. A second form of the task is the completion of a text. Subjects are asked to read a written dialogue and a brief summary statement. Then, they are asked to complete the dialogue. Another form is an SLA completion task: the Second Language Oral Production English (SLOPE Test). This test is a parody of the Berko morphology test, which was invented by Berko (1958). He gave a child a nonsense word, e. g. "wug", and then showed the child a picture of a "wug". Next the child was shown a picture of two wugs and was told: "This is a picture of…" If the child completed the sentence successfully, the researcher could determine that the child had the ability to extend morphological rules to new cases. That means he has acquired the plural rule for English nouns.

7.1.5.4 Elicited imitation

The usual way of doing elicited imitation is to read or to play a taped reading of a particular set of sentences, which contain examples of the structure under study, to the subject, who is asked to imitate each sentence after it is read. This is based on the assumption that if the sentence is long enough, the subject will be pushed beyond the limit of his short-term memory, and consequently the subject will be unable to repeat the sentence by rote. What the subject has to do is to understand the sentence and to reconstruct it using his or her own grammar. In this way, the natural data could be gained.

7.1.5.5 Elicited translation

Subjects are given a sentence in their first language and then asked to translate it into the second language or vice versa. Researchers believe that such a method requires both the decoding of the stimulus sentence and the encoding of the translation. Collected in this way, the subjects' performance is close to natural speech production.

7.1.5.6 Guided composition

In response to some organized stimuli, subjects may be asked to produce an oral or written composition. Stimuli may take different forms. For example, they may be some picture sequences which tell a story; they may also be an arrangement of content words provided for the subjects to write a composition.

7. 1. 5. 7   Question and answer

A very common way of collecting SLA data is to conduct a question-and-answer session. Subjects look at a picture or a sequence of pictures and answer the questions which are designed to elicit particular structures under study.

7. 1. 5. 8   Reconstruction

This method is also called "story retelling" and "paraphrase recall". Subjects read, listen to a story or watch a film, and then are asked to retell or reconstruct the story orally or in writing.

7. 1. 5. 9   Communication games

Subjects contribute their data by participating a game designed by a researcher. For example, in the research conducted by Lightbown et al (1980), each subject was given ten sets of cards. Each set consisted of four pictures which minimally differed from each other. The subject was asked to choose one of the four and to describe it to the researcher so the researcher would know which picture the subject had selected. The pictures were specifically designed to provide contexts in which the structures under study would be most likely to occur.

7. 1. 5. 10   Role play

Role play may be used as a useful means to study learners' pragmatic competence. In order to determine how the subject will behave, researchers must recognize the importance of various relevant contextual features, such as the status of speaker and listener, urgency of the message, speaker-listener relationship, the sexes and ages between speaker and listener. In a role play, the speech act can be kept constant, but the contextual features vary. In such a way, many dimensions of a learner's pragmatic competence can be explored.

7. 1. 5. 11   Oral interview

There are different ways to elicit data using oral interview. Some exercises exert control over the topics with the intention that they can steer the conversation in a way that learners will be encouraged to produce a certain structure under study. Other researchers acknowledge that an oral interview is constrained in some ways, and allow learners freedom in choosing what topics should be discussed. In this way, it is hoped that subjects will tend to become involved in the subject matter of the conversation, producing more spontaneous speeches.

7. 1. 5. 12 Free conversation

Free conversation may perhaps be the least controlled of all elicitation methods. Except establishing a topic, a researcher exerts no intervention upon the learners. It is true that a topic itself can encourage the production of certain structures rather than others. For instance, if a researcher wants to investigate how well the learners have mastered past tense morphemes, he may require that they have to relate the past experience in their writing. This may give the researcher sufficient data to study the acquisition of how the learners expressed past time.

7. 1. 6 Non-linguistic information elicitation

In addition to the above linguistic data elicitation devices, there are also some non-linguistic information collection devices in second language acquisition research. Studies investigating attitude, motivation, learning styles and personality characteristics often use non-linguistic data, whose elicitation instruments are borrowed from the field of psychology. In this part, we will introduce a few non-linguistic data elicitation methods: questionnaires, interview, and diaries.

7. 1. 6. 1 Questionnaires

Questionnaires may be one of the most widely-used information elicitation methods in social science. Questionnaires are often used to obtain information about attitudes learners who may have toward language learning. The question types that can be asked are numerous. Gardner and Lambert have listed a sampling of the types of questions, which are presented below (Gass and Selinker, 2008: 70 – 71):

I am studying French because:

_____*a. I think it will someday be useful in getting a good job.*

_____*b. I think it will help me to better understand French people and their way of life.*

_____ *c. It will allow me to meet and converse with more and varied people.*

_____ *d. A knowledge of two languages will make me a better educated person.*

_____ *e. Any other personal reason.*

Another kind of question involves completing a sentence:

a. One thing I like about this activity is _____

b. I found this activity _____

Attitudinal ratings are also used in research on motivation and attitudes. Respondents are given polar opposites and asked to judge their impressions of a group of people on an evaluation scale:

a. interesting ____ : ____ : ____ : ____ : ____ : ____ : ____ *boring*

b. prejudiced ____ : ____ : ____ : ____ : ____ : ____ : ____ *unprejudiced*

c. happy ____ : ____ : ____ : ____ : ____ : ____ : ____ *sad*

d. hardworking ____ : ____ : ____ : ____ : ____ : ____ : ____ *lazy*

7. 1. 6. 2 Interviews

Interviews are often conducted orally and one-on-one. They can either have fixed questions or they can be less structured, which allows the interviewer to tailor the questions according to the responses of the interviewee.

7. 1. 6. 3 Diaries

Diaries refer to the journals that a learner keeps, either by his own choice or following a teacher's assignment. Diaries are often a good source of information about attitudes and motivation and provide a more open-ended forum for such information without the constraints of specific questions.

7. 2 Data Analysis and Interpretation

A good understanding of the process of second language acquisition is gained by hands-

on experience in data analysis and data interpretation. In this part we will discuss how to analyze and interpret data. In analyzing and interpreting data, we may follow a few steps:

First, know your purpose of data analysis. For example, a supposed purpose of data analysis is to describe the ESL learners' interlanguage patterns of plural usage.

Second, collect data and focus on the noun phrases (those italicized noun phrases) used by these learners. For example, the following data are the utterances collected from three adult native speakers of Cairene Arabic, ranging from intermediate to advanced speakers of English, after they arrived in the United States of America. The data were elicited from compositions and conversations.

(1) There are also *two deserts*.

(2) I bought *a couple of towel*.

(3) So, when I like to park my car, there is no place to put it, and *how many tickets* took.

(4) There *is many kind of way* you make Baklawa.

(5) *The streets* run from east to west, *the avenues* from north to south.

(6) I go to university *four days* a week.

(7) Just a *few month* he will finish from his studies.

(8) Egypt shares *its boundaries* with the Mediterranean.

(9) There is *a lot* of *mosquito*.

(10) *Many people* have *ideas* about Jeddah and other cities located in Saudi Arabia.

(11) When he complete *nine month*…

(12) He can spend *100 years* here in America.

(13) There are about *one and half-million inhabitant* in Jeddah.

(14) *How many month or years* have been in his mind?

(15) There are *many tents—and goats* running around.

(16) There are *two mountains*.

(17) *How many hour*?

(18) There are more than *200, 000 telephone lines*.

(19) Every country had *three or four kind of bread*.

(Gass and Selinker, 2008: 41 –42)

Third, categorize the data according to whether they are English-like or non-English-like patterns of plural usage. For example, the noun phrase in sentence 1, *two deserts*, is English-like, but the noun phrase in sentence 2, *a couple of towel*, is non-English-like. In categorizing the data, make sure whether the choice is clear or not. Sometimes data are often ambiguous.

Fourth, make a list of sentences according to the criteria of English-like or non-English-like. That is, a sentence, which contains an -s plural marker on the plural noun, is English-like; if there is no plural marker on the noun, the sentence is non-English-like. For example, by studying the data, it can be found that some sentences are English-like and some others are not, as is shown in Table 7.3.

Table 7.3　Possible Categorization of Plurals in Arabic-English Interlanguage
(Gass and Selinker, 2008: 43)

English-like	Non-English-like
1. two deserts 5. the streets, the avenues 6. four days 8. its boundaries 10. many people, ideas 12. 100 years 15. many tents—and goats 16. two mountains 18. 200, 000 telephone lines	2. a couple of towel 3. how many ticket 4. many kind of way 7. a few month 9. a lot of mosquito 11. nine month 13. one and half-million inhabitant 14. how many month or years 17. how many hour 19. three or four kind of bread

There is no doubt that the analysis of the sentences on the left column is clear. Through a further study of the data on the right column, we may find the analysis of sentence 14 is not clear. It contains both a singular and plural noun. The form *month* is non-English-like while the form *years* is English-like. As can be seen, there is interlanguage variation in the same sentence. Therefore, there is a choice in terms of analysis. One is that when any element of the plural phrase is non-English-like, then the whole phrase is non-English-like. Another choice is to put it in a third category— "ambiguous". Thus, there emerges

another way of data categorization, as shown in Table 7. 4.

Table 7. 4 Possible Categorization of Plurals in Arabic-English Interlanguage (ibid)

English-like	Non-English-like	Ambiguous
1. two deserts 5. the streets, the avenues 6. four days 8. its boundaries 10. many people, ideas 12. 100 years 15. many tents—and goats 16. two mountains 18. 200, 000 telephone lines	2. a couple of towel 3. how many ticket 4. many kind of way 7. a few month 9. a lot of mosquito 11. nine month 13. one and half-million inhabitant 17. how many hour 19. three or four kind of bread	14. how many month or years

Fifth, set up a hypothesis. A close look at the categorized data will bring us such a finding: there are frequently quantifying phrases, such as *kind of*, and *how many*, in those non-English-like phrases. Thus, an initial hypothesis might be formed:

Whenever there is a quantifying phrase or a non-numerical quantifying word before the noun, there is no overt marking on the plural of that noun. (ibid: 44)

Sixth, test the initial hypothesis. From the data of non-English-like phrases in Table 7. 3, we can easily find out that phrases 2, 3, 4, 7, 9, 13, 17, 19 all support the above generalization, though sentence 13 is written differently from the TL form (*one and a half-million*). Thus the above hypothesis seems to be supported by these data. However, we have still not accounted for all the data. When taking all those data into consideration, we now can formulate another interlanguage hypothesis:

Mark all plural nouns with -s except those that are preceded by a quantifying phrase or a non-numerical quantifying word. (ibid)

Finally, consider the exceptions. Despite the above hypothesis, there are still possible exceptions to deal with. ①One exception is sentence 11. According to the rule, it should be *months*. This exception can be explained by the difficulty in pronunciation, that is, the /nths/ cluster at the end of the word. This may be the result of simplification. Even many native English speakers simplify this cluster by pronouncing the end of the word /ns/ rather than /nths/. The Arabic speakers just simplify it in their own way. ②Sentence 14 is also an exception. We have already discussed that the analysis is not clear. It might be that the learners have created a special rule that relates plural marking to the type of conjunction. This is not clear yet since one example cannot lead us to draw such a conclusion. ③Still another exception is sentence 10, which may also be rather ambiguous. It could be a special "irrelevant" category in that we can view this as an unanalyzed chunk. It could also be said to support the hypothesis, if we believe that the learner categorizes it as a non-plural form.

Dealing with exceptions is as important as dealing with the majority of the data. If exceptions are in sufficient quantity, they may suggest that the initial hypothesis is incorrect, or they may reflect another rule at play. Here comes an important question: when you have achieved the best possible analysis with the limited data at your disposal, and when there is still some uncertainty, what further data would you like from the learners to test your hypothesis? One type has been mentioned regarding sentence 13: more data that differentiate oral from written production, because the interlanguage rules constructed may differ along this dimension. Another type of data has been suggested. If you are trying to understand an individual's IL generalization, you must only consider that individual's utterances. On the other hand, if the data are gathered from different subjects, counterexamples will be expected to show up. Therefore, for some purposes, we need to gather data where plural phrases are marked individual by individual, because large individual differences sometimes characterize second language acquisition.

Assignment

1. Questions for self-study.

(1) How can second language data be categorized?

(2) What is a longitudinal study? What are its characteristics?

(3) What is a cross-sectional study? How does it differ from a longitudinal study?

（4）How can linguistic data be elicited? Give a few examples.

（5）How can non-linguistic information be collected? Give a few examples.

2. Fill in the blanks in the following passage.

Free Conversation

Free conversation may perhaps be the _____ controlled of all elicitation methods. Except establishing a topic, a researcher exerts no _____upon the learners. It is true that a topic itself can encourage the _____of certain structures rather than others. For instance, if a researcher wants to investigate how well the learners have mastered past tense morphemes, he may require that they have to relate the _____ experience in their writing. This may give the researcher sufficient data for him or her to study the _____of how the learners express past time.

3. Open discussion for pair or group work.

（1）Study an article from a journal which deals with longitudinal data, and answer the following questions：

—What is the time frame of data collection?

—How often are the data collected?

—How much detail is given about the participants?

—In what environment does learning take place?

—What method is used in collecting the data?

（2）Suppose you were to design a second language acquisition study to investigate each of the following topics, what method would you use?

—English articles

—The structure of tense/aspect

—Fluency

Appendix 1   A Glossary of English Terms in This Book

Access to UG（通达 UG）The claim that the innate LAD is operative in second language learning and it constrains the learners' grammars.

Accessibility hierarchy（递进阶）A series of relative clause types in which the presence of one type suggests the presence of other types on the hierarchy.

Accommodation theory（调和理论）A social-psychological model of language use proposed by Giles to account for the dynamic nature of variation within the course of a conversation. Speakers can converge or diverge.

Acculturation model（文化移入模式）A model of second language acquisition which consists of social and affective variables, and which is based on the assumption that second language learners need to adapt to the target language culture in order to gain a successful acquisition.

Accuracy order（准确度顺序）It is believed by some researchers that the accuracy in using a grammatical feature indicates that it is acquired first; less accurate use of another grammatical feature indicates that it is acquired later.

Acquisition order（习得顺序）See Unit 2 for definition.

Acquisition-learning hypothesis（习得—学得假说）One of the hypotheses in the Monitor Model. See Unit 3 for definition.

Affective filter（情感过滤）One of the five hypothesis in the Monitor Model. It is claimed that affect is an important factor affecting the learning process. If the affective filter is up, learning will be difficult; if it is lowered, learning becomes easy.

Affective strategies（情感策略）A type of learning strategy. See Unit 4 for more information.

Anxiety（焦虑）One of the affective factors that have been found to affect L2 acquisition. Different types of anxiety have been identified: trait anxiety, state anxiety, situation-specific anxiety.

Apperceived input （统觉输入） See Unit 4 for detailed definition.

Aptitude （学能） See Unit 4 for definition.

Associative memory capacity （联想记忆能力） See Unit 4 for definition.

Automatic processing （自动加工） A kind of processing that occurs quickly, and does not consume, or consumes little amount of attention and effort.

Avoidance （回避） This is the result of L1 influence. Learners are likely to avoid structures or words they find difficult as a result of differences between their native language and the target language.

Backsliding （倒退） A phenomenon in which L2 learners are likely to manifest correct target-language forms on some occasions but deviant forms on other occasions. Backsliding involves the use of a rule belonging to an earlier stage of development. It can occur when learners are under some pressure.

Behaviourism （行为主义） A school of psychology, according to which learning is regarded as the formation of habits. Habits are formed when a learner is confronted with stimuli which lead to responses, which are reinforced by rewards or corrected. Behaviourism emphasizes environmental factors in opposition to internal, mental factors.

Bilingualism （双语） The use of two languages by an individual or a speech community. There are various types of bilingualism. In the case of additive bilingualism, a speaker adds a second language without any loss of competence to the first language. This can lead to balanced bilingualism. In the case of subtractive bilingualism, the addition of a second language leads to gradual erosion of competence in the first language.

Broca's area （布罗卡区） The area of the brain located at the base of the motor cortex in the left hemisphere that controls the production of spoken language.

Cognitive ability （认知能力） See Unit 4 for detailed definition.

Cognitive mechanism 认知机制 It refers to the mechanism in the mind that enables learners to extract information about the L2 from input and build their own language system.

Competence （语言能力） It refers to knowledge of language, or the linguistic capacity of a fluent speaker of a language.

Competition model （CM） （竞争模式） A functional model of language use and language acquisition. It views the task of language learning as that of discovering the particular form-function mappings that characterize the target language. These mappings are viewed as having varying "strengths" in different languages.

Comprehended input （被理解输入） The language that a learner understands.

Comprehension （理解） Understanding.

Connectionism （连通主义） A theory of cognition which draws inspiration from the way the billions of neutrons in the brain are interconnected in complex ways to produce a network of associations. According to connectionism, the complexity of language emerges from associative learning processes being exposed to a massive and complex environment.

Consciousness-raising （增强意识） It is used by some researchers with much the same meaning as "formal instruction". Rod Ellis used this term with a narrower meaning. "Consciousness raising" is contrasted with "practice". It refers to attempts to help learners understand a grammatical structure and learn it as explicit knowledge.

Constructions （构式） The recurrent patterns of linguistic elements that serve some well-defined linguistic function. They can be at sentence level or below. Emergentist account of L2 acquisition views acquisition as a process of internalizing and subsequently analyzing constructions.

Contrastive analysis hypothesis （CAH）（对比分析假说） The prediction that the similarities between two languages do not require learning and that the differences are what should be learned.

Controlled processing （控制加工） A kind of processing which occurs when a learner is accessing information that is new or rare or complex. It requires mental effort and takes attention away from other controlled processes.

Co-reference （共指） The situation in which two expressions refer to the same person, event, or thing. For example, in the sentence *Mike told me a story about himself*, *Mike* and *himself* are co-referential because they refer to the same person.

Corrective feedback （纠正反馈） A feedback to a learner that his utterance is incorrect.

Critical period hypothesis （关键期假说） A theory that in child language development there is a period of time after which successful language learning cannot take place.

Cross-sectional data （典型数据） See Unit 7 for definition.

Deductive processing （演绎加工） See Unit 4 for definition.

Definitizer （限定词） A word that definitizes another word.

Ego permeability（自我渗透性）L2 learners may be uneasy because they perceive their L1 to have fixed and rigid boundaries. Or they may feel free if they perceive their L1 to have permeable and flexible boundaries.

Emergentism（浮现主义）In the context of SLA, it refers to theories that assume that language use and acquisition emerge from basic processes that are not specific to language.

Error（差错）Incorrect forms learners produce.

Error analysis（差错分析）A procedure for analyzing L2 data that begins with errors made by learners, and then tries to explain why there are errors.

Explicit instruction（显性教学）Explicit instruction involves "some sort of rule being thought about during the learning process". Learners are encouraged to develop metalinguistic awareness of the rule. It can be achieved by means of deductive or inductive instruction.

Explicit knowledge（显性知识）Knowledge about language that the learner is aware of and can talk about to others.

Extraversion/introversion（外向/内向）These terms describe the dimension of personality which has been most thoroughly interested in SLA research. They reflect a continuum: at one end are learners who are sociable and risk-takers, while at the other end are learners who are quiet and avoid excitement.

Field dependence/independence（场依赖/场独立）Each of them constitutes one kind of cognitive style. Field-dependent learners are believed to operate holistically, while field-independent learners operate analytically.

Final state（最终状态）See Unit 3 for relative information.

Focus on form（关注形式）A type of form-focused instruction; it overtly draws students' attention to linguistic elements as they arise incidentally in lessons whose overriding focus is on meaning or communication.

Focus on meaning（关注意义）A kind of instruction that focuses on understanding of meaning instead of linguistic forms.

Form-focused instruction（**FFI**）（关注形式教学）It involves some attempt to focus learners' attention on specific properties of the L2 so that they will learn them. Different types of form-focused instruction can be distinguished, including explicit instruction and implicit instruction.

Fossilization （僵化）Incomplete L2 acquisition. Progress in a certain aspect of the L2 stops，and the learner's language becomes fixed at an intermediate state.

Frequency of input （输入频率）See Unit 4 for detailed definition.

Functional practicing （功能训练）Practice by which learners make attempts to maximize exposure to language through communication.

Functional typology （功能类型学）See Unit 3 for definition.

Global error （结构错误）In the learner's interlanguage，there may be an error that violates the overall structure of a sentence. It may bring problems in understanding the meaning of the whole sentence. For example，the error in the sentence *That computer you want to use now is impossible* is a global one.

Grammatical sensitivity （语法敏感性）See Unit 4 for definition.

Implicit instruction （隐性教学）It is directed at enabling learners to infer rules without awareness. It contrasts with explicit instruction.

Implicit knowledge （隐性知识）Knowledge about language that the learner is not aware of.

Impulsivity （冲动）A kind of cognitive style as opposed to reflectivity. When one is impulsive，he tends to make a quick or gambling guess at an answer to a problem.

Inductive language learning ability （归纳语言学习能力）See Unit 4 for definition.

Inductive processing （归纳加工）See Unit 4 for definition.

Inflectional morphemes （曲折词素）Morphemes that serve a grammatical function，not creating a new word，but only a different form of the same word.

Information processing （信息加工）See Unit 4 for definition.

Initial state （起始状态）The starting point of learning a language.

Input （输入）The language that is available to the learner；the exposure to target language.

Input modification （输入调节）The input which is modified for the convenience of L2 learning.

Input-based instruction （基于输入的教学）Opposed to output-based instruction. See Unit 6 for definition.

Instrumental motivation （工具性动机）See Unit 4 for definition.

Intake （吸收）The process in which part of input is internalized by learners and goes into temporary memory. Intake may subsequently be accommodated in the learner's interlanguage system.

Integration（整合）The process that takes place after intake, which has two forms, either development of grammar or storage.

Integrative motivation（融入性动机）See Unit 4 for relevant information.

Intention-reading skill（意图—阅读技能）A human-unique form of social learning. Early skills of intention-reading emerge near the end of the first year of life. Intention-reading skill serves as a prerequisite of language learning.

Interaction hypothesis（交互假说）See Unit 5 for detailed definition.

Interactional modification（交互调节）It occurs when some kind of communication problem arises and the participants engage in interactional work to overcome it. It takes the form of discourse functions such as comprehension checks, requests for clarification, and requests for confirmation.

Interactionist learning theory（交互学习理论）This theory emphasizes the importance of both linguistic environment and the learners' internal cognitive mechanisms in explaining second language acquisition. It is held that learning results from an interaction between learners' mental abilities and the linguistic input.

Interlanguage（中介语）The language system that is produced at an intermediate stage of second language learning, and that is different from both the first language and the target language.

Interlanguage pragmatics（中介语语用学）See Unit 2 for detailed definition.

Interlocutor（对话者）A person with whom one is speaking.

Internalization（内化）The process in which grammar has been accepted as part of a learner's own language system.

Intrinsic motivation（内在动机）See Unit 4 for relevant information.

Investment（投资）A metaphor in Bonny Peirce's socio-cultural view of SLA. It holds that one who learns an L2 participates in a kind of "struggle" and "investment". The learner is a combatant and fights to assert himself; he is an investor and expects a good return on his efforts.

Language acquisition device（**LAD**）（语言习得机制）A language faculty in human minds that constrains and guides the language acquisition process.

Lateralization（脑部偏侧性）It refers to the specialization of the two halves of the brain. When a child's brain matures, different functions became lateralized to the left or right hemisphere. See 4. 1 for detailed definition.

ENG

Local binding（局部约束）A principle which states an expression in a dependent clause refers to another expression inside the clause. For example, in the sentence *Tom knew Gary blamed himself*, *himself* refers to *Gary*, not *Tom*; it is locally "bound" to *Gary*.

Local error（局部错误）In a learner's interlanguage, a sentence may have one or two grammatical errors, which may not affect communication. Such an error is called a local error. For example, in the sentence *He standed beside me*, *standed* is a local error.

Long-distance binding（远距离约束）It refers to a situation in which an expression co-refers to a subject in another clause. "Long distance binding" is prohibited in English, but is allowed in Japanese. For example, in the English sentence *Tom knew Gary blamed himself*, *himself* is only locally bound to Gary. But in Japanese, *himself* is bound to *Tom*, as well as *Gary*.

Longitudinal data（纵向数据）Data which are collected from one or more learners over a long period of time in order to gather information about change over time.

Mediation（中介）See Unit 5 for detailed definition.

Mentalism（心灵主义）A psychological, as well as a philosophical term picked up and developed by Chomsky, which describes the internal language mechanism that provides the basis for the creative aspect of language development and use.

Mimicking（模仿）A behaviourist way of learning, by imitating the way someone speaks.

Minimalist program（最简方案）A theory of grammar introduced by Chomsky (1995) as an advance on Government/Binding theory, according to which grammars should make use of the minimal theoretical apparatus necessary to provide a characterization of linguistic phenomena that meets the criterion of descriptive adequacy. This goal is motivated in part by the desire to minimize the acquisition burden faced by children and account for the fact that children will acquire any language they are exposed to.

Miscommunication（交际失败）Failure to make oneself understood, or to understand others in communication.

Mistake（错误）Nonsystematic errors which are correctable by learners. See Unit 2 for more information.

Monitor model（监察模式）A model of second language acquisition based on the concept that learners have two systems: acquisition system and learning system; the latter monitors the former.

Morphology（形态学）The study of word structure.

Multilingualism（多语现象）The use of three or more languages by an individual or within a speech community. Frequently, multilingual people do not have equal control over all the languages they know and also use the languages for different purposes.

Natural order hypothesis（自然顺序假说）One of the hypotheses in the Monitor Model. See Unit 3 for definition.

Negative evidence（负面证据）Information which is provided to the learner, informing him or her that a form is incorrect.

Non-interface（非接口）The claim that explicit knowledge is different from implicit knowledge, and that one type of knowledge cannot be converted directly into the other type.

Output（输出）Produced spoken or written language.

Output-based instruction（基于输出的教学）Opposed to input-based instruction. See Unit 6 for definition.

Overgeneralization（过度概括）Extensions of some general rule to items not covered by the rule in the target language. For example, errors like 'comed' produced by L2 learners belong to overgeneralization.

Overproduction（过度产出）One of the results of L1 influence. L2 learners tend to produce too many certain kinds of structures, which is like their L1, in their output.

Parameter setting（参数设定）Based on the theory of Universal Grammar. It refers to the process by which children determine what setting of a parameter is appropriate for the one they are learning. In SLA, it is considered parameter-resetting, since learners already have parameter-settings initially established for their first language.

Pattern-finding skill（类型发现技能）See Unit 4 for detailed definition.

Performance（语言使用）Opposed to competence. It refers to the actual use of language in real communications.

Phonemic coding ability（音素编码能力）See Unit 4 for definition.

Phonology（音系学）The study of sound system of a language. It is about how the particular sounds contrast in each language to form an integrated system for encoding information and how such system differs from one language to another.

Pidginization（皮钦语化）The development of a grammatically reduced form of a target language in SLA. It is usually a temporary stage in language learning. The learners' interlanguage may have a limited system of auxiliary verbs, simplified question and negative forms, and reduced rules for tense, number, and other grammatical categories.

Positive evidence（正面证据）Evidence that something is possible in the language being learned. For example, if a learner of Spanish encounters sentences that have no subject, this is positive evidence that subjects do not have to be overtly expressed in Spanish.

Positive reinforcement（正面强化）According to behaviorism, the strengthening of a response as a result of repetition followed by a positive reward.

Pragmatics（语用学）The study of the use of language in communication. Among other aspects of language use, it includes the study of illocutionary acts.

Principles and parameters（原则与参数）See Unit 3 for detailed definition.

Processing instruction（加工教学）See Unit 6 for detailed definition.

Production（产出）Act of speaking or writing a language.

Reflectivity（深思）A kind of cognitive style as opposed to impulsivity. Before a learner makes a final decision, he tends to think carefully.

Regulation（调节论）See Unit 5 for definition.

Restructuring（重构）Changes or reorganization of one's grammatical knowledge.

Schematization（图式化）See Unit 4 for detailed definition.

Second language acquisition（第二语言习得）The learning of another language after the mother tongue has been learned.

Semantic formulas（语义套语）In interlanguage pragmatics, semantic formulas refer to the means by which a particular speech act is accomplished in terms of the primary content of an utterance.

Semantics（语义学）The study of the meaning of words and sentences.

Sequence of acquisition（习得顺序）See Unit 2 for relevant information.

Social identity（社会身份）The relationship between the individual and the larger social world, as mediated through institutions such as families, schools, workplaces, social services, and law courts. Social identity is multiple and dynamic.

Speech act（言语行为）An utterance that performs a locutionary and an illocutionary meaning in communication. For example, "I like your dress" is a locutionary speech act concerning a proposition about a person's dress with the illocutionary force of a compliment.

Spontaneous speech（自发言语）The natural speech produced without being planned in advance.

Structured input （结构性输入） This is input that has been specially designed to expose learners to exemplars of a specific linguistic feature. It is a technique in form-focused instruction.

Suppletive form （不规则词形曲折形式） A type of irregularity in which there is a complete change in the shape of a word in its inflected forms. For example, *go-went* does not follow the normal pattern as in *play-played* but uses a different form for the past tense form of the verb *go*.

Syntax （句法） Known as grammar, syntax concerns the ways in which words combine to form sentences and the rules which govern the formation of sentences.

Systemic linguistics （系统语言学） Developed by Halliday, systemic linguistics sees language in a social context.

Teachability hypothesis （可教性假说） See Unit 6 for definition.

Token （词次/形符） See Unit 4 for detailed definition.

Token frequency （型符频率） See Unit 4 for detailed definition.

Topicalization （话题化） The tendency of putting topics at the beginning of a sentence.

Transfer （迁移） The carrying over of learned behavior from one situation to another. In SLA, there are two types of transfer, positive transfer and negative transfer.

Type （词型/类符） See Unit 4 for detailed definition.

Type frequency （类符频率） See Unit 4 for detailed definition.

Typological universals （类型普遍性） Universals derived from an exploration of the similarities of world languages. See Unit 3 for detailed information.

Universal grammar （UG） （普遍语法） A set of innate principles which are common to all languages. It is claimed that every one knows a set of principles which apply to all languages and also a set of parameters which vary from one language to another within certain limits.

U-shaped pattern （U－型发展模式） See Unit 2 for definition.

Wernicke's area （韦尼克区） An area of the brain found in the left half which controls language comprehension.

Wild grammar （野语法） A grammar that contains rules that contravene UG. It is argued that children do not in fact construct wild grammar.

Willingness to communicate （交际意愿） This is the extent to which learners are prepared to initiate communication when they have a choice. It constitutes a factor believed to lead to individual differences in language learning.

Zone of proximal development（最近发展区）The distance between the actual development level as determined by independent problem solving and the level of potential development as determined through adult guidance or in collaboration with more capable peers.

Appendix 2   Reference Key to Some Questions in the Assignment

Chapter One

2. naturalistic; meaning; culture; formal; forms; competence; performance

3. (1) b; (2) a; (3) d; (4) c

4. (3) a. F   b. T   c. T   d. F   e. T   f. T   g. T   h. F

        i. F   j. F   k. T   l. T   m. F   n. F   o. F   p. T

Chapter Two

2. slips; mistake; systematic; system; universal

Chapter Three

2. (1) c; (2) e; (3) f; (4) a; (5) b; (6) d

3. acquisition; learning; acquired; learned; functions; uses; meanings; realization

4. (1) a—lexicon; b—phonology; c—syntax; d—morphology

Chapter Four

2. (1) instrumental;

   (2) integrative;

   (3) field-independent;

   (4) field-dependent;

   (5) Deductive; inductive;

   (6) Cognitive; Affective; Sociocultural-interactive

Chapter Five

2. stimulus; response; device; input; processing; environment

Chapter Six

2. (1) b; (2) c; (3) a

3. practice; structures; feedback; representation; explicit; rule

Chapter Seven

2. least; intervention; production; past; acquisition

References

Abraham, R. *The Relationship of Cognitive Style to the Use of Grammatical Rules by Spanish-speaking ESL Students in Editing Written English*. Champaign-Urbana, University of Illinois, 1981.

Ammar, A. and N. Spada. One Size Fits All? Recasts, Prompts, and L2 Learning. *Studies in Second Language Acquisition*, 2006 (28).

Anderson, J. *Language, Memory, and Thought*. Hillsdale, N. J.: Lawrence Erlbaum, 1976.

Ard, J. and Homburg, T. Verification of Language Transfer. In S. Gass and L. Selinker (eds.). *Language Transfer in Language Learning*, 2nd ed. . Amsterdam: John Benjamins, 1992.

Bailey, K. Competitiveness and Anxiety in Adult Second Llanguage Learning: Looking at and through the Diary Studies. In H. Seliger & M. Long (eds.). *Classroom Oriented Research in Second Language Acquisition*. Rowley, MA: Newbury House, 1983.

Bardovi-Harlig, K. *Tense and Aspect in Second Language Acquisition: Form, Meaning, and Use*. Language Learning Monograph Series. Malden, Mass,: Blackwell, 2000.

Bardovi-Harlig, K and Z. Dörnyei. Do Language Learners Recognize Pragmatic Violations? Pragmatic vs. Grammatical Awareness in Instructed L2 Learning. *TESOL Quarterly*, 1998 (32).

Bardovi-Harlig, K. Evaluating the Empirical Evidence—Grounds for Instruction in Pragmatics? In K. R. Rose and G. Kasper (eds.): *Pragmatics in Language Teaching*. Beijing: World Book Publishing House, 2006.

Bardovi-Harlig, K. Exploring the Interlanguage of Interlanguage Pragmatics: a Research Agenda for Acquisitional Pragmatics. *Language Learning*, 1999 (49).

Bardovi-Harlig, K. *Pragmatic competence of the advanced learner*. Indiana University manuscript, 2004.

Beebe, L. , T. Takahashi, and R. Uliss-Weltz. Pragmatic Transfer in ESL Refusals. In R. Scarcella, E. Andersen, and S. Krashen (eds.). *Developing Communicative Competence in a Second Language*. New York: Newbury House, 1990.

Berko, J. The Child's Learning of English Morpheme. *Word*, 1958 (14).

Bialystok, E. A Theoretical Model of Second Language Learning. *Language Learning*, 1978 (28).

Bialystok, E. Achieving Proficiency in a Second Language: AProcessing Description. In R. Phillipson et al. (eds.). *Foreign/Second Language Pedagogy Research*. Clevedon: Multilingual Matters, 1991.

Birdsong, D. (eds.). *Second Language Acquisition and the Critical Period Hypothesis: Second Language Research and Methodological Issues*. Mahwah, NJ: Lawrence Erlbaum, 1999.

Blackledge, A. and A. Creese. *Multilingualism: A critical perspective*. New York: Continuum Press, 2010.

Bloom, L. M. *Language Development: Form and Function in Emerging Grammars*. Cambridge, Mass. : MIT Press, 1970.

Bloom, L. Why not Pivot Grammar? *Journal of Speech and Hearing Disorders*, 1971 (36).

Bloomfield, L. *Language*. New York: Holt, Rinehart and Winston, 1993.

Brown, H. D. *Principles of Language Learning and Teaching* (3rd edition). Beijing: Foreign Language Teaching and Research Press, 2002.

Brown, H. D. , *Principles of Language Learning and Teaching* (6th edition). Beijing: Foreign Language Teaching and Research Press, 2021.

Brown, R. *A First Language: The Early Stages*. Harmondsworth: Penguin Books, 1973.

Bybee, J. L. *Frequency of Use and the Organization of Language*. Oxford: Oxford University Press, 2007.

Canale, M. From Communicative Competence to Language Pedagogy. In J. Richards and R. Schmidt (eds.). *Language and communication*. London: Longman, 1983.

Carroll, J. The Prediction of Success in Foreign Language Training. In R. Glaser (eds.). *Training, Research, and Education*. New York: Wiley, 1965.

Chomsky, N. *The Minimalist Program*. Cambridge. Mass. : MIT Press, 1995.

Chaudron, C. A Descriptive Model of Discourse in the Corrective Treatment of Learners'

Errors. *Language Learning*, 1977, 27 (1).

Cohen A and Olshtain E. Developing a Measure of Sociocultural Competence: The Case of Apology. *Language Learning*, 1981, 31 (1).

Cook, V. *Second Language Learning and Language Teaching.* 2nd edtion. London: Edward Arnold, 1996.

Cook V. *Inside Language.* London: Edward Arnold, 1997.

Corder, S. P. "Error analysis" in Allan and Corder (eds.). *The Edinburgh Course in Applied Linguistics Volume 3.* London: Oxford University Press, 1974.

Corder S. P. *Error Analysis and Interlanguage.* Oxford: Oxford University Press, 1981.

Corder, S. P. The Significance of Learners' Errors. *International Review of Applied Linguistics*, 1967 (5).

Dabrowska, E. & Lieven, E. Towards a Lexically Specific Grammar of Children's Question Construction. *Cognitive linguistics*, 2005 (16).

Dagut, M., and B. Laufer. Avoidance of Phrasal Verbs—A Case for Contrastive Analysis. *Studies in Second Language Acquisition*, 1985 (7).

Derwing, T. Information Type and Its Relation to Non-native Speaker Comprehension. *Language Learning*, 1989 (39).

Dewaele, J. and A. Furnham. Extraversion: The Unloved Variable in Applied Linguistic Research. *Language Learning*, 1999 (49).

Dickerson, L. The Learner's Interlanguage as a System of Variable Rules. *TESOL Quarterly*, 1975 (9).

Diesel, H. *The Acquisition of Complex Sentences.* Cambridge: Cambridge University Press, 2004.

Doron, S. *Reflectivity-impulsivity and Their Influence on Reading for Inference for Adult Students of ESL.* University of Michigan, 1973.

Dörnyei, Z. On the Teachability of Communication Strategies. *TESOL Quarterly*, 1995 (29).

Dulay, H. and M. Burt. "You can't learn without goofing" in Richards (ed.). *Error Analysis.* London: Longman, 1974.

Dulay, H., M. Burt, and S. Krashen. *Language Two.* Oxford: Oxford University Press, 1982.

Dunn, W. and J. P. Lantolf. i + 1 and the ZPD: Incommensurable Constructs; Incommensurable Discourses. *Language Learning*, 1998 (48).

DeKeyser, R. Beyond Focus on Form: Cognitive Perspective on Learning and Practicing Second Language Grammar. In C. Doughty and J. Williams (eds.). *Focus on Form in Classroom Second Language Acquisition*. Cambridge: Cambridge University Press, 1998.

DyKeyser, R. M. Implicit and Explicit Learning. In C. J. Doughty and M. H. Long (eds.). *Handbook of Second Language Acquisition*. Malden, Mass.: Blackwell, 2003.

Eckman, F. Markedness and the Contrastive Analysis Hypothesis. *Language Learning*, 1977 (27).

Elley, W. Grammar Teaching and Language Skill. In Asher, R. E. (eds.). *The Encyclopedia of Language and Linguistics*. Oxford: Pergmon Press, 1994.

Ellis, N. Constructions, Chunking, and Connectionism: The Emergence of Second Language Structure. In C. Doughty and M. Long (eds.). *Handbook of Second Language Acquisition*. Malden, Mass.: Blackwell, 2003.

Ellis, N. C., and D. Larsen-Freeman. (eds.) *Language as a Complex Adaptive System*. Boston, MA: Wiley-Blackwell, 2009.

Ellis, N. Rules and Instances in Foreign Language Learning: Interactions of Explicit and Implicit Knowledge. University College of North Wales, 1991.

Ellis, N. Frequency Effects in Language Processing: AReview with Implications for Theories of Implicit and Explicit Language Acquisition. *Studies in Second Language Acquisition*, 2002 (24).

Ellis, R. Learning to Communicate in the Classroom. *Studies in Second Language Acquisition* 1992 (14).

Ellis, R. Sources of Variability in Interlanguage. Paper presented at the Interlanguage Seminar in Honor of Pit Corder, Edinburgh, 1984.

Ellis, R., H. Basturkmen, and S. Loewen. Learner Uptake in Communicative ESL Lessons. *Language Learning*, 2001 (51).

Ellis, R., S. Loewen, and R. Erlam. Implicit and Explicit Corrective Feedback and the Acquisition of L2 Grammar. *Studies in Second Language Acquisition*, 2006 (28).

Ellis, R. *The Study of Second Language Acquisition*. Shanghai: Shanghai Foreign Language Education Press, 1994.

Ellis, R. Interpretation Tasks for Grammar Teaching. *TESOL Quarterly*, 1995 (29).

Ellis, R. *Understanding Second Language Acquisition*. Shanghai: Shanghai Foreign Language Education Press, 1999.

Ellis, R. *Second Language Acquisition*. Shanghai: Shanghai Foreign Language Education Press, 2000.

Ellis, R. The Differential Effects of Corrective Feedback on Two Grammatical Structures. In A. Mackey (eds.). *Conversational Interaction and Second Language Acquisition: A Series of Empirical Studies*. Oxford: Oxford University Press, 2007.

Ellis, R. Explicit Form-focused Instruction and Second Language Acquisition. In B. Spolsky and F. Hult (eds.). *The Handbook of Educational Linguistics*. Oxford: Blackwell, 2008.

Ellis, R. *The Study of Second Language Acquisition* (Second Edition). Shanghai: Shanghai Foreign Language Education Press, 2013.

Eysenck, S., and J. Chan. A Comparative Study of Personality in Adults and Children: Hong Kong vs. England. *Personality and Individual Differences*, 1982 (3).

Ferguson, C. Absence of Copula and the Notion of Simplicity: AStudy of Normal Speech, Baby Talk, Foreigner Talk and Pidgins. In D. Hymes (eds.). *Pidginization and Creolization of Languages*. Cambridge: Cambridge University Press, 1971.

Fotos, S. and R. Ellis. Communicating about Grammar: ATask-based Approach. *TESOL Quarterly*, 1991 (25).

Fotos, S. Consciousness-raising and Noticing through Focus-on-form: Grammar Task Performance vs. Formal Iinstruction. *Applied Linguistics*, 1993 (14).

Freed, B. Foreigner Talk, Baby Talk, Native Talk. *International Journal of the Sociology of Language*, 1981 (28).

Fries, C. Forward. In R. Lado. *Linguistics Across Culture*. Ann Arbor: University of Michigan Press, 1957.

Gan, Z., G. Humphreys, and L. Hamp-Lyons. Understanding Successful and Unsuccessful EFL Students in Chinese Universities. *Modern Language Journal*, 2004 (88).

Gao, Wei. *A Usage-based Approach to Second Language Acquisition of Collocations*. Beijing: Science Press, 2016.

Gardner, R. *Social Psychology and Second Language Learning: The Role of Attitudes and Motivation*. London: Edward Arnold, 1985.

Gass, S. and L. *Selinker. Second Language Acquisition: An Introductory Course* (3rd *edition*). New York and London: Routledge, 2008.

Gass, S. Second Language Acquisition: Past, Present, and Future. *Second Language Research*, 1993 (9).

Gass, S. *Selected Works of Susan Gass on Applied Linguistics.* Beijing: Foreign Language Teaching and Research Press, 2009.

Gass, S. and A. Mackey. *Data Elicitation for Second and Foreign Language Research.* Mahwah, NJ: Lawrence Erlbaum Associates, 2007.

Gass, S. Input and Interaction. In C. Doughty and M. Long (eds.). *The Handbook of Second Language Acquisition.* Malden, Mass. : Blackwell, 2003.

George, H. *Common Errors in Language Learning: Insights from English.* Rowley, Mass. : Newbury House, 1972.

Giles, H. and J. Byrne. An Intergroup Approach to Second Language Acquisition. *Journal of Multicultural and Multilingual Development*, 1982 (3).

Gleitman, L. and E. Wanner. Language Acquisition: The State of the Art. In E. Wanner and L. Gleitman. (eds.). *Language Acquisition: The State of the Art.* Cambridge, UK: Cambridge University Press, 1982.

Goldberg, A. E. *Constructions: A Construction Grammar Approach to Argument Structure.* Chicago: University of Chicago Press, 1995.

Goldberg. A. E. *Constructions at Work: The Nature of Generalization in Language.* Oxford: Oxford University Press, 2006.

Halbach, A. Finding out about Students ′ Learning Strategies by Looking at Their Diaries: ACase Study. *System*, 2000 (28).

Halliday, M. A. K. *Learning How to Mean: Explorations in the Development of Language.* London: Arnold, 1975.

Halliday, M. A. K. The Functional Basis of Language. In B. Bernstein (eds.). *Class, Codes and Control, Volume* II. London: Routledge and Kegan Paul, 1973.

Han, Z. Persistence of the Implicit Influence of NL: The Case of the Pseudo-passive. *Applied Linguistics*, 2000 (21).

Harley, B. Functional Grammar in French Immersion: A Classroom Experiment. *Applied Linguistics*, 1989 (19).

Hatch, E. Discourse Analysis and Second Language Acquisition. In E. Hatch (ed.).

Second Language Acquisition. Rowley, Mass.: Newbury House, 1978b.

Hatch, E. Psycholinguistics: *A Second Language Perspective*. Rowley, MA: Newbury House, 1983.

Havranek, G. When is Corrective Feedback Most Likely to Succeed? *International Journal of Educational Research*, 2002 (37).

Hawkins, E. Language Awareness. In Asher, R. E. (ed.). *The Encyclopedia of Language and Linguistics*. Oxford: Pergmon Press, 1994.

Housen, A. and M. Pierrard. Investigating Instructed Second Language Acquisition. In A. Housen and M. Pierrard (eds.). *Investigations in Instructed Second Language Acquisition*. Berlin: Mouton de Gruyter, 2006.

Horwitz, E. Foreign and Second Language Anxiety. *Language Teaching*, 2010 (43).

Hudson, R. Grammar. In M. Berns (ed.). *Concise Encyclopedia of Applied Linguistics*. New York: Elsevier, 2010.

Hymes, D. H. On Communicative Competence. In J. B. Pride and J. Holmes (eds.). *Sociolinguistics* (pp. 269 – 293). Baltimore, USA: Penguin Books Ltd., 1972.

Hymes, D. H. On Communicative Competence. In Brumfit, C. and Johnson, K. (eds.). *Communicative Approach to Language Teaching*. Oxford: Oxford University Press, 1979.

Izumi, S. Processing Difficulty in Comprehension and Production of Relative Clauses by Learners of English as a Second Language. *Language Learning*, 2003 (53).

Jeon, E. and T. Kaya. Effects of L2 Instruction on Interlanguage Pragmatic Development: AMeta-analysis. In J. Norris, L. Norris and L. Ortega (eds.). *Synthesizing Research on Language Teaching and Learning*. Amsterdam: John Benjamins, 2006.

Johnson, K. *Language Teaching and Skill Learning*. Oxford: Blackwell, 1996.

Jourdenais, R., M. Ota, S. Stauffer, B. Boyson, and C. Doughty. Does Textual Enhancement Promote Noticing? A Think – aloud Protocol Analysis. In R. Schmidt (ed.). *Attention and Awareness in Foreign Language Learning*. Honolulu: University of Hawai'i Press, 1995.

Kasper, G. Classroom Research on Interlanguage Pragmatics. In K. Rose and G. Kasper (eds.). *Pragmatics in Language Teaching*. Cambridge: Cambridge University Press, 2001.

Kasper, G. Pragmatic Comprehension in Learner-native Speaker Discourse. *Language*

Learning, 1984a (34).

Kasper, G. and K. R. Rose. *Pragmatic Development in a Second Language*. Oxford: Blackwell, 2002.

Kasper, G. and S. Blum-Kulka. *Interlanguage Pragmatics*. Oxford: Oxford University Press, 1993.

Kellerman, E. *Aspects of Transferability in Second Language Acquisition*. Unpublished doctoral dissertation, Katholieke Universiteit te Nijmegen, 1987.

Khalil, A. Communicative Error Evaluations: Native Speakers' Evaluation and Interpretation of Written Errors of Arab EFL Learners. *TESOL Quarterly*, 1985 (19).

Klein, W. The Acquisition on English. In R. Dietrich, W. Klein and C. Noyau (eds.). *The Acquisition of Temporality in a Second Language*. Amsterdam: John Benjamins, 1995.

Kramsch, C. *The Multilingual Subject: What Foreign Language Learners Say about Their Experience and Why It Matters*. Oxford, UK: Oxford University Press, 2009.

Krashen, S. Individual Variation in the Use of the Monitor. In W. Ritchie (ed.). *Second Language Acquisition Research*. New York: Academic Press, 1978.

Krashen, S. Some Issues Relating to the Monitor Model. In H. Brown, C. Yorio, and R, Crymes (eds.). *On TESOL'77*. Washington D. C. : TESOL, 1977.

Krashen, S. *The Input Hypothesis: Issues and Implications*. London: Longman, 1985.

Krashen, S. *Principles and Practice in Second Language Acquisition*. London: Pergamon, 1982.

Krashen, S. , M. Long, and R. Scarcella. Age, Rate and Eventual Attainment in Second Language Acquisition. *TESOL Quarterly*, 1979 (13).

Lado, R. *Linguistics Across Cultures: Applied Linguistics for Language Teachers*. Ann Arbor, Michigan: University of Michigan, 1957.

Langacker, R. W. 1987. *Foundations of Cognitive Grammar (Vol. 1)*. Stanford, CA: Stanford University Press, 1987.

Langacker, R. W. An Overview of Cognitive Grammar. In B. Rudzka-Ostyn (ed.). *Topics in Cognitive Linguistics*. Amsterdam: John Benjamins Publishing Company, 1988.

Lantolf, J. Sociocultural and Second Language Learning Research: An Exegesis. In E. Hinkel (ed.). *Handbook of Research on Second Language Teaching and Learning*. Mahway, N. J. : Lawrence Erlbaum, 2005.

Lantolf, J. and S. Thorne. *Sociocultural Theory and the Genesis of Second Language Development*. Oxford: Oxford University Press, 2006.

Lardiere, D. *Ultimate Attainment in Second Language Acquisition: A Case Study*. Mahwah, N. J.: Lawrence Erlbaum, 2007.

Larsen-Freeman, D. Complexity Theory: The Lessons Continue. In L. Ortega and Z. H. Han (eds.). *Complexity Theory and Language Development: In Celebration of Diane Larsen-Freeman*. Amsterdam: John Benjamins, 2017.

Larsen-Freeman, D. Second Language Development in Its Time: Expanding Our Scope of Inquiry. *Chinese Journal of Applied linguistics*, 2019 (3).

Larsen-Freeman, D. An Explanation for the Morpheme Accuracy Order of Learners of English as a Second Language. In E. Hatch (ed.). *Second Language Acquisition: A Book of Readings*. Rowley, MA: Newbury House, 1978.

Larsen-Freeman, D. and M. Long. *An Introduction to Second Language Acquisition Research*. Beijing: Foreign Language Teaching and Research Press, 2000.

Laufer, B. and N. Girsai. Form-focused Instruction in Second Language Vocabulary Learning: A Case for Contrastive Analysis and Translation. *Applied Linguistics*, 2008 (29).

Laufer, R. and S. Eliasson. What Causes Avoidance in L2 Learning: L1 – L2 Differences, L1 – L2 Similarity, or L2 Complexity? *Studies in Second Language Acquisition*, 1993 (15).

Lenneberg, E. *The Biological Foundations of Language*. New York: Wiley, 1967.

Li, S. The Effectiveness of Corrective Feedback in SLA: A Meta-analysis. *Language Learning*, 2010 (16).

Lightbown, P. , N. Spada, and R. Wallace. Some Effects of Instruction on Child and Adolescent ESL Learners. In R. Scarcella and S. Krashen (eds.). *Research in Second Language Acquisition*. Rowley, Mass. : Newbury House, 1980.

Lightbown, P. Can They Do It Themselves? A comprehension-based ESL Course for Young Children. In R. Courchene et al. (eds.). *Comprehension-based Second Language Teaching*. Ottawa: University of Ottawa Press, 1992.

Lightbown, P. Exploring Relationships between Developmental and Instructional Sequences in L2 Acquisition. In H. Seliger and M. Long (eds.). *Classroom-oriented Research in Second Language Acquisition*. Rowley, Mass. : Newbery House, 1983.

Lightbown, P. Great Expectations: Second Language Acquisition Research and

Classroom Teaching. *Applied Linguistics*, 1985, 16 (2).

Lightbown, P. M. and Spada, N. Focus-on-form and Corrective Feedback in Communicative Language Teaching: Effects of Second Language Learning. *Studies in Second Language Acquisition*, 1990 (12).

Lightbown, P. and N. Spada. *How Languages are Learned. Oxford*: Oxford University Press, 2006.

Littlewood, W. *Foreign and Second Language Learning*. Beijing: Foreign Language Teaching and Research Press, 2000.

Liu, M. and J. Jackson. An Exploration of Chinese ESL Learners' Unwillingness to Communicate and Foreign Language Anxiety. *Modern Language Journal*, 2008 (92).

Loewen, S. Focus on Form. In E. Hinkel (ed). *Handbook of Research in Second Language Teaching and Learning*. New York: Routledge, 2011.

Loewen, S. *Introduction to Second Language Acquisition*. New York: Routledge, 2015.

Loewen, S. and T. Nabei. Measuring the Effects of Oral Corrective Feedback on L2 Knowledge. In A. Mackey (ed.), *Conversational Interaction in Second Language Acquisition*. Oxford: Oxford University Press, 2007.

Long, M. Does Second Language Instruction Make a Difference? A Review of the Research. *TESOL Quarterly*, 1983 (17).

Long, M. and S. Ross. Modifications that Preserve Language and Content. In M. tichoo (ed.). *Simplification: Theory and Application*. Singapore: SEAMEO Regional Language Centre, 1993.

Long, M. H. Focus on Form: ADesign Feature in Language Teaching Methodology. In K. de Bot, R. Ginsberg, and C. Kramsch (ed.). *Foreign Language Research in Cross-cultural Perspective*. Amsterdam: John Benjamins, 1991.

Long, M. H. The Role of the Linguistic Environment in Second Language Acquisition. In W. C. Ritchie and T. K. Bhatia (ed.). *Handbook of Second Language Acquisition*. New York: Academic Press, 1996.

Long, M. Native Speaker/Non-native Speaker Conversation and the Negotiation of Comprehensible Input. *Applied Linguistics*, 1983a (4).

Long, M. Questions in Foreigner Talk Discourse. *Language Learning*, 1981b (31).

Lyster, R. The Effect of Functional-analytic Teaching on Aspects of FrenchImmersion Students' Sociolinguistic Competence. *Applied Linguistics*, 1994 (15).

Lyster, R. and L. Ranta. Corrective Feedback and Learner Uptake: Negotiation of Form in Communicative Classrooms. *Studies in Second Language*, 1997, 19 (1).

Macaro, E. and L. Masterman. Does Intensive Grammar Instruction Make all the Difference? *Language Teaching Research*, 2006, 10 (3).

Mackey, A. Feedback, Noticing and Instructed Second Language Learning. *Applied Linguistics*, 2006 (27).

Mackey, A. Stepping up the Pace—Input, Interaction and Interlanguage Development: An Empirical Study of Questions in ESL, University of Sydney, Australia, 1995.

Mackey, Oliver and Leeman. Interactional Input and the Incorporation of Feedback: An Exploration of NS-NNS and NNS-NNS Adult and Child Dyads'. *Language Learning*, 2003 (53).

MacWhinney, B. Emergentism-Use often and with Care. *Applied Linguistics*, 2007 (27).

MacWhinney, B., E. Bates, and R. Kligell, Cue Validity and Sentence Interpretation in English, German and Italian. *Journal of Verbal Learning and Verbal Behavior*, 1984 (23).

Matsumara, S. Modelling the Relationships among Interlanguage, Pragmatic Development, L2 Proficiency, and Exposure to L2. *Applied Linguistics*, 2003 (24).

McKay, S and S. Wong. Multiple Discourses, Multiple Identities: Investment and Agency in Second Language Learning among Chinese Adolescent Immigrant Students. *Harvard Educational Review*, 1996 (3).

McLaughlin, B. *Theories of Second Language Learning*. London: Arnold, 1987.

McLaughlin, B. and J. L. C. Heredia. Information Processing Approaches to Research on Second Language Acquisition and Use. In Ritchie, W. C., Bhatia, T. (ed). *Handbook of Second Language Acquisition*. New York, NY: Academic, 1996.

Meisel, J. Linguistic Simplification. In S. Felix, (ed). *Second Language Development: Trends and Issues*. Tübingen: Gunter Narr Verlag, 1980.

Mohamed, N. Teaching Grammar through Consciousness-raising Tasks. MA thesis, University of Auckland, 2001.

Morris, C. *Foundations of the Theory of Signs*. Chicago: University of Chicago Press, 1938.

Muranoi, H. Focus on Form through Interaction Enhancement: Integrating Formal

Instruction into a Communicative Task in EFL Classrooms. *Language Learning*, 2000 (50).

Murphy, B. and J. Neu. My Grade's Too Low: The Speech Act Set of Complaining. In S. Gass, and J. Neu (eds.). *Speech Acts across Cultures*. Berlin: Mouton de Gruyter, 1996.

Nassaji, H. and S. Fotos. *Teaching Grammar in Second Language Classrooms: Integrating Form-focused Instruction in Communicative Contexts*. New York: Routledge, 2011.

Nation, P. Teaching and learning vocabulary. In E. Hinkel (ed.). *Handbook of Practical Second Language Teaching and Learning*. New York: Routedge, 2023.

Nemser W. Approximative Systems of Foreign Language Learners. *IRAL*, 1971 (9).

Norris, J. and L. Ortega. Effectiveness of L2 Instruction: AResearch Synthesis and Quantitative Meta-analysis. *Language Learning*, 2000 (50).

Norton, B. *Identity and Language Learning: Extending the Conversation* (2nd Edition). Bristol, UK: Multilingual Matters, 2013.

Norton, B. Language, Identity, and the Ownership of English. *TESOL Quarterly*, 1997 (31).

Norton, B. and K. Toohey. Identity, Language Learning, and Social Change. *Language Teaching*, 2011 (44).

Obler, L. Right Hemisphere Participation in Second Language Acquisition. In K. Diller (ed.), *Individual Differences and Universals in Language Learning Aptitude*. Rowley, MA: Newbury House, 1981.

O'Grady, W. *How Children Learn Language*. Cambridge, UK: Cambridge University Press, 2005.

O'Malley, J., et, al. Learning Strategy Applications with Students of English as a Second Language. *TESOL Quarterly*, 1985 (19).

O'Malley, J., A. Chamot, and L. Kupper. Listening Comprehension Strategies in Second Language Acquisition. *Applied Linguistics*, 1989 (10).

Oxford, R. Strategies for Learning a Second or Foreign Language. *Language Teaching*, 2011 (44).

Oxford, R. *Language Learning Strategies: What Every Teacher Should Know*. New York: Newbury House, 1990.

Oxford, R. Use of Language Learning Strategies: A Synthesis of Studies with Implications for Teacher Training. *System*, 1989 (17).

Pavlenko, A. and J. Lantolf. Second Language Learning as Participation in the Reconstruction of Selves. In J. Lantolf (ed.), *Sociocultural Theory and Second Language Learning*. Oxford, UK: Oxford University Press, 2000.

Pavesi, M. Markedness, Discoursal Modes and Relative Clause Formation in a Formal and Informal Context. *Studies in Second Language Acquisition*, 1986 (8).

Peirce, B. Social Identity Investment and Language Learning. *TESOL Quarterly*, 1995 (29).

Pica T. The Selective Impact of Instruction on Second Language Acquisition. *Applied Linguistics*, 1985 (6).

Pica, T. The Textual Outcomes of Native Speaker-nonnative Speaker Negotiation: What do They Reveal about Second Language Learning. In C. Kramsch and S. McConnell-Ginet (eds.). *Text and Context: Cross-disciplinary Perspective on Language Study*. Lexington, Mass. : D. C. Heath and Company, 1992.

Pienemann, M. Learnability and Syllabus Construction. In K. Hyltenstam and M. Pienemann (ed.). *Modelling and Assessing Second Language Acquisition*, Clevedon: Multilingual Matters, 1985.

Pienemann, M. An Introduction to Processability Theory. In M. Pienemann (eds.). *Cross-linguistic Aspects of Processability Theory*. Amsterdam: John Benjamins, 2005a.

Pienemann, M. Psychological Constraints on the Teachability of Languages. *Studies in Second Language Acquisition*, 1984 (6).

Pienemann, M. Learnability and Syllabus Construction. In K. Hyltenstam and M. Pienemann (eds.). *Modelling and Assessing Second LanguageAcquisition*. Clevedon: Multilingual Matters, 1985.

Plonsky, L and J. Zhuang. A Meta-analysis of Second Language Pragmatics Instruction. In N. Taguchi (ed.), *Routledge Handbook of SLA and Pragmatics*. New York: Routledge, 2019.

Porter, P. How Learners Talk to Each Other: Input and Interaction in Task-centered Discussion. In R. Day (ed.). *Talking to Learn: Conversation in Second Language Acquisition*. Rowley, Mass. : Newbury House, 1986.

Prabhu, N. S. *Second Language Pedagogy*. Oxford: Oxford University Press, 1987.

Reber, A. S. Kassin. , S. Lewis and G. Cantor. On the Relationship Between Implicit and Explicit Modes in the Learning of a Complex Rule Structure. *Journal of Experimental*

Psychology: Human Learning and Memory, 1980 (6).

Ritchie, W. and T. Bhatia (eds). *Handbook of Language Acquisition*, New York: Academic Press, 1996.

Rogoff, B. Observing Sociocultural Activity on Three Planes: Participatory Appropriation, Guided Participation, and Apprenticeship. In J. V. Wertsch, P. Del Rio, and A. Alvarez (ed.). *Sociocultural Studies of Mind*. Cambridge: Cambridge University Press, 1995.

Rosa, E. and D. O'Neill. Explicitness, Intake, and the Issue of Awareness: Another Piece to the Puzzle. *Studies in Second Language Acquisition*, 1999 (21).

Rose, K. and C. Kwai-fun. Inductive and Deductive Teaching of Compliments and Compliment Responses. In K. Rose and G. Kasper (eds.). *Pragmatics in Language Teaching*. Cambridge: Cambridge University Press, 2001.

Rubin, J. What the "Good Language Learner" Can Teach Us. *TESOL Quarterly*, 1975 (9).

Santors, T. Markedness Theory and Error Evaluation: An Experimental Study. *Applied Linguistics*, 1987 (8).

Sato, C. Phonological Processes in Second Language Acquisition: Another Look at Interlanguage Syllable Structure. *Language Learning*, 1984 (34).

Saville-Troike, M. *Introducing Second Language Acquisition*. Beijing: Foreign Language Teaching and Research Press, 2008.

Schachter, J. Second Language Acquisition: Perceptions and Possibilities. *Second Language Research*, 1993, 9 (2).

Schachter, J., and W. Rutherford. Discourse Function and Language Transfer. *Working Papers in Bilingualism*, 1979 (19).

Schmidt, R. Awareness and Second Language Acquisition. *Annual Review of Applied Linguistics*, 1993 (13).

Schmidt, R. Interaction, Acculturation and Acquisition of Communication Competence. In M. Wolfson and E. Judd (ed.). *Sociolinguistics and second language acquisition*. Rowley, Mass.: Newbury House, 1983.

Schumann, J. The Acculturation Model for Seond Language Acquisition. In R. Gingras (ed.). *Second Language Acquisition and Foreign Language Teaching*. Arlington, Va.: Center for Applied Linguistics, 1978.

Scovel, T. Foreign Accents, Language Acquisition and Cerebral Dominance. *Language Learning*, 1969 (19).

Scovel T. *A Time to Speak*. New York: Newbury House, 1988.

Selinker, L. and D. Douglas. Wrestling with Context in Interlanguage Theory. *Applied Linguistics*, 1985 (6).

Selinker, L. Interlanguage. *International Review of Applied Linguistics*, 1972 (10).

Shinttani, N, S. Li, and R. Ellis. Comprehension-based Versus Production-based Grammar Instruction: A Meta-analysis of Comparative Studies. *Language Learning*, 2013 (63).

Skehan, P. *A Cognitive Approach to Language Learning*. Oxford: OUP, 1998.

Skehan, P. *Individual Differences in Second Language Learning*. London: Edward Arnold, 1989.

Slobin, D. I. *Psycholinguistics*. 2nd Edition. Glenview: Scott, Foresman, 1979.

Slobin, D. (ed.). *The Crosslinguistic Study of Language Acquisition: Vol. 5: Expanding the Contexts*. Mahwah, NJ: Lawrence Erlbaum Associates, 1997.

Spada, N and P. M. Lightbown. Second Language Acquisition. In N. Schmitt (ed.). *An Introduction to Applied Linguistics*. Beijing: World Book Inc. , 2008.

Stevick, E. *Teaching and Learning Languages*. New York: Cambridge University Press, 1982.

Strong, M. Social Styles and Second Language Acquisition of Spanish-speaking Kindergarteners. *TESOL Quarterly*, 1983 (17).

Swain, M. and S. Lapkin. Problems in Output and the Cognitive Processes they Generate: AStep towards Second Language Learning. *Applied Linguistics*, 1995, 16 (3).

Swain, M. Manipulating and Complementing Content Teaching to Maximize SecondLanguage Learning. *TESL Canada Journal*, 1988 (6).

Sykes, J. M. Multiuser Virtual Envioronment: Apologies in Spanish. In N. Taguchi and J. M. Sykes (eds.). *Technology in Interlanguage Pragmatics Research and Teaching*. Amsterdam: John Benjamins, 2013.

Taguchi, N. Instructed Pragmatics at a Glance: Where Instructed Studies were, are, and should be Going. State-of-the-art Article. *Language Teaching*, 2015 (48).

Taguchi, N. Teaching and Learning Pragmatics. In E. Hinkel (ed.), *Handbook of Practical Second Language Teaching and Learning*. New York: Routledge, 2023.

Takahashi, S. Pragmatic Transferability. *Studies in Second Language Acquisition*, 1996 (18).

Tang, X. and N. Taguchi. Digital Game-based Learning of Formulaic Expressions in L2 Chinese. *Modern Language Journal*, 2021 (105).

Taylor, G. Errors and explanations. *Applied Linguistics*, 1986 (7).

Tarone, E. On the Variability of Interlanguage Systems. *Applied Linguistics*, 1983 (4).

Tarone, E. and M. Swain. A Sociolinguistic Perspective on Second Language Use in Immersion Classroom. *ModernLanguage Journal*, 1995 (79).

Thomas, J. Cross-cultural Pragmatic Failure. *Applied Linguistics*, 1983 (4).

Tode, T. Durability Problems with Explicit Instruction in an FFI Context: the Learning of Copula be before and after the Introduction of Auxiliary be. *Language Teaching Research*, 2007 (11).

Tomasello, M. Acquiring Linguistic Constructions. In W. Damon, et al. (ed.). *Handbook of Child Psychology (Volume 2): Cogniion, Perception, and Language*. Hoboken. New Jersey: John Wiley & Sons, Inc., 2006.

Tomasello, M. *Constructing a Language: A Usage-based Theory of Language Acquisition*. Cambridge, MA: Harvard University Press, 2003.

Tomiyana, M. Grammatical Errors and Communication Breakdown. *TESOL Quarterly*, 1980 (14).

Trahey, M. and L. White. Positive Evidence and Preemption in the Second Language Classroom. *Studies in Second Language Acquisition*, 1993 (15).

Van Lier, L. Language Learning: An Ecological-semiotic Approach. In E. Hinkel (ed.). *Handbook of Research in Second Language Teaching and Learning: Volume II*. New York: Routlege, 2011.

VanPatten, B. and T. Cadierno. Explicit Instruction and Input Processing. *Studies in Second Language Acquisition*, 1993 (15).

VanPatten, B. and W. Wong. Processing Instruction and the French Causative: Another Replication. In B. VanPatten (ed.). *Processing Instruction: Theory, Research, and Commentary*. Mahwah, NJ: Lawrence Erlbaum Associates, 2004.

VanPatten, B. *From Input to Output—A Teacher's Guide to Second Language Acquisition*. Beijing: World Book Inc., 2007.

VanPatten, B. Input Processing and Second Language Acquisition: on the Relationship Between Form and Meaning. In P. Hashemipour, R. Maldonado, and M. van Naerssen (eds.). *Festschrift in Honor of Tracy D. Terrel.* New York: McGraw-Hill, 1995.

VanPatten, B. Processing Instruction. In C. Sanz (ed.). *Mind and Context in Adult Second Language Acquisition.* Washington DC: Georgetown University Press, 2007b.

VanPatten, B. Processing Matters in Input Enhancement. In T. Piske and M. Young-Scholten (eds.). *Input matters.* Clevedon: Multilingual Matters, 2008.

Varonis, E., and S. Gass. Miscommunication in Native/non-native Conversation. *Language in Society*, 1985 (14).

Vygotsky, L. S. *Mind in Society: The Development of Higher Psychological Processes.* Cambridge, MA: Harvard University Press, 1978.

Wagner-Gough, J. Comparative Studies in Second Language Learning. MA thesis, UCLA, California, 1975.

Wells, G. The Complementary Contributions of Halliday and Vygotsky to a "Language Based Theory of Learning". *Linguistics and Education*, 1994a (6).

Whinnom, K. Linguistic Hybridization and the "special case" of Pidgins and Creoles. In D. Hymes (ed). *Pidginization and Creolization of Languages.* New York: Cambridge University Press, 1971.

White, J. Getting Learners' Attention: ATypographical Input Enhancement Study. In C. Doughty and J. Williams (eds.). *Focus-on-form in Classroom Second Language Acquisition.* Cambridge: Cambridge University Press, 1998.

White, L. Adverb Placement in Second Language Acquisition: Some Effects of Positive and Negative Evidence in the Classroom. *Second Language Research*, 1991 (7).

White, L. The Adjacency Condition on Case Assignment: Do Learners Observe the Subset Principle? In S. Gass and J. Schachter (eds.). *Linguistic Perspectives on Second Language Acquisition.* Cambridge: Cambridge University Press, 1989.

White, L., N. Spada, P. Lightbown, and L. Ranta. Input Enhancement and Question Formation. *Applied Linguistics*, 1991 (12).

White, L. *Second Language Acquisition and Universal Grammar.* Cambridge: CUP, 2003.

Whiteman, R., and K. Jackson. The Unpredictability of Contrastive Analysis. *Language Learning*, 1972 (22).

Williams, J. Memory, Attention and Inductive Learning. *Studies in Second Language Acquisition*, 1999 (21).

Williams, J. and J. Evans. What Kind of Focus and on which Forms? In C. Doughty and J. Williams (eds). *Focus on Form in Classroom Second Language Acquisition*. Cambridge: CUP, 1998.

Wolfram, W. Systematic Variability in Second-language Tense Marking. In M. Eisenstein (ed.). *The Dynamic Interlanguage*: *Empirical Studies in Second Language Variation*. New York: Plenum Press, 1989.

Yoshimura, F. Does Manipulating Foreknowledge of Output Tasks Lead to Differences in Reading Behavior, Text Comprehension and Noticing of Language Form? *Language Teaching Research*, 2006 (10).

Zobl, H. A Direction for Contrastive Analysis: the Comparative Study of Developmental Sequences. *TESOL Quarterly*, 1982 (16).

Zobl, H. The Formal and Developmental Selectivity of L1 Influence on L2 Acquisition. *Language Learning*, 1980 (30).

王初明. 学相伴用相随: 外语学习中的学伴用随原则. 中国外语, 2009, 16 (5).

王建勤. 第二语言习得研究. 北京: 商务印书馆, 2009.

郑超. 当代语言学导论. 重庆: 重庆大学出版社, 2006.